A REGIONAL HISTORY OF
THE RAILWAYS OF GREAT BRITAIN

General Editor: DAVID ST JOHN THOMAS

VOLUME VI
SCOTLAND: THE LOWLANDS AND THE BORDERS

Frontis: *Convenience*. A poster in the famous Caledonian Railway
'The True Line' series, 1915

A REGIONAL HISTORY OF
THE RAILWAYS OF GREAT BRITAIN

Volume VI

SCOTLAND:
THE LOWLANDS
AND THE BORDERS

by

John Thomas

WITH 29 PLATES
10 ILLUSTRATIONS IN TEXT
8 MAPS
AND FOLDING MAP

DAVID & CHARLES : NEWTON ABBOT

ISBN 0 7153 5408 6

Set in Baskerville, 11pt, 1pt leaded
and printed in Great Britain by
Latimer Trend & Company Limited Plymouth
for David & Charles (Publishers) Limited
South Devon House   Newton Abbot   Devon

Contents

Illustrations

IN TEXT

MAPS

*The jacket illustration is from a print in the Edinburgh Library, and
is reproduced by kind permission of the Librarian.*

An Introduction to the Region

The territory covered by this volume includes the whole of central Scotland from the Forth–Clyde valley to the Border. The book traces the story of railways in the region from the first waggonways, through the rousing pioneer days and the rumbustious peak years to the period of decline that followed the wars; and back again to the railway renaissance of the 1970s.

The railways of Scotland evolved independently of the English railways; the country had its own railway system before it had a rail link with England. The Scottish railways had a *flavour*. It is true that English engineers had a hand in the making of some of them, but most of the important ones were fashioned by native engineers. And Scottish mechanical engineers produced locomotives with a look that came to be accepted as the Scottish look. The country even had its own Father of Railways. He was Charles Maclaren who in 1824 advanced the theory that the little waggonways and tramroads of the eighteenth and early nineteenth centuries might be welded into a network of *public* railways over which *locomotive engines* would haul people and goods. His pamphlet on the subject was published internationally. Northumberland received it with scepticism but Maclaren lived to see his prophecy fulfilled.

The region is full of evocative names, every one with significance in the rich story of the railway. *Beattock*; *the Waverley route*; *the Flying Scotsman*; *Cowlairs incline*; *The Tourist*; *Carstairs Junction*; *the Port road*; and many more. Action and incident abound as the story unfolds. Take any weekday of the year, and picture the trains of rival railway companies racing for twenty miles out of Glasgow on parallel courses on opposite banks of the River Clyde. Picture next the passengers decanted brusquely (two minutes only allowed) from train to ship so that the contest can be continued on water. Then there was the fun and fury of the competition on the inter-city routes between Glasgow and Edinburgh. There was a time when progressive fare-cutting got so badly out of hand that the company accountants would have been happy to *pay* passengers not to travel at all. At fixed times every day and night there would be three or four Anglo-Scottish expresses being urged towards the Border by their various routes. And while these and other glamorous trains performed in the public eye, the goods engines, the company workhorses, would be labouring in the rich coalfields of Lanarkshire and Ayrshire earning money in plenty to pay for the excitements and extravagances that were part of the lives of the old companies.

The great stations of the region were, and some still are, community centres. The Caledonian's Central Station in Glasgow with its seventeen platforms (four of them underground) handled at its peak 22,000,000 passengers a year; 260 steam trains a day passed through its underground platforms alone. At quieter Buchanan Street (also Caledonian) the destination boards exhibited names like Stirling, Perth, Aberdeen; Blair Atholl, Aviemore and Inverness; Balquhidder, Strathyre, Dalmally and Oban. From Queen Street the North British dispatched trains to Edinburgh and London via the East Coast route, to Dundee and Aberdeen via the Forth and Tay bridges, to the little towns of the Fife coast, to Fort William and Mallaig, and to a host of local destinations. If you were in Queen Street at the right time you could see on a single train carriages labelled Harwich (Parkeston Quay), Southampton and Penzance. St Enoch of the Glasgow & South Western Railway housed the elegant trains that went to London by the Midland route as well as sending Glaswegians by the hundred thousand to the bracing resorts of the Ayrshire coast. In Edinburgh the North British Waverley station was the second largest in Britain.

It was sometimes said that a railway was as good as the engines that hauled its trains. Glasgow was the world centre of the locomotive trade. There were five great railway works within its boundaries, and another at Kilmarnock. The region could produce all the engines it needed. The bronze green engines of the North British, the apple green of the Glasgow &

South Western and the brilliant blue of the Caledonian were part of the landscape and much loved by people who knew or cared nothing about their mechanical make-up. Today representatives of their breed stand silent in the Glasgow Transport Museum, bright symbols of a brave era in the country's transport history.

The aim of this book is to bring the story of the nation's railways to life in smooth, narrative prose, at the same time giving as much solid information as possible within the space allowed. The danger in describing an area so rich in railway interest is that the story might well be lost in a dreary welter of opening and closing dates. Most important dates are given in the text, and a more comprehensive list appears as an appendix. In this way the author hopes to satisfy both the railway lover who enjoys a good read, and the reader whose main concern is to find a reference easily and quickly.

CHAPTER I

'Hurray! Hurray! the Railway!'

THE WAGGONWAYS

In the turbulent summer of 1745 the clans were 'out' and marching south towards the English border—5,000 rebels with the Young Pretender, Charles Edward Stuart, at their head. By the night of 20 September the Highland army was ten miles east of Edinburgh and Sir John Cope, with only 2,000 Government troops, was told to stem the Jacobite flood. That night Cope picked a defensive position at Prestonpans and mounted his artillery on what he himself described as 'a narrow cart road'. Perhaps it was too much to expect a soldier hurriedly preparing for an unequal battle to notice that the cart road was equipped with two parallel strips of wood set 3ft 3in apart. Alexander Carlyle, a local doctor, was more explicit when he came to describe how the Camerons overran the Government position at dawn on the 21st. 'The rebel army had before day marched in three divisions one of which went straight down the wagon way to attack our cannon.'

The Tranent waggonway was twenty-three years old when it entered the history books as the first railway to be used strategically in battle. It was planned at the London headquarters of the York Buildings Company, an organisation which specialised in exploiting the estates confiscated from Scottish proprietors who had supported the earlier Jacobite rising in 1715. Tranent estate was an interesting property. On the coast was the little port of Cockenzie, and two miles inland were the Tranent coal pits while in between were the salt pans of Prestonpans which supplied the whole of eastern Scotland with salt. Ships brought in rock salt from Scandinavia and took away Tranent coal. It was to simplify the transport of coal from pit to port that the waggonway was made.

The Tranent waggonway was laid with wooden rails on stone blocks, and was single track with two passing places. The line sloped gently from Tranent to the sea, and the loaded waggons made the journey by gravity with a man running alongside to sprag the wheels when necessary. Horse haulage was used on the return trip.

When the Tranent waggonway was built the railway age was still a century away. Just 119 years before, Scotland had been a completely separate kingdom and only fifteen years had passed since a fully-fledged Scottish parliament had sat in Edinburgh. Scotland was striving to escape from a period of domestic strife and establish herself as a modern, forward-looking nation. There were two Scotlands. The Highlanders in their mountain fastnesses in the north for the most part hankered after the old Scottish regime, and twice in thirty years they had tried to put a Stuart on the British throne by force. The Lowlanders, from the central plains to the Border, were by and large reconciled to the Hanoverian succession and were eager to take advantage of the commercial and industrial opportunities offered by the Act of Union.

If the country was short of material things it was not lacking in brain power, actual or latent. Scotland had four ancient universities compared with the two of her rich southern co-partner, and a school system that soon was to expand to cater for all classes of the community. Scotland's educational system was to ensure that her youth was amply prepared to play a part in the dawning industrial age. James Watt was a nine-year-old schoolboy in Greenock in 1745. Thomas Telford was born in 1756, John Loudon Macadam a year later. Scattered through the Lowlands were obscure families with names like Neilson and Grainger, Stirling and Drummond whose sons were to make their mark in the coming Scottish transport revolution.

Thomas Allan Croal writing of conditions in 1745 said, 'If the civilisation of a country were to be measured by the condition of its communications Scotland would present a problem of a mixed kind.' Roads were little more than hard-beaten paths, rutted and dusty in summer, quagmires in winter. When, in 1748, Provost Andrew Cochrane of Glasgow and two of his magistrates found it necessary to go to London to negotiate for Government compensation for the ravages of the Jacobite rebels, no transport was available nor was there a direct road from Glasgow to the Border. The Town Council had to buy a post-chaise at a cost of £28 2s 6d (£28.12½) and dispatch the travellers via Edinburgh and the Great North Road. The journey took twelve days and cost £25 2s (£25.10).

Until 1709 the mail between Edinburgh and Glasgow had been handled by one man on foot, but after that date a pony was used. Various attempts to establish inter-city stages failed until, in 1747, the Edinburgh and Glasgow Caravan Company offered a twice weekly service at a fare of 5s (25p) for the single journey. Glasgow also sent out stage coaches to Greenock, Ayr, Hamilton and other points usually at a frequency of once or twice a week. By 1764 a daily stage coach was serving the Glasgow–Edinburgh route (taking nine hours to the journey) and freight was handled by an irregular service of heavy wagons.

Edinburgh and Glasgow, the political and commercial capitals of Scotland, faced each other 45 miles apart at opposite ends of Scotland's narrow waistbelt. By the third quarter of the eighteenth century Glasgow was emerging as the country's greatest manufacturing centre and seaport. The Clyde ran through its heart and lay open to the trade routes of the world. Edinburgh with its port of Leith faced east and traded mainly across the German Ocean with the countries of Europe, the Forth providing an internal trade highway as far west as Stirling. The bulk of Scotland's trade was waterborne. Manufacturers in Glasgow found it easier (and sometimes cheaper) to send their products to the Americas than to transport them over the fifty miles or so of dismal roads to the other side of Scotland.

Glasgow was in urgent need of improved transport if the new industries were not to be stifled. A quick means of getting coal in quantity from the Monkland pits, 10 miles to the east, was the first priority, with an adequate east-west transport system a close second. The situation drove Scotland into the canal age. The Monkland Canal started in 1761 and partially brought into operation in 1778, gave much needed relief to the city. The Forth & Clyde Canal, begun in 1768 had by 1790 opened up a magnificent sea-to-sea passage from the Clyde to the Forth. The Union Canal, linking the Forth & Clyde at Falkirk with Edinburgh was begun in 1818 and finished in 1822 to give

B

direct water communication between Glasgow and Edinburgh. The Glasgow, Paisley & Ardrossan Canal, an attempt to provide an inland water transportation system between Glasgow and the Ayrshire coast (thus by-passing the Clyde) was in use between Glasgow and Johnstone by 1812.

The success of the new canal system was reflected in the population figures. In 1801 Glasgow had a population of 77,058; by 1811 the figure was 103,224 and in the next decade, as people poured in from country and Highland areas the population rose to 140,432. For Lanarkshire as a whole, including Glasgow, the figures for 1801, 1811 and 1821 were 147,692, 191,291 and 244,387 respectively.

Proprietors whose properties lay off the canal and river system, in some cases built waggonways to link their estates with the nearest traffic artery. In 1768 John, Earl of Mar, built the Alloa Railway, 2½ miles long to take coal to a bottle works on the Forth. It was perhaps the most substantially constructed of all the early railways. The rails were bars of foreign fir of 4in section overlaid with a second wooden rail the running surface of which was reinforced with a strip of malleable iron, the whole being firmly embedded in clay. The first *Statistical Account of Scotland* (1793) had this to say of the railway:

> To the west of the ferry stands a glass house for making bottles which is thought to be the most conveniently situated of any in Britain. It can have whatever quantity of coals it requires at a very easy rate, as they are conveyed from the pits to the very doors of the glass house by a wagon way.

In 1767 the Charlestown Railway was opened by the fifth Earl of Elgin to carry coal from his pits near Dunfermline to the north bank of the Forth near Rosyth. The line dropped from the high ground above the river on two rope-worked inclined planes. On occasion the wagons were used to convey passengers to join the Granton–Stirling packet boats. These, the first 'boat trains' in Scotland, handled some 23,000 passengers a year. Not far from the Charlestown Railway, the Halbeath tramway carried coal from the Halbeath colliery to Inverkeithing. Sir John Hope built a short waggonway at Pinkie near Musselburgh, a line which earned a place in history by being the first railway to use wrought-iron rails.

On 1 January 1760 the first of the famous Carron blast furnaces was blown in at Falkirk and six years later a railway was laid down between Kinnaird colliery and the works. The first rails were of wood covered with thin strips of hoop iron, but after a year these were replaced with cast-iron rails from Coalbrookdale. The first cast-iron rails ever made were turned out at Coalbrookdale on 13 November 1767 and it seems probable that the Carron Railway was allotted rails from this batch.

The Kilmarnock & Troon was a much more sophisticated waggonway than its eighteenth-century predecessors. It had the hallmarks of a real railway and indeed was the first line in Scotland for which an Act of Parliament was obtained. The line began as an idea of the Duke of Portland's in 1807. The duke's problem was the standard one of moving coal from the pits to navigable water, in this case from Kilmarnock 10 miles west to the harbour of Troon. Assured of financial support from his fellow landowners he commissioned William Jessop to survey a railway. An Act was obtained on 27 May 1808, and the railway was opened from St Marnock's depot, Kilmarnock, to Troon harbour on 6 July 1812.

The line followed an easy course down the valley of the Irvine Water. There were no outstanding engineering works except for a stone arched bridge spanning the river at Drybridge. The railway was 9 miles 6 furlongs in length and cost £38,167 10s (£38,167.50). It was double-tracked throughout, the gauge being 4ft. Cast-iron plate rails were used with a flange on their inner edge; the 4in running surface was sunk flush with the ground. A contemporary sketch describes the space between the rails as the 'horse path' and the space between the two tracks as the 'attendant path'. There was some difficulty at first through the horses kicking stones and gravel on to the rails thus making the running surface rough and bumpy, and men had to be employed to keep the rails swept clean of ballast. Ordinary road carts were allowed to use the railway on payment of a toll, and passengers were conveyed in two coaches *Caledonia* and *The Boat* for a shilling a head for a through journey.

The Kilmarnock & Troon had been functioning for about five years when the Duke of Portland decided to try a steam locomotive. The name of Stephenson was hardly known outside Northumberland, but Portland had heard of the two locomotives built at Killingworth by the colliery engineer, and he had the second Killingworth engine and its creator brought to Troon. By all accounts the engine could pull a train all right, but it damaged the cast-iron track. Archibald McKay, who saw the engine himself, spoke of its 'very rude appearance'. The *New Statistical Account of Scotland* said, 'From its defective construction and ill-adaption to flat rails, it only drew ten tons at a rate of five miles an hour.' The locomotive was more successful after wooden wheels had been fitted, and it remained in use until 1848. Not only was it the first steam engine in Scotland, but it was the only one for fourteen years. A representation of it is to be seen to this day in the coat of arms of the Burgh of Troon.

CHARLES MACLAREN

Charles Maclaren has been described as a moral and mechanical philosopher, 'one of the most useful, though one of the most unseen men of his time and country'. He it was who first painted a clear picture of the coming railway age for his fellow Scots. In 1824 Maclaren was editor of *The Scotsman* and in December of that year he devoted the whole of the front page of four issues of his paper to a dissertation on the future of railways. Maclaren maintained that railways should not be mere feeders of canals but great transportation networks in their own right, and that steam locomotives should be used to power them. He explained to his readers that he had given deep thought to his subject for a year before he had written his essays. Among the books he had studied were Professors Leslie's *Elements*, Playfair's *Outlines*, Vine and Coulomb's reports on their experiments with the laws of friction, the *Journal de Physique* and *Philosophical Transactions*. He had turned to contemporary engineers and scientists for guidance and had found little.

'Writers on science', Maclaren explained, 'generally travel on beaten tracks, and as railways are a recent innovation we have scarcely found a single article which would throw light on the theory of their use and construction; nor do the authors of the works in question seem to have any adequate idea of their importance. We are quite satisfied that the introduction of the *locomotive steam power* has given a decided superiority to railways. Indeed, we are convinced, and we hope by and by to convey some share of the conviction to the minds of our readers that the general use of railways and steam carriages for all kinds of internal communication opens up prospects of almost boundless improvement and is destined perhaps to work a greater change in the state of civil society than even the grand discovery of navigation.'

Charles Maclaren made his affirmation of faith in railways and the steam locomotive nearly four years before George Stephenson *publicly* acclaimed the locomotive. *The Scotsman* essays were widely copied by the British press and in 1825 were published in pamphlet form in England and America. They were translated into French and German. There were many who scorned Maclaren's views, among them Nicholas Wood of Killingworth. But opinion in Scotland was swinging powerfully in favour of railways. The Royal Highland Society awarded a prize to the Edinburgh civil engineer Robert Stevenson for an essay on railways, in which the writer reached the same conclusions as Maclaren. The *Edinburgh Association for Railway Experiments* was formed for the purpose of collecting a pool of knowledge on railways.

The mechanically-minded people of Glasgow had their eyes on the steam locomotive.

'Although the locomotive engine is a late invention and not generally understood,' said the *Glasgow Herald* of 5 November 1824, 'it seems to be nearly perfect in construction, and it is efficient almost beyond belief in operation. The power employed is only that of eight horses and in compass it does not much exceed the size of a single horse. A cart of coals is more than sufficient to supply the engine for twelve hours so that beyond the original cost there are very few attendant expenses.'

The *Herald* concluded that one engine in charge of one man and a boy would do the work of ten canal boats, ten horses and twenty men.

The most significant event of 1824 was the passing, on 17 May, of the Act authorising the construction of the Monkland & Kirkintilloch Railway. The Monkland tableland, lying to the east of Glasgow and south of the Forth & Clyde Canal concealed a marvellously rich accumulation of minerals as yet little exploited. There were pits and iron mines dotted over the plateau, and some of them made use of waggonways to help with their transport problems. William Dixon, a Monkland ironmaster, built a waggonway about 1800 to connect his Legbrannock collieries with the east end of the Monkland Canal. Another linked the pits at Newarthill with the Omoa Ironworks, and a line ran from the Calderbank Ironworks to the Monkland Canal. The canal, fed by waggonways and cart roads, was the main coal route from the Monklands to Glasgow.

Edinburgh, too, was a steady customer for Monkland coal. A coal barge for Edinburgh, 35 miles east of the coalfield, had to start its journey on the Monkland Canal travelling *west*. It had to thread its way through the Glasgow canal system, negotiating the congested basins at Townhead and Port Dundas before turning eastwards along the Forth & Clyde Canal. By the end of a week it might have reached Kirkintilloch, 6¾ miles north of its starting point. The Monkland & Kirkintilloch was planned to run direct from the coalfield to Kirkintilloch thus providing a striking short cut for Edinburgh-bound coal and an alternative route for Glasgow-bound coal. It was a conventional waggonway sloping from the coal field to the canal and designed to be gravity-assisted in one direction and power worked in the other. Where it differed from other waggonways was in that its far-seeing promoters specified the use of steam locomotives. The Monkland & Kirkintilloch was the first railway to obtain an Act authorising the use of locomotives. (The original Stockton & Darlington Act specified horse haulage and a subsequent amending Act had to be obtained to permit the use of locomotives.)

The invention by James Beaumont Neilson in 1828 of the hot blast method of smelting iron ore sparked off a blaze of activity in the Monklands. Already in 1805 David Mushat, manager of a Monklands ironworks had found veins of blackband ironstone from 14 to 18in thick lying under 10 square miles of the Monklands. The ironstone contained 35 per cent of iron 'and so much coal as nearly to burn itself'. It was the perfect fodder for the new blast furnaces. There was a stampede of ironmasters eager to stake claims to every available acre of the ironfield. Coatbridge, the main town of the Monklands, blossomed from a village into a great iron centre. 'Fire smoke and soot are its leading characteristics,' said a local gazetteer. 'The flames of its furnaces cast on the midnight sky a glow as if of some vast conflagration.' Railways were built to serve the new pits and ironworks to such an extent that eventually there were 280 miles of running lines within a 7 mile radius of the centre of Coatbridge.

The promoters of the little railways that spread end-on-end through the Monklands in the 1830s were coal and ironmasters rather than transport men. Their prime concern was to move their own materials to the markets or the blast furnaces. Their job as they saw it was to provide a medium on which traders, if they wished, could convey their own goods in their own vehicles. The railway company would on occasion carry goods in its vehicles using its own staff, but the practice was to be discouraged. The Wishaw & Coltness was very specific about this. 'The Committee recommend that if possible the carriage and leading should be performed by the traders as this is not the proper business of a railway company, but the company must provide accommodation of both descriptions so far as necessary.' The railway proprietors had canal and toll-road minds. The lines, crudely engineered at first, were built to the peculiar 'Scotch' gauge of 4ft 6in. They abounded in sharp curves and steep inclines, some self-acting, some worked by stationary engine. These inclines were analogous to the locks on the canals.

With one exception the Monklands railways failed to fulfil the vision of Charles Maclaren. The exception was the Garnkirk & Glasgow which was opened between the Monkland & Kirkintilloch near Gartsherrie and the Townhead of Glasgow in September 1831. The Garnkirk & Glasgow was the first railway in Scotland to operate independently of a waterway. It ran roughly parallel to the Monkland Canal and was in open competition with the canal for the Monklands–Glasgow traffic. It was managed and functioned as a railway in its own right, and offered regular passenger and goods services both steam and horse hauled. Yet it fell far short of being a trunk line. It was no accident that its title put the name of an obscure Monkland village first and the first city of Scotland second. Basically, the Garnkirk & Glasgow was built to carry Monkland coal to Glasgow.

TRUNK LINES

The trunk line era dawned on 15 July 1837 when the Glasgow, Paisley Kilmarnock & Ayr and the Glasgow, Paisley & Greenock got their Acts. A year later, on 4 July 1838, the Edinburgh &

Glasgow was authorised, and the railways were opened in 1840, 1841 and 1842 respectively. In each case the promoters exploited routes pioneered with great success by waterway and road transport operators. A rail link between the two most important cities in Scotland could not fail to pay. The promoters had an eye on, among other things, the 40,000 tons of Lothian grain that came to Glasgow annually via the Union and the Forth & Clyde canals. The GPK & A replaced the scheme to take a canal to Ayrshire, a project now stuck permanently at Johnstone.

The prospects for the Glasgow, Paisley & Greenock were bright indeed. From the coming of the *Comet* in 1812 the accepted way of getting from Glasgow to Greenock and the Clyde resorts was by packet steamer. Steam navigation made mass travel for Glaswegians possible for the first time, and generated an enormous amount of traffic on the river. By the 1830s steamer services were so frequent that the boats could not find room to berth in the ordinary manner, but were stacked paddle box to paddle box at an angle to the quay wall. The density of traffic was so great that in the seasons 1838 and 1839 there were no fewer than sixty-nine collisions altogether on the river. Here was a river for the railways to plunder. It was no wonder that rival companies pushed lines along both banks of the river each striving to secure a railhead and pier seaward of its competitors from which it could despatch steamers to the Firth resorts. It was as exciting an episode as can be found in the pages of British transport history. By the end of the century the London *Daily News*, in a survey of boat train services, was to say of the Clyde arrangements, 'Each of the three services with its minor ramifications is worked with a smartness almost beyond description; within two minutes of the arrival of the boat train the passengers are on board and the steamer is gliding off. The fares are ridiculously low and overcrowding is reduced to a minimum, thanks to the liberal supply of railway trains always forthcoming. The whole, in fact, is an eyeopener to the southerner. Would that we could have something approaching it between London and the South Coast.'

In 1843 Mr C. R. Porter, FRS, made an investigation into what he called the locomotive habits of the British people, and his findings give an interesting picture of the pattern of railway travel in England and Scotland at a time when the railways of the two countries had no physical link. England then had 1,852¼ miles of railway for a population of 15,911,725, Scotland 227¼ miles for a population of 2,620,610. England had one mile of line for every 8,596 persons, Scotland one mile for 11,544 persons. For every 1,000 of the population 1,149 railway journeys were made in England, 1,182 in Scotland, but distances travelled in Scotland were, on average, less than in England. Distribution of the classes, too, varied between the countries. In England 22·98 per cent travelled first class, in Scotland only 9·27. English second-class passengers amounted to 52·99 per cent of the whole, Scottish second-class passengers to 33·06 per cent. In England only 24·03 per cent of the total travelled third class while the corresponding figure in Scotland was 57·67 per cent. These figures could have been a reflection of the relative economic health of the two countries. (Two years earlier the Edinburgh & Dalkeith had reported that a rise in fares of *one farthing* per mile had resulted in a loss of 1,400 passengers per week.) In the year up to 30 June 1843 the Scottish railways, most of which were at this date confined to the region covered by this volume, produced a passenger revenue of £169,833 and a goods revenue of £114,839—a total of £284,672.

By 1840 the campaign to link the English and Scottish railway systems was in full blast. Intrepid entrepreneurs searched for ways through the passes of the Southern Uplands or round the coasts to unite at the Border or thereabouts with corresponding English enterprises being pushed north. In 1841 a Government decision that Anglo–Scottish traffic justified the building of only one railway served to intensify the struggle between the rival factions.

One of the projected international lines was the National Railway of Scotland. This scheme had its headquarters in Peebles and was planned to run from Lancaster through Carlisle to Peebles with forks to Glasgow and Edinburgh. On 12 February 1841 William Turnbull of Peebles wrote to an English fellow-promoter, John Rooke of Wigton in Cumberland, 'This is entre nous and should only have been made in words, but burn my letter.' Rooke did not burn the letter. One hundred and seventeen years later it turned up in a stamp collection in Slough; its contents give an unusually intimate glimpse of the political intrigue and chicanery which surrounded railway promotion in the 1840s.

> 'I certainly agree with you,' wrote Turnbull, 'if we can raise funds by respectable and powerful Committees in Edinburgh and Glasgow we should employ such influential Gentlemen as Messrs Walker and McDougall. All are alike to me except my distant relation Sir John Rennie. You are right however to bring your friends in view, yet if Mr. Stewart and his friend or brother-in-law, the great Mr. Gladstone MP, know some of equal influence as conjunct with their nephew you and I won't destroy our own Union of purpose by differing among ourselves. Last but not least by him we have the Ministerial interest on our side he being Whiggish and has supported them; and, mark ye, we may be said to be double armed for if a change of the Cabinet take place to the Conservatives then the great Gladstone etc gain us then the Conservative interest, so cheer up.'

It was important not to frighten away potential subscribers by making the line seem too expensive or too long, so judicious juggling with figures and mileage was called for in the prospectus.

> I am glad in your last letter you have agreed to make Berwick forty miles. Our rivals, I hope, will not falsify or catch that. You say it will cause you to alter your estimates. I do not think your remark 'cheapest in construction' enough in the first report. I omitted the £4,140,000 cash and extension to Lancaster. Even deducting the seventy miles at price £1,150,000, your estimate £3,150,000 is £1,150,000 above what our rivals state theirs at. Let us avoid estimates and keep by generalities at present to prevent controversy.

The correspondence gave an insight into the preparation of a railway prospectus. The promoters pondered over the problem whether to describe the line as running from Carlisle to Glasgow with a branch to Edinburgh or from Carlisle to Edinburgh with a branch to Glasgow. Either way they were bound to offend one city. In the end they settled on the phrase 'continuing on to Edinburgh and Glasgow'. Galashiels was described as an extensive manufacturing town 'to gain their friendship'. The promoter of the £4,000,000 railway concluded by describing how pennies could be saved in postage. Turnbull suggested that the letter announcing the National Railway of Scotland be printed in such a way that 'a space may be left at the end of the letter unprinted where, if sending to a friend or an acquaintance you may make remarks etc on its superiority to all others, which after showing to all friends around they can refold and re-address with an additional penny and penny label so as to get either to the Lands End or Jonny [*sic*] Groat's House. The repeated address may increase the circulation greatly. Such are the benefits of the National postage system.'

The schemes to link England and Scotland were temporarily lost sight of when, in the summer of 1845, Scotland was engulfed in the maelstrom of the Railway Mania. By the autumn of that year the newspapers contained announcements of new railways in almost every issue. A glowing future was held out for the many Scottish schemes advertised. 'It is the happy privilege of the prospectus', said the *Scottish Railway Gazette*, 'to look at all its objects through a rose-coloured spectrum.' Most of them took full advantage of the privilege. There was a great scramble for scrip and shares changed hands at fancy prices. The shares of the General Terminus Railway, a perfectly sound Glasgow scheme later successfully completed, were selling at a £25 premium. The Edinburgh engravers, famous for their maps, turned to producing railway plans. A visitor to an engraving establishment found that craftsmen had been on the premises continuously for eleven days snatching what sleep they could under their benches. Every issue of the daily papers ran pages of railway news, and commentators gave their opinions of the various railway schemes after the style of racing tipsters. Journals devoted solely to railway topics commanded a ready sale, among them *Scottish Railway Gazette*, *North British Railway and Shipping Journal*, *Steam Times* and the *Railway King*, the latter edited by the late editor of the *Glasgow Argus* who had seen fit to resign his important charge to devote his talents exclusively to railway journalism. On one page of one issue of the *Argus* thirteen new Southern Scottish companies were announced; their titles give an idea of their geographical scope.

Glasgow & Lesmahagow Railway Company.
The Lanark, Dumfries, Ayr & Galloway Junction Ry.
The Sanquhar, Muirkirk & Glasgow Ry.
The Ayr & Dumfries Junction Railway.
Lesmahagow, Dalserf & Coatbridge Mineral Junction Ry.

Edinburgh & Hamilton Direct Railway.
Glasgow, Partick & Dumbarton Direct Railway.
East Lothian Central Railway.
Carnwath & West Linton Railway.
Lochryan Harbour & Stranraer General Terminus Ry.
Glasgow & Stirling Direct Railway.
Hamilton & Strathaven Railway.
Edinburgh & Perth Railway.

The bubble had burst by the spring of 1846, and by the end
of the year the railways of the region had settled down to a
steady pattern of development. The 1841 commissioners, who
had taken two years to decide that one railway between Scotland and England was enough, were wrong. By 1850 there were
three Anglo-Scottish routes in operation, and with them came
the great names that were to dominate the railway scene for
three quarters of a century. The North British ran from Edinburgh round the coast to Berwick to link up with the East Coast
lines. The Caledonian came up through the heart of the
country from Carlisle to Carstairs, Edinburgh and Glasgow.
The Glasgow & South Western (formed by an amalgamation
of the Glasgow Paisley Kilmarnock & Ayr and the Glasgow,
Dumfries & Carlisle) swept through the south western counties
to join the Caledonian at Gretna on the Border. Rivalry between the three great companies was an important factor in the
shaping of the railway map of the region. Each company had
its zone of influence which it defended with ferocity against
enemy encroachment. The Caledonian, its trunk line secure in
its great central valley, thrust branches through the transverse
valleys, east towards North British territory, west towards
Glasgow & South Western preserves. The North British and
Glasgow & South Western likewise ran branches inwards towards the Caledonian sphere of influence. Occasionally rival
lines met—the Caledonian and Glasgow & South Western at
Muirkirk, for instance, and the Caledonian and the North
British at Peebles. Lines were built into unfruitful valleys
merely to keep rivals out. Sometimes glib railway lawyers persuaded parliamentary committees that there was traffic for two
railways in an area and wasteful duplication of services resulted. When independent companies appeared with schemes

their promoters were wooed by one or more of the big three and usually passed under the control of the major company by lease, interlocking directorships or outright amalgamation.

By 1870 the main features of the regional railway pattern had appeared on the map, and there followed an inevitable slowing down of development. By the turn of the century the pattern was all but complete.

THE SUBURBAN ERA

The last great spurt of railway building took place in the 1890s and opening years of the twentieth century round the main cities as rival companies struggled to gain control of the expanding suburban traffic. When the Garnkirk & Glasgow opened in 1831 the population of Glasgow was 193,030. In 1891 it was 658,198. The steady growth of the city had been matched by an expansion of the railway system serving it and in 1890 the prospects for suburban traffic could not have appeared brighter. The Caledonian-backed Glasgow Central Railway embarked on a difficult and expensive scheme to make a 6 mile railway under Glasgow, already heavily built up, from east to west. A contemporary Caledonian scheme to put a steam underground line beneath Edinburgh's Princes Street was thwarted by public opinion. In Paisley the Glasgow & South Western and the Caledonian were locked in combat over who should serve the growing town and its environs.

The promoters of the new suburban railways had not reckoned with the electric tram. Everywhere the suburban trains went the electric trams were snapping at their heels. The newest and cheapest novelty in urban transport took the public by storm. In 1902 Glasgow was the scene of the first massive capitulation of railways to trams when a formerly lucrative Glasgow & South Western local service, that to the busy shipbuilding suburb of Govan, was abandoned. There was consternation in board rooms (notably the Great Eastern) where millions had been sunk in suburban railway development. In the Glasgow area several almost new stations closed—starved of passengers. A circular service opened by the Glasgow & South Western in 1902 to serve the Paisley area was abandoned in 1907. Worst of all, the rival circle line built round Paisley by the Caledonian, provided with six passenger stations in the lavish Caledonian style, was jettisoned without a passenger coach wheel ever having turned on its metals.

The Light Railways Act of 1896 conferred insignificant benefit on the region mainly because vigorous promotion had left little ground worthy of exploitation. The Caledonian pushed a light railway from its main line at Elvanfoot into the bleak, bare hills encircling the villages of Leadhills and Wanlockhead. The Glasgow & South Western put a line round the sparsely-populated coast between Ayr and Girvan and another from near Dumfries up the Cairn Valley to Moniaive. The North British revived an earlier, unfulfilled standard railway scheme to run a line from Ormiston to Gifford and Garvald. It got as far as Gifford as a light railway, but the extension to Garvald was never completed. The Lauder Light Railway ran from Fountainhall to Lauder. All of the light railways suffered an early demise.

The Lothian Lines, the last railway scheme promoted in the region, began as a curious throw-back to early nineteenth-century railway thinking. The Lothian coalmasters, perturbed about the perennial problem of getting their coal to water, and dissatisfied at the service offered by existing railways, decided to build their own line from pit to port. The railway was to be entirely independent of the big companies. It was to be 12¾ miles long and was to link certain Lothian pits with Leith docks. The promoters intended to provide the railway only, and expected the traders to provide their own motive power and rolling stock after the fashion of the pioneer mineral railways. And this was in 1912! The North British opposed the scheme successfully, and promptly produced a similar (and successful) scheme of its own. The opening of the Lothian Lines on 26 September 1915 marked the end of an era.

The Scots loved their railways. True, there were adventurers whose only aim was to squeeze every possible penny out of the railway industry—like the Monkland landowners who made the railway companies pay for the coal under the strip of land occupied by the lines, or the Glasgow property owner who way-laid the messenger boys taking the Glasgow, Central & Subur-ban plans from the engraver to the engineer, and stole a plan in which he had a vested interest. But there were gentlemen, and even whole communities, who gave every possible help and encouragement to the railway promoters. Rigby Wason, a landowner who was active in railway management in South Ayrshire, wrote thus in a local newspaper.

> As there can be no doubt that such a railway would increase the value of my property far beyond any fair price which could be placed on the land which would be required, I request you to intimate to the promoters that they are very welcome to the land required for the railway without any cost, for I have always maintained that it is highly discreditable, if not absolutely unjust, for a proprietor to require payment for the land used by a railway when such railway will increase the value of his estate far beyond the value of the land. I would strongly recommend the promoters to insist upon the adoption of this principle, or to abandon the undertaking, publishing the names of those who agree to act on it, as also those who refuse, leaving the latter to be dealt with by their neighbours.

The arrival of a railway in a community was an occasion for public rejoicing. On the day in 1849 when the Slamannan Railway merely announced its intention to construct a paltry $4\frac{1}{2}$ mile extension to Borrowstounness (Bo'ness) on the Forth the inhabitants held an impromptu celebration in the local inn. 'The firing of cannon, and a rich display of flags from the vessels in the harbour, the Town House and every prominent place testified to the delight of one and all.' As late as 1875 the advent of a straggling rural line in the Isle of Whithorn inspired the local laureate to compose a poem which speaks more eloquently of the hopes and aspirations of the railway builders than pages of board room reports.

> Oor new clock lichted shows the oor,
> The parish kirk has got a toor,
> And better still, up to our door,
> Has come the Wigtown Railway.
>
> Lord Galloway, gude worthy man,
> The enterprise at first did plan,
> An' great and sma' put to their han',
> To help to mak the Railway.
>
> A while it stood at Sorbie Mill,
> For want of cash to mount the hill,

But Johnston Stewart with rich guidwill,
Has brocht us up the Railway.

What gudes we noo may hae to spare
Be't kintra growth or merchant ware,
Is sure to find a sale somewhere
Thanks to the Wigtown Railway.

What gudes we want, be't coarse or fine
At price accordin' to its kin'
We'll get by cotch or English line,
And doon the Wigtown Railway.

Now fill us up nae skimpet sip,
But fill your glasses to the lip
Three hearty cheers—Hurray! Hip! Hip!
Hurrah! Hurrah! the Railway!

When the First World War ended there was no indication
that the omnipotence of the railway was threatened. In 1918 a
Government committee recommended the construction of 78½
miles of rural railways in the region. The committee saw no
threat at all in the motor-car; only *railways* would solve the
country's transport problems. Motor transport was described as
'a rudimentary form of branch line'. Of the road services
pioneered by the Great North of Scotland Railway the report
said, 'While their motor omnibuses and steam lorry services
have improved the means of transport they do not allow of the
traffic being fully developed, and probably have only post-
poned the demand for railways.' The role of the motor-car, as
the report saw it, was to develop traffic to the stage when construction of a railway would be justified.

The soldiers who came home from the war brought new
mechanical skills with them. And among the flotsam of war
were many thousands of trucks and lorries. Enterprising ex-
service men bought army vehicles and organised local transport
services. New passenger vehicles appeared operated singly or in
small fleets. For the first time since the stage coach days people
in rural areas were offered door-to-door transport—and at
tramcar frequency and prices. A Clyde Valley operator who
named his two buses IKANOPIT and SOKANI caught the new
cavalier spirit of the road. By the mid 1920s there were thirty

Page 33 Rock cutting at Bishopton. Glasgow, Paisley &
Greenock Railway

Page 34 The Townhead (Glasgow) terminus of the Garnkirk & Glasgow Railway. Tennant's chemical works are on the left, and the Monkland Canal in the middle distance

bus operators on the Glasgow–Paisley road. A local man who started a bus service between Annan and Carlisle in 1925 carried 54,750 passengers in his first year.

When the three Scottish companies lost their identities in the 1923 groupings, and the region was henceforward served by two London-based companies, effective competition almost disappeared. Only on the Anglo-Scottish routes was something of the old fighting spirit retained. The London & North Eastern began non-stop runs with the Flying Scotsman between Edinburgh and King's Cross in 1928 using corridor tender engines for exchange of crews en route. The London Midland & Scottish retaliated with a nominal non-stop run from Glasgow to Euston by the Royal Scot, although a service stop was made during the journey. The edge was taken off enterprise by the companies agreeing to allow their trains 8¼ hours for their trip between capitals. Much more exciting was the work of the 1937 Coronation of the LNER which made the Edinburgh–King's Cross run in 6 hours and the LMS Coronation Scot which did the Glasgow–Euston journey in 6½ hours. The railways were poised for an all-round speed-up of their services when the outbreak of war in September 1939 put paid to the enterprise.

Both the London Midland & Scottish and the London & North Eastern took the opportunity to close ailing branches, a process that went on for the next two decades as road services won passengers and freight from the railways. The years following nationalisation in 1948 saw the elimination of more and more branch lines and duplicated routes, then in the 1960s came the massive planned obliteration that left important towns and even whole areas rail-less. The descendants of the people who had shouted *Hurray! Hurray! the Railway!* no longer wanted the railway. The closures were paralleled by unprecedented innovations and improvements to the services in those areas where the railway was to play a vital part in the life of the community. The new railway took shape.

At Cockenzie, where the Tranent waggonway reached the sea, there now stands a modern, coal-fired electricity generating station, and a railway links it with Monktonhall colliery. Trains of twenty-eight wagons glide under vast bunkers at the colliery. At the touch of a button five wagons are each filled with 32 tons of coal in 60 seconds. At the power station the train moves across bunkers and drops its load without stopping; then it goes back for more coal. With their capacity to move 3,600 tons of coal a day the Monktonhall merry-go-round trains are a far cry from the crude wooden hutches that rumbled down the Tranent waggonway with a few hundred-weights of coal 249 years ago.

CHAPTER II

The Monklands: Cradle of the Scottish Railways

There were fortunes to be made in the Monklands in the first half of the nineteenth century as landowners discovered that the soil they had tilled, often for scant reward, hid vast mineral riches. The Monklands had everything needed for the foundation of a great iron industry—coal in plenty, rich veins of blackband ironstone, limestone, and fireclay said to withstand higher temperatures than any other Scottish fireclay in beds up to 19ft thick. It only needed James Beaumont Neilson's hot blast to bring into being the iron industry that was to make the Monklands famous.

Most of the products of the Monklands went to Glasgow 10 miles to the west. By the 1820s the Monkland Canal was no longer able to cope easily with the traffic; and Monkland production was continuing to rise. The time was ripe for a railway.

THE MONKLAND & KIRKINTILLOCH

Coalmasters, ironmasters and canalmen united to promote the Monkland & Kirkintilloch. The line was to run from the Palacecraig pit a mile south-west of Airdrie to the nearest point on the Forth & Clyde canal passing on the way Coatbridge and Gartsherrie. With two short branches (to Kipps and Rosehall) the total mileage was 10½. The railway was visualised as a canal feeder; as the Act (obtained on 17 May 1824) put it 'the opening of an easy and cheap means of conveyance of coal &c in the neighbourhood of the railway to the said canals'. The line was opened on 1 October 1826.

The engineer of the M & K was Thomas Grainger who was to become the doyen of Scottish railway engineers. Grainger was instructed 'to fit the road for locomotive engines'. Nevertheless, he bored a tunnel with only 9ft headroom under the Cumbernauld road at Bedlay. The track was crudely laid with 28lb, fish-bellied rails on whinstone blocks from under which muddy water spurted when they took the weight of the trains. The track was single throughout, although the roadbed was made to take double track.

The M & K proprietors were not distressed by the line's imperfections. They had no intention meantime of employing the locomotives allowed them in their Act, and conventional horse haulage was a great improvement on transport by road. The line dropped 127ft between its southern terminus and the Kirkintilloch canal basin, and the favourable gradient eased the working of loaded trains. An engraving in Hill's *Views of Glasgow* shows the horse *Dragon* owned by Thomas Johnston of Langloan pulling a 55 ton train consisting of fourteen wagons between Gartsherrie and Kirkintilloch in 1827. The text explains that the trip took 1 hour 43 minutes. The railway raised Kirkintilloch's status as a canal port and provided an easy outlet for Monkland coal to Edinburgh and an alternative route to Glasgow and, via Bowling, to the Clyde.

THE UPLAND RAILWAYS

Between 1828 and 1844 three railways were threaded east and south through the Monklands. All fed traffic to the M & K whose managers habitually referred to them as 'the upland railways'.

The Ballochney Railway, opened in 1825 was an extention from Kipps on the M & K through Rawyards and Arbuckle to Ballochney, a colliery district north-east of Airdrie. The main line was 3¾ miles long, and with a branch from Rawyards to Clarkston the total mileage was only 5. But the line was important in that it tapped new pits and sent more coal down to the M & K and the canals. The prudent little company bought thirty-five sets of wagon wheels and axles from Newcastle before construction even started. Bodies were built locally and the wagons hired to the contractors as required. As soon as the line was ready the vehicles were made available for hire to the traders.

The Wishaw & Coltness was a continuation southwards of the Monkland line of communication from the Monkland & Kirkintilloch at Dundyvan Basin, Whifflet to the mineral fields round Motherwell and the Coltness Iron Works. The first section, Whifflet to Holytown, was opened on 23 January 1834. On 31 March 1834 the line was opened to Newarthill and on 9 March 1844 to its terminus.

Meanwhile the Slamannan Railway had been constructed and opened (31 August 1840) between Airdriehill on the Ballochney and Causewayend on the Union Canal, 12½ miles to the east. The line climbed steeply away from Airdrie, crossed the plain in the centre of which stood Slamannan village and then dropped abruptly down to the canal at Causewayend. The Slamannan Railway brought Monkland coal to within 24 miles of Edinburgh; a coal basin with arrangements for trans-shipping cargo from wagons to canal barges was a feature of Causewayend. The canal terminus was only 4½ miles from the Forth. The Slamannan directors, conscious of the fact that Charlestown on the northern side of the river was exporting 180,000 tons of Fife coal annually, had visions of establishing a rival coal port on the south bank of the Forth. The line was in fact extended to Bo'ness on 17 March 1851 (Chapter III).

The Monkland railways were built to a gauge of 4ft 6in. They had certain engineering peculiarities including two self-acting inclined planes on the Ballochney, and two stationary engine inclined planes on the Slamannan. The climb out of Airdrie on the Slamannan (the Commonhead incline) varied from 1 in 23 to 1 in 27, and the drop to Causewayend was at 1 in 23 for half a mile.

The lines were a law unto themselves, with their proprietors conducting their affairs in their own way with scant regard for the standard gauge railway world that was growing up all round them. The companies were separate and independent, although the directors of one were apt to crop up on the board of another, and eventually the railways shared a common secretary. The companies held their official meetings on the same day at the same place but at times so spaced that interested shareholders could attend all the meetings in turn.

The Monkland proprietors did not consider themselves *railwaymen*. They provided a means of communication, and charged traders for the use of it. They preferred the traders to provide their own vehicles and haulage, although they were prepared, but not too willingly, to supply wagons and motive power for their customers. A note of disdain crept into the Ballochney report of 1831 which began, 'In regard to the carrying trade in which the Company have found it necessary to engage,' and went on, 'This branch of the business the Committee are, however, now anxious to give up, as it adds greatly to the trouble of management. The business of the Company will then be restricted to the maintenance of the road, the working and passage of the inclined planes and the supply of wagons to the traders, and this last, *viz*, the supply and maintenance of wagons, the Company trust soon to have it in their power to discontinue.'

Traders using the Monklands railways were faced with a complicated scale of charges. All the lines had identical scales, but when the traffic passed over more than one line the complete journey, for rate computation purposes, was regarded as having taken place over one railway. Traders who provided their own wagons and haulage were charged a toll of 1d per ton for any distance not exceeding half a mile. Thenceforth charges were on a sliding scale up to 6d per ton for three miles. Every successive quarter mile was charged at $\frac{1}{8}$d per ton mile. These rates were for first class traffic which included the Monkland staples, coal, dross, ironstone, pig iron, limestone and fireclay. Second class traffic (malleable iron, slates, lime, peat, coke and ashlar) was charged the same rate as first class traffic for the first three miles and $\frac{1}{4}$d per ton for every succeeding quarter mile. Third class traffic (cotton, wool, grains and general merchandise) was charged a flat rate of 2d per ton mile.

A trader who hired wagons from any of the companies was charged an additional 2d per ton up to the first three miles and $\frac{1}{4}$d per ton for every succeeding mile. If he also required the company to provide haulage there was a further charge of 2d per ton up to three miles and $\frac{1}{4}$d for each additional mile. The pattern was still further complicated by the fact that a surcharge of 1d per ton mile was made for the first three miles of 'ascending haulage' plus $\frac{1}{2}$d for each additional mile. The self acting and stationary engine inclines imposed yet more supplementary charges. These ranged from $1\frac{1}{2}$d per ton for coal to 3d per ton for groceries. The Ballochney accounts indicate that a self-acting incline was a good investment: in 1831 the company

MONKLAND RAILWAYS—

THE MONKLAND & KIRKINTILLOCH, THE BALLOCHNEY & THE SLAMANNAN RAILWAYS.

TONNAGE DUES.

FIRST CLASS.—*Coals, Dross, Ironstone, Char, Pig-Iron, Limestone, Whinstone, Manure, Rubble, Sand, Ashes, Slag, Fire Clay, Bricks and Tiles.*

For any Distance not exceeding Half a-Mile,				1*d.*	per Ton.
—	½ Mile, and not exceeding	¾	—	1½*d.*	—
—	¾ — —	1	—	2*d.*	—
—	1 — —	1¼	—	2½*d.*	—
—	1¼ — —	1½	—	3*d.*	—
—	1½ — —	1¾	—	3½*d.*	—
—	1¾ — —	2	—	4*d.*	—
—	2 — —	2¼	—	4½*d.*	—
—	2¼ — —	2½	—	5*d.*	—
—	2½ — —	2¾	—	5½*d.*	—
—	2¾ — —	3	—	6*d.*	—

Every succeeding Quarter of a-Mile, ⅛ of a-Penny per Ton.

SECOND CLASS.—*Malleable Iron, Slates, Lime, Peats, Coke and Ashlar Stone.*
The same Rates as Charged on First Class for the First Three Miles.
Every succeeding Quarter of a-Mile, ¼*d.* per Ton.

THIRD CLASS.—*Cotton, Wool, Yarn, Cloth, Grain, Timber and all Goods not above specified.*
Twopence per Ton per Mile.

HAULAGE.

For the First Three Miles,..1*d.* per Ton per Mile.
Every succeeding Mile, ...¼*d.* —
Ascending Haulage, for First Three Miles, 1*d.* per Ton per Mile, every succeeding Mile, ½*d.* except on Limestone, to be charged the same as Descending.

WAGGON HIRES.

For all Distances under Three Miles,..2*d.* per Ton.
Every succeeding Mile,..¼*d.* —
Dross, Limestone, Whinstone, Manure, Rubble, Sand, Ashlar, Bricks, Tiles, Fire Clay and Slag, ¼*d.* per Ton per Mile.

All Waggons detained at the Works, Pits or Basins, to the interruption of the Trade, to be charged Ninepence per Waggon per day.
These Charges for Haulage and Waggons to extend over the Monkland Amalgamated Railways, and also over the Adjoining Railways.

SELF-ACTING INCLINE PLANE DUES, BALLOCHNEY RAILWAY.

Coals and Dross, using any part of One or Both Inclines,..1½*d.* per Ton.
Pig-Iron, Limestone, Whinstone, Ironstone and Iron-Char, using any part of One or Both Inclines, 2*d.* —
Bar-Iron, Timber, Bricks, Tiles, Slates and other Building Materials, except Whinstone, also Cotton, Wool, Grain, Flour, Groceries and other Merchandise, using any part of One or Both Inclines, 3*d.* per Ton.

STATIONARY ENGINE INCLINE PLANE DUES, SLAMANNAN RAILWAY.

Same Rates as for Self-Acting Incline Planes.

STATIONARY ENGINE INCLINE PLANE DUES, ROCHSOLES BRANCH RAILWAY.

Goods of any Description Descending the whole or any part of the Incline,..................2*d.* per Ton.
Goods of any Description Ascending the whole or any part of the Incline,..................4*d.* —

CRANE DUES, for Loading and Unloading, if done by the Companies, 2*d.* per Ton for Loads under One Ton, and 4*d.* for all Loads up to Four Tons. Extra Lifts charged according to expense, except for Coal and Limestone, which are not to be charged for at Causewayend Basin.
Loading and Unloading Horse Haulage and Wharfage at Kirkintilloch, 1½*d.* per Ton.

Note.—This Table is applicable to each of the Three Railways separately, but when the Traffic passes over more than One the Rates will be charged on the Total Distance Travelled, as if the whole Three were One Railway.

GRAHAM, PRINTER.

Tables of tonnage dues and hire charges, Monkland Railways

spent £1,000 maintaining and operating its inclines, and drew £1,900 in revenue.

The peculiar physical characteristics of the Monkland lines were reflected in the titles of the company employees—inclinemen, bankheadmen, travelling porters. The bankheadmen prepared the trains for the descent of the system's formidable inclines. After he had secured the drag ropes and safety chains, inspected the couplings and applied 'snibbles' to the wheels he handed the train over to the inclineman whose job it was to ensure its cautious passage down the incline. The travelling porter was in effect a human single line tablet—a pilotman.

The Monkland proprietors were canal minded; they knew that the success of their railways depended on the prosperity of the canals they fed. Thomas and William Grahame of Kilsyth, who were on the boards of the M & K and the Ballochney, were enthusiastic canal men. When the Forth & Cart Canal was promoted the Monkland proprietors supported it financially—the Ballochney bought the theodolite used in the survey—for they saw in it a means whereby Monkland coal could reach the textile mills of Paisley. The Forth & Cart, a short cut linking the main stem of the Forth & Clyde with the Clyde near Kilbowie, created an all water route from Kirkintilloch to the heart of Paisley. In 1836 the M & K agreed to support a branch canal from the Forth & Clyde to Stirling. The directors had in view the establishment of a peculiar two way traffic in coal. Monkland coal, which was 3s (15p) a ton cheaper than Stirlingshire coal, would find a ready market in the area served by the new canal. On the other hand Stirlingshire coal which 'was well adapted for some particular branches of manufacture' might well make its way westward and up the Monkland railways to feed local industries. The Stirling Canal was never built.

In 1833 Thomas Grahame suggested the commissioning of a wagon ferry on the Forth & Clyde Canal to run in conjunction with M & K coal trains. The vessel was an ordinary barge fitted with rails and a turnplate. Loaded coal wagons arriving at Kirkintilloch were run directly on board and the barge was towed to its destination when the wagons were run ashore over lines laid into consumers' premises. Since double trans-shipment was no longer necessary time was saved, and deterioration of the cargo through excessive handling was avoided. Export coal was taken direct to ocean going vessels at Bowling. In 1836 the 'coal waggon boat' earned £540 17s 8d (£540.88).

THE GARNKIRK & GLASGOW

The Garnkirk & Glasgow was the nigger in the Monkland woodpile. Its promoters set out from the start to run the line as a *railway* in direct opposition to the Monkland Canal and the Monkland railways. The Tennant brothers, whose large chemical work adjoined the canal basin at Townhead, Glasgow, were the chief sponsors of the Garnkirk. The Monkland Canal could no longer bring coal in sufficient quantity to the Tennant works. The railway was planned to start from a point close to the works and run east for 8 miles to form a junction with the M & K at Gartsherrie, thus providing a direct all-rail route from the Monklands to Glasgow.

The Garnkirk & Glasgow enlisted the help of the leading railway lights of the day. George Stephenson was asked to provide two steam engines of his latest design. The railway was planned as a double line system capable of carrying passengers and goods at high speeds. The Act was obtained in 1826 and by May 1831 goods trains were operating; beginning on 1 June a passenger coach was attached to the goods trains. The directors won wide publicity for the line by staging an elaborate ceremonial opening on 27 September 1831. In front of invited civic dignitaries and leaders of industry and commerce, the Tennants and their friends gave a convincing demonstration of what steam locomotives could do on a well-planned railway. Both Stephenson engines were functioning that day. While one took the distinguished passengers out to Coatbridge at speeds hitherto undreamed of, the other, in charge of George Stephenson himself, came in from the Monklands with a long train loaded with typical Monkland products.

The Garnkirk advertised rates 25 per cent below those of the M & K. The Monkland Canal cut its rates to one-third of pre-railway level, an inducement which attracted traders to the water route in substantial numbers, to the detriment of both railways. But the convenience and speed of the Garnkirk service earned the line a steadily rising flow of traffic. The M & K board had the disconcerting experience of seeing trains coming

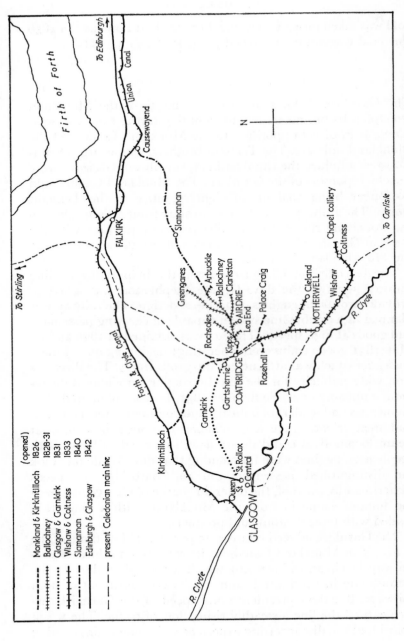

	(opened)
Monkland & Kirkintilloch	1826
Ballochney	1828-31
Glasgow & Garnkirk	1831
Wishaw & Coltness	1833
Slamannan	1840
Edinburgh & Glasgow	1842
present Caledonian main line	

Sketch of early railways in the Monklands, based on an original in Lewin's *The British Railway System*

down from the upland lines and taking the left-hand fork at
Gartsherrie instead of the right-hand fork to Kirkintilloch.

M & K anger at the new railway was vented in a series of
pamphlets and in reports to shareholders which were remark-

RAILWAY PLEASURE TRIPS.

SELECT FIRST-CLASS TRAIN,
AT ONE O'CLOCK,
DURING THE SUMMER MONTHS.

ON Saturday the 20th June current, and daily thereafter during Summer, or till farther notice, a
STEAM ENGINE and TRAIN of FIRST-CLASS
COACHES will leave the RAILWAY DEPOT, Townhead,
at One o'Clock, for GARTSHERRIE, *without stopping at
intermediate stations*; and will RETURN at half-past Two,
reaching Glasgow, at THREE. A limited number of Passengers will only be taken, so as to ensure additional comfort and speed.

FARE, ONE SHILLING.

This arrangement is intended to obviate the objections
made by many to the crowds in the ordinary Trains, and
to the stoppages for Passengers at the intermediate places
on the line of Railway. Genteel Parties will find the trip
an agreeable and healthful mode of spending part of the
day.

THE ORDINARY TRAINS

Continue to run with Passengers to Airdrie, Gartsherrie,
and intermediate places, at *half-past Seven, Eleven, Two*,
and *Five o' Clock*, returning from Airdrie at half-past
Eight, Twelve, Three, and Six; and from Gartsherrie, at
Nine, half-past Twelve, half-past Three, and half-past
Six.—Fare, Sixpence or Ninepence.

The Evening Coach, during June and July, to GART-
SHERRIE, (drawn by a Horse,) starts at a *quarter past
Seven*, and returns at half-past Eight.—Fare, Eightpence
or One Shilling.

Railway Office, 10th June, 1835.

The patrons of this excursion offered by the Garnkirk &
Glasgow Railway in 1835 were expected to derive their
pleasure from the journey itself, only one hour being allowed
at the destination

able for their vituperation. The M & K office was still more alarmed when it became plain that the G & G office supported an expansionist policy. When a Bill was announced for a railway from the eastern end of the Garnkirk to run all the way to Edinburgh, the M & K directors informed their shareholders,

> The object of this Bill is very different from what its title purports. It consists merely of an extension towards the east of a very unimportant railway called the Garnkirk and Glasgow Railway Company. The Projectors of the scheme, and Promoters of the Bill are the Garnkirk Railway Company; and the principal object of it is to effect a sale of their Railway (which had turned out a losing speculation) to a new set of subscribers, under the cover and pretence of promoting a Railway between Edinburgh and Glasgow. In order to obtain leave to bring in the said Bill the promoters of it deposited in the Private Bill Office a fictitious List of Subscribers containing the names of a number of respectable persons who are *not* subscribers, and even of a number of deceased persons and of others who were bankrupt.

With the Monklands booming there was enough trade to bring prosperity to the canals and the railways. The following table illustrates the steady increase in Garnkirk & Glasgow revenue over the first full five years' operations. The drop in tonnage in 1836 was due to 'frequent suspension of work by colliers'.

	Tons	Passengers	Revenue	
1832	114,144	62,605	£6,476 6s 5d	(£6,476.32)
1833	112,471	96,003	£7,234 18s 4d	(£7,234.92)
1834	132,675	117,743	£8,413 11s 3d	(£8,413.56)
1835	143,520	136,724	£9,311 0s 6½d	(£9,311.02½)
1836	137,827	145,703	£10,324 0s 4d	(£10,324.02)

M & K accounts showed that the advent of the Garnkirk & Glasgow did not halt the upward trend of the company's revenue.

1826	£704 2s 11d (704.15)	1831 £3,602 1s 6d (£3,602.07½)
1827	£2,020 0s 0d (£2,020.0)	1832 £4,114 8s 0¼d (£4,114.40)
1828	£2,837 13s 11d (£2,837.70)	1833 £4,578 18s 8¾d (£4,578.94)
1829	£3,480 5s 0d (£3,480.25)	1834 £5,332 1s 1d (£5,332.05)
1830	£3,538 4s 1d (£3,538.20)	1835 £6,260 3s 9d (£6.260.19)

The railways owed much more to the canal than vice versa. The Forth & Clyde accounts for 1836 show a total revenue of £55,593 18s 8d (£55,593.93½). But only £1,624 4s 5d (£1,624.22) of this accrued from M & K railway trade.

THE COMING OF THE LOCOMOTIVE

The news that the Garnkirk on its opening would employ steam locomotives forced the M & K to think in terms of steam power. One can picture the meeting of the Committee of Management when the momentous decision was taken to use locomotives. It is unlikely that any members of the committee had seen a locomotive; they would be relying on the opinion and advice of their engineer, George Dodds. The publicity given to the Rainhill trials of 1829 and the recent success of locomotives on the Liverpool & Manchester Railway prompted some members to press for English-built engines. Dodds, determined to pursue an independent line from the Stephensons, assured the board that the L & M-type engine was liable to damage at 'the high speeds at which they (the proposed M & K engines) had been calculated'.

The committee forthwith 'devolved the whole form and plan' of the engines to Dodds, and Murdoch and Aitken of Glasgow built them. The first was delivered on 10 May 1831—the month that the Garnkirk opened for goods, and the second was put in traffic on 10 September of the same year. They were the first engines built in Glasgow, a city that was to become the world centre of the locomotive trade. The M & K found itself with engines more akin to the early Killingworth engines than to the latest locomotives from the Stephenson stable. However, in the next report to the shareholders the committee *boasted*, 'Mr Dodds in his plans and specifications adopted none of the newest improvements.'

Prior to the arrival of the locomotives the M & K spent £5,925 8s 10d (£5,925.44) in making the line fit to receive them. The engines were intended for the through coal traffic from the Monklands to Kirkintilloch basin, but the low tunnel at Bedlay thwarted this scheme. One engine was placed north of the tunnel, the other south. Each worked its traffic to the tunnel portals, the actual passage of the tunnel being undertaken by horse haulage. The tunnel was opened out, and through working began in January 1832. A locomotive could take a coal train down the line at 5 miles an hour and return the empties at from 3 to 4 miles an hour. If committee members

quibbled at the slow speeds of the new locomotives they were
assured by Dodds that higher speeds would cause great wear
and tear 'and moreover hurt the coals'.

In their report to the shareholders the M & K committee wrote
of the engines in glowing terms and at the same time took the
opportunity to comment on the alleged poor performance of
the neighbouring Garnkirk engines.

> They proved themselves the most efficient engines of their kind ever
> made in the kingdom, being capable of taking ten tons more on a level
> railway than any engine yet made of the same size of cylinder with a
> pressure of fifty pounds to the square inch upon the boiler. The loco-
> motives never required a single horse to assist them, and they were
> never off the road for one day except on two occasions when injured by
> the malice or carelessness of certain waggoners of the road. On the
> other hand the engines procured from England by an adjoining railway
> company have repeatedly been taken off the road on account of need-
> ing repairs. Hundreds of people about Glasgow have frequently seen
> this engine standing hard fast on the Garnkirk Railway with a load
> which one horse could have taken away with ease. It may be asked,
> where was the power of the other three and twenty horses at the time?
> In the stable, it is presumed.

The M & K improvements included doubling of the line. The
Garnkirk used 1½ miles of M & K metals south of Gartsherrie
junction and great confusion arose because much of the Garnkirk traffic was horse-hauled, while the M & K was steam hauled.
The M & K protested that the slower Garnkirk trains delayed
their own traffic on the section of line used jointly. The committee also asserted that careless drivers detached horses and
allowed unbraked wagons to run into and damage the M & K
locomotives. The M & K solved the difficulty by directing that
one line was to be used by steam engines only irrespective of
direction of travel and the other line was to be reserved for
horse-drawn traffic. The double line was, in fact, worked as two
single lines. The Garnkirk objected to this arrangement if only
because it increased the efficiency of its rival, and the working
arrangement became the concern of Parliament, although in a
rather roundabout way.

In 1833 the M & K decided to construct branches to Gunnie
and Rosehall pits and to double the remainder of the main line.
These improvements were not opposed by the Garnkirk as a

corporate body but some of the shareholders, led by Charles Tennant, did object as individuals. Tennant went to London with Thomas Grainger the engineer and began to canvass MPs to oppose the M & K Bill. This obliged the M & K to send representatives to London to 'undeceive' the MPs. The Parliamentary Committee that met to hear Tennant's case described it as 'nugatory and groundless' and at that point most of the members left the committee room. With only seven MPs present Tennant proposed that the following clause be inserted in the M & K Bill. 'That wherever a double line of rails are now or shall be laid down by the said Company one line of such rails shall be set apart and be used by carriages going in one direction, and the other line of rails set apart and used by carriages going in the opposite direction.' By four votes to three the remnants of the committee approved Tennant's suggestion.

When next day the M & K accused Tennant of sharp practice he blandly assured members that he only sought to have applied to the M & K a rule already sanctified on the Stockton & Darlington. This was bluff. The S & D operated steam and horse haulage on separate lines. The M & K well knew this and immediately offered to have a clause inserted in their Bill agreeing to work the line according to the established rules of the S & D. Tennant rejected the suggestion and declared that such a clause would be acceptable only if the M & K agreed to operate according to Liverpool & Manchester principles. The L & M, of course, observed ordinary double line working.

The Bill duly reached a second reading and the House solemnly debated operating procedures on the distant Monkland railways. Argument centred on whether the offending clause should stay or be removed. Mr Joseph Pease (a good railway name) MP for South Durham said,

I can only say that this appears to me to be a clear case. Nothing would tend so much to crush a spirit of enterprise than for this House to impose restrictions on the free use of public works which they had previously authorised to be made without any such restrictions. Here is a rival railway which has already to a certain extent destroyed the revenues of the Monkland and Kirkintilloch which the present Bill proposes to improve, and I think it is rather too much for this House to interfere to enable them to take away the remainder of the revenues of those who are the promoters of the Bill.

The M & K won the day, but Tennant was nothing if not persistent. He got an MP to move the re-insertion of the clause when the Bill came up for a third reading. The move was rejected and the Bill again passed without a division. Tennant then gave notice that he would fight the Bill in the House of Lords and proceedings in the upper chamber were delayed to await the arrival of fresh Garnkirk witnesses from Glasgow. They never turned up, and the M & K got its Act. The relevant operating clause read,

> The Monkland and Kirkintilloch Railway Company shall forthwith make regulations for passing along the said railway similar to those now established or from time to time to be established on the Stockton and Darlington Railway so long as both locomotive engines and horses are used at the same time on the Stockton and Darlington Railway and on the Monkland and Kirkintilloch Railway, and similar to those now established on the Liverpool and Manchester Railway when the trade on the Monkland and Kirkintilloch Railway shall be confined to locomotive engines alone.

The arrival of the locomotive resulted in a complete reversal of operating policy. A locomotive could not be hired out to Tom, Dick or Harry. The companies had to maintain and operate the engines themselves. Soon they were buying back wagons they had sold to the traders, and the Monkland lines began to look like conventional railways.

The Wishaw & Coltness stuck to horse haulage until 1838 when pressure from local traders led to the committee agreeing to allow Garnkirk and M & K engines to work over their line. George Dodds designed three engines for the Wishaw & Coltness, *Wishaw*, *Coltness* and *Cleland*; they were built by James M. Rowan of Glasgow, and came into service in November and December 1840. The Wishaw & Coltness was as pleased with its acquisition as the other Monkland lines had been with their engines. 'When received', said a W & C report, 'they were forthwith applied to the purpose of the traffic, and they have provided the advantages to be derived on this as on the adjoining railways from the more general employment of engines instead of horse haulage. In all cases they have been found to be of great service to the prosperity of the Company's revenue.'

The M & K was the first Scottish railway to build its own locomotives. The work was carried out at first in a workshop rented

Page 51 (*above*) Queen Street station, Glasgow, in 1845; (*below*) the Travel Centre, Queen Street station, Glasgow, in 1970

Page 52 (*above*) Paisley (Gilmour Street) about 1888; (*below*) a Glasgow–Edinburgh express passing Bishopbriggs about 1937

from the Ballochney by William Dodds, son of George Dodds. He was at the same time manager of the Ballochney and engineer of the Monkland. In 1837 the Ballochney workshop was found to be too small for the work offered and the M & K built a new factory at Kipps, opposite the old workshop. An explanatory note on the company's building policy appeared in the report to shareholders for 1838. 'You are aware that the company have for many years been in the practice of making and repairing and adjusting the locomotive engines, wagons etc at a manufactory of their own. The constant recurrence of repairs in wood and ironwork, the distance of the undertaking from Glasgow and the fluctuation of labour and prices in that city, render such a manufactory not only necessary but profitable to the Company.'

Like their kind in other parts of the country the Monkland engines had their detractors. Mrs Drysdale demanded and got £500 before she would allow steam engines to pass through her property on the Wishaw & Coltness. The trustees of the Motherwell turnpike road flatly refused to raise a low bridge to accommodate W & C engines, and the company had to lower the track. The road trustees throughout the Monklands complained of engines fouling the roads with oil at level crossings, and the railway companies had to employ men to see that the crossings were kept clean.

PASSENGER TRAFFIC

'Can General Pasley (of the Board of Trade) really have sanctioned this rickety thing as a passenger railway?' asked a Monkland passenger in a letter to the editor of the *North British Railway and Shipping Journal*. 'Again and again has this company (the Ballochney) had their mineral trains dashed to pieces by the breaking up of the rope or other mishaps upon the incline. Limbs have been lopped off, and lives too sacrificed on the same spot.'

It was a common sight to see a passenger train being pulled slowly up a self-acting incline by a train of loaded coal wagons coming down the adjoining track. The parallel lines converged on to single track at the foot of the incline. There was an occasion on a dark winter night when a rope broke and carriages and coal wagons plunged down their respective slopes to pile up in a heap at the points.

D

From the opening of the Ballochney a horse-drawn passenger coach was run from Leaend, Airdrie to Kirkintilloch. The Garnkirk also ran a passenger service to Leaend from Glasgow —locomotive hauled to Gartsherrie and horse-hauled for the remainder of the journey.

With the opening of the Slamannan Railway a through, if somewhat tortuous, rail link was created between Townhead and Causewayend on the Union Canal, a distance of 25½ miles. Mr Martin, a civil engineer of Glasgow, was commissioned to report on the possibility of running an express passenger service between Glasgow and Edinburgh using the Monkland railways and the Union Canal. Martin reported that only the Garnkirk was fit to take fast trains. Sharp curves and steep gradients were a disadvantage on the other lines but since the Ballochney and the M & K expressed willingness to improve their track Martin suggested that the service be started. He thought that a joint committee of railway and canal interests should be formed with power to own their own engines, rolling stock and canal boats and operate with their own staff. Martin's lack of confidence in the route was shown by his recommendation that a police-man (who was really a lengthman) be appointed to patrol every two miles of track and that these men should be 'well paid and well housed to render them more careful and attentive to their duties'.

The report stated that 333 passengers a day could be carried in two first class and four second class carriages and four canal boats to yield an annual profit of £8,368. Martin worked out distances and travelling times over the route.

	Miles	Minutes
Garnkirk and Glasgow	8	20
M & K	1½	5
Ballochney	3¾	23
Slamannan	12½	40
Union Canal	24	150
Total	49¾	238

Fifteen minutes were added for service stops and interchange at Causewayend making a total time between the cities of 4 hours 13 minutes.

The service which materialised at the opening of the Slamannan Railway was not quite what Martin had visualised. The companies organised the service without establishing an independent committee. The new route was advertised as serving 'Edinburgh and Glasgow and Linlithgow by the Slamannan and Intervening Railways and the Union Canal'. There were two trains each way a day, the combined rail and canal journey taking 4 hours 5 minutes. The eastern part of the inter-city journey could be completed by coach which reduced the total time by 30 minutes, giving the fastest time hitherto achieved between the cities. Fares were 8s (40p) first class and cabin, 5s 6d (27½p) second class and steerage. Coach and rail fares were 10s (50p) first class and inside and 6s (30p) second class and outside.

The railway and canal route had been in operation for less than two years when the opening of the Edinburgh & Glasgow Railway gave a swift, direct railway passage between the cities for the first time. The standard gauge Edinburgh & Glasgow swept in a wide arc north of the Monklands, crossing the M & K by a viaduct near Kirkintilloch and coming within a mile of the eastern terminus of the Slamannan at Causewayend. (When the Slamannan was extended to Bo'ness the extension passed under the E & G at Manuel.) The E & G expected to get traffic from the Monklands, but the break in gauge prevented the through movement of vehicles. However, a 4ft 6in spur was run down from the E & G to the M & K at Kirkintilloch (Garngaber) and an exchange platform established. A passenger service from Airdrie to Glasgow Queen Street began on 25 December 1845, the passengers changing trains at the break in gauge.

The Slamannan trains provided a welcome service for the villages along the line which previously had been very isolated. Regular train trips down to Airdrie became a feature of village life.

In March 1843 the Garnkirk announced that it had opened a station at Coatbridge and that there were 'engine trains plying thereto.' What had happened was that the Garnkirk had built a branch of its own from Gartsherrie into Coatbridge thus by-passing the M & K. The Garnkirk horse coach from Gartsherrie to Airdrie was discontinued on 18 May 1843. By an Act of 1844 the Garnkirk changed its name to Glasgow, Garnkirk &

Coatbridge Railway and extended its avoiding line to Whifflet, thus giving the Garnkirk a route of its own between Gartsherrie and the Wishaw & Coltness at Whifflet. A service began on this line on 14 July 1845.

From 8 May 1843 the Wishaw & Coltness ran a mixed train from Morningside (dep 7.40 am) to Coatbridge (arr 8.50 am) calling at Stirling Road, Overtown Road, Wishaw, Mother-well, Holytown and Carnbroe Iron Works. A through coach from Glasgow (Townhead) was taken on from Coatbridge by the Garnkirk, and there was a corresponding return service late in the afternoon. An omnibus was run from Lanark to Stirling Road in connection with these trains, through tickets being issued from Lanark to Glasgow. Contemporary advertisements indicate that the Garnkirk and its associates made an attempt to generate *tourist* traffic on the mineral railways. The Garnkirk put on a special connection for Stirling Road leaving Townhead at 9 am to connect with the Lanark bus, and urged its patrons to 'Visit the Falls of Clyde'. The advertisement went on, 'Travellers and others will find the above route to the Falls of Clyde at Lanark to be both cheap and expeditious and superior to the present conveyance.' From 16 May 1846 Croall, the Edinburgh stage coach proprietor, ran his *Luck's All* coach from Edinburgh via East, Mid and West Calder to Longridge on the Wilsontown, Morningside & Coltness Railway where a connection was made with a train for Glasgow. The coach left Edinburgh at 11.15 am and the train arrived at Townhead, Glasgow at 3.0 pm. By 1847 the Garnkirk was offering three through trains a day via the Wishaw & Coltness to the WM & C serving Daviedykes, Headlesscross, Crofthead and Longridge. The journey took two hours.

THE GLASGOW, AIRDRIE & MONKLANDS JUNCTION

Between 1836 and 1846 the number of furnaces in blast in and around Coatbridge increased from ten to sixty, and the existing railways were proving inadequate. At one time production was stopped at the ironworks because of a shortage of transport. In 1846 several Monkland ironmasters, among them J. B. Neilson, John Wilson of Dundyvan, William Dixon and Colin Dunlop, promoted a new direct railway to Glasgow. It was to be 11 miles long and to run via Shettleston to a terminus in the heart of Glasgow. It was a Monklands production; £328,000 of the £400,000 capital was held by 117 Monkland shareholders.

The Act of 26 August 1846 that sanctioned the Glasgow, Airdrie & Monklands Junction was one of the most curious railway documents ever to demand the attention of Parliament. The railway depended on getting access to a central goods station in Glasgow. At that time the north bank of the Clyde was served by Townhead station and by Queen Street, both badly placed and cramped for space. The narrow, closely-packed streets of the city seemed to offer no scope to the railway builders.

However, the Monkland promoters had heard that the University of Glasgow in the High Street was contemplating moving to a new site, and High Street was an excellent place for a station. The Monklands Junction undertook to purchase a 23 acre site at Woodlands in the west end of Glasgow and build a new university on it. On an agreed date four years later the railway company would hand over the completed university and receive the old one in exchange. The new university was to consist of a hall, lecture and class-rooms, laboratories, a dissecting room, museum, chapel, library, administrative offices and thirteen houses for staff. In addition the railway company agreed to contribute £10,000 towards the cost of a new hospital. It also agreed to remove all books and equipment from the old university to the new together with stonework of historical or archaeological interest. This curious arrangement appeared in the Act as follows:

> An Act to enable the College of Glasgow to effect an exchange of the present lands and buildings belonging to and occupied by the said College for other sufficient and adequate lands and buildings more advantageously situated and for other purposes relating thereto.

An architect, John Baird, drew up the plans for the new university and contracts to the value of £147,000 were provisionally let. In April 1847 the Lords of the Treasury rejected the plans and returned them to the architect for amendment. It was July 1848 before the plans were approved and by that time the Monkland promoters had abandoned their scheme. They feigned surprise when the university authorities inquired when they were going to start on the building. The university took the railway to court and extracted £12,000 in compensation for breach of contract. The site at Woodlands was sold to Glasgow Corporation in 1852, and was used partly for dwelling houses and partly for the formation of Kelvingrove Park.

THE MONKLAND RAILWAYS COMPANY

In 1844 the Edinburgh & Glasgow opened negotiations with the Monkland lines with a view to taking them over as soon as an Act could be obtained. As a preliminary the Monkland lines handed over all their plant to the E & G on 31 December 1845 and an interim working agreement was reached, the benefit of which was to depend on the uniform operation of the lines. The Monkland companies also undertook to apply for permission to change to standard gauge. The Edinburgh & Glasgow take-over plans were shattered when in May 1846 permission for the amalgamation was refused on the grounds that the district was insufficiently developed for the parliamentary committee to decide whether it was suitable for an amalgamation. The E & G announced that it would withdraw from the Monkland lines on 31 December 1846.

Meanwhile the Caledonian, coming up from Carlisle, was seeking a way through the Monklands into Glasgow. It lured the Wishaw & Coltness into its net by offering a dividend of 10½ per cent on its capital, and the Garnkirk, too, fell to the Caledonian. The major company thus not only obtained a ready-made route into Glasgow but effectively barred the E & G's path into the rich coalfields of Lanarkshire.

The partition of the Monkland railways resulted in the M & K, the Ballochney and the Slamannan drawing closer together. During 1845 and 1846 they separately got Acts to change their lines to standard gauge, and this operation was carried out on 26 and 27 July 1847. On 14 August they got powers to amalgamate to form the Monkland Railways Company. The MRC, with its main line running from Kirkintilloch to Causewayend was a more businesslike concern than the former loosely-knit triumvirate, and it was to survive for seventeen years while the great trunk lines spread and multiplied round it.

The events of 1846–7 gave rise to a railway anomaly that was to exist for almost a hundred years. As well as coming into Glasgow the Caledonian built a 10 mile branch line to link with the Scottish Central at Greenhill. To get access to the branch the Caledonian trains had to leave the Garnkirk at Gartsherrie and traverse 52 chains of the M & K. The Caledonian was granted running powers for all types of traffic for a down payment of £750 and tollage on all traffic proceeding west over the line to points west of Gartsherrie station.

As the railway system developed the North British and the Caledonian became the two contenders in the area. The mighty Caledonian stretched all the way from Carlisle to Aberdeen (240¾ miles) but for 52 chains of the route its trains had to use North British (ex-M & K) metals. The owning company ran only mineral and goods traffic over the section but the Caledonian ran its principal expresses over those 52 chains. Moreover, the North British was 'required to keep the said Portion of Railway clear of all other traffic for a reasonable time before each of such Passenger trains and Mixed trains shall from time to time be due theron'. The Monkland anomaly persisted through LMS and LNE days and the 52 chains did not come into common ownership until nationalisation in 1948.

On 30 December 1907 the Caledonian was authorised to make a spur of its own from Gartsherrie to Glenboig on its north line, the spur to be opened on 15 May 1911, the expiry date of the original running powers agreement. But the spur was never built.

The MRC amalgamated with the E & G on 31 July 1865 and on the following day the North British absorbed the E & G. The Monkland system thus became a part of a 700 mile major railway. To the end it remained a mineral line. The final year's figures showed that the MRC earned £71,544 from minerals, £7,359 from general goods and parcels and £8,125 from passengers.

The main stem of the Monkland railways remained unaltered through the years, but the branches and sidings changed course like the shifting channels of a deltaic river as pits and ironmines opened and closed. Every issue of the OS maps showed a different pattern; indeed the maps became obsolete between the survey and the printing. The high peak of prosperity in the Monklands had passed by the eighties when the best of the ore had been worked out, and supplies were coming in from Cumberland and Spain. The centre of the iron industry then shifted south into the Clyde basin.

Into the early thirties passenger trains were still ambling leisurely through the Monklands on railways built in the canal age. The pioneer proprietors could never have guessed that their property would one day be London-owned. The oldest coaches were relegated to the Monkland lines as were aged drivers to finish their working lives in this quiet byway. The decline in freight traffic was followed by a decline in passenger traffic. Buses now took people from the Slamannan line villages down to Falkirk, and there was less need for the trains to Airdrie. Passenger services on the Slamannan were withdrawn on 1 May 1930.

Today the Monklands, criss-crossed with grass-grown road-beds, often barely traceable and dotted with ruins of long-abandoned installations, make an industrial archaeologist's paradise. The once proud Monkland & Kirkintilloch is little more than a mere branch to Bedlay Colliery. But where the old Monkland lines were incorporated into main lines the original routes survive.

CHAPTER III

Inter-City

A railway to connect a country's two principal cities was bound to attract speculators, especially since both cities were seaports and the 45 miles between them presented few serious engineering difficulties. Glasgow in 1831 had a population of 193,548 and Edinburgh with its port of Leith 162,383; and both had great growth potential. (By 1891 the respective figures were 638,198 and 322,353.) Most of the commerce between the cities was handled by the Forth & Clyde and Union canals. The wave of interest in railways in 1824 produced a proposal for the Edinburgh, Leith, Glasgow, Paisley, Ardrossan & Troon Railway, a line to run 'from the East to the West seas' with trains 'propelled by steam or gas engines'. The Duke of Hamilton and Brandon presided over the first meeting of subscribers on 13 November 1824, but nothing came of the scheme. But with the successful promotion of the Garnkirk & Glasgow, inter-city railway schemes were thick on the ground. Much money, especially English money, was expended on surveys and engineers' reports. There was Charles Tennant's proposal to extend the Garnkirk to Edinburgh. An Edinburgh-based company explored the possibility of running a line westwards along the shores of the Forth and then across the country by Falkirk and Kilsyth to Glasgow. Some of the most prominent English engineers of the day were lured across the Border to take part in the quest for a railway route between the cities, among them George Stephenson, Rastrick and Vignoles.

THE EDINBURGH & GLASGOW RAILWAY

The route that won the day made a sweeping parabola between the cities following fairly closely the path of the Forth & Cydel and Union canals. That was good commercial and engineering sense. The Edinburgh & Glasgow Railway obtained its Act on 4 July 1838. It was English-financed and Scottish-managed. According to the *Railway Times* 90 per cent of the shareholders were domiciled in England, but of the eleven original directors only two were English. There was a high concentration of shareholders in Lancashire. They held regular meetings in Manchester or Liverpool where the prospects and difficulties of their Scottish railway, which few of them had seen, were explained to them in terms of the Liverpool & Manchester. Very soon the Lancashire shareholders were to become thorns in the flesh of the Scottish directors.

Shareholders and management alike expected that the new inter-city railway would, like the L & M, cream off the lucrative local canal traffic. The current Forth & Clyde Canal accounts must have made interesting reading in the E & G board room. In 1836 the canal had earned £55,593 8s 8d (£55,593.43) and had carried 177,593 passengers in its day boats and 20,117 in its night boats.

Falkirk, with a population of 8,209, and half-way along the railway route, was a key point in the transport system of Central Scotland. Lock 16, on the Forth & Clyde Canal just west of the town was a meeting place of land and water routes. Shipping converged on Lock 16 from Grangemouth, Glasgow and Edinburgh, and connecting coaches served Stirling, Perth and the North. Here was a ready-made site for a railway junction of the first importance. Falkirk, too, was the home of the Carron Foundry, one of the most important in Britain. It had made its name manufacturing the species of cannon known as the carronade, but in 1836 it was within twenty years of forsaking armament production for highly profitable domestic ironwork.

The E & G was engineered as a high speed trunk line. Valleys were crossed by viaducts, deep cuttings or tunnels were cut through rock formations. The most spectacular single engineering feature was Robert Telford's magnificent thirty-six arch viaduct across the Almond Valley. At Croy there was a deep cutting through a mile of solid rock. East of Philpstoun the line ran through 3 miles of rock cuttings while at Bishopbriggs at the approaches to Glasgow there was a third major rock cutting. There were tunnels at Falkirk and Winchburgh. The result was an almost completely level route beautifully aligned from Haymarket, Edinburgh to Cowlairs, a distance of 44½ miles. The company had intended to drop the line gently down the remaining 1½ miles into the heart of Glasgow. This involved bridging the Forth & Clyde Canal Port Dundas extension and the canal authorities forced the railway company to take the line in a steep gradient mostly in tunnel under the canal to emerge at the platform ends of its station at Queen Street. The perfection of the high speed railway was thus marred by Cowlairs Incline, a costly and time-wasting feature that had to be worked by stationary engine and cable. The 46 miles of the E & G were completed at a cost of £1,200,000 which compared favourably with £1,407,172 for the 30½ miles of the Liverpool & Manchester.

The opening of the Edinburgh & Glasgow Railway on 21 February 1842 began a new era in the social history of the two cities. For the first time citizens could exchange visits with ease and convenience. The first timetable showed four trains in each direction daily. These left Glasgow and Edinburgh at 7 and 11 am and 3 and 5 pm. Three trains stopped at all stations— Bishopbriggs, Kirkintilloch, Croy, Castlecary, Falkirk, Polmont, Linlithgow, Winchburgh, Ratho, and Corstorphine— and took 2½ hours to the journey. The forenoon train in each direction stopped only at Castlecary, Falkirk and Linlithgow and took 2¼ hours to the journey. Through fares between the cities were 8s (40p) first class, 6s (30p) second class and 4s (20p) third class. Third class passengers were carried by the 6 am luggage trains in both directions at a fare of 2s 6d (12½p).

Passenger traffic exceeded the company's expectations. In their prospectus the directors had estimated the number of passengers at 340,000 per year. Up to 30 June 1842 the E & G trains carried 205,268 passengers. The following table shows the number of passengers and passenger receipts for the years 1844 to 1848.

Year ending	No of passengers	Receipts
31 July 1844	666,206	£80,619
31 July 1845	877,902	£92,837
31 July 1846	1,021,659	£106,456
31 July 1847	1,069,980	£114,181
31 July 1848	1,051,872	£109,888

The most spectacular increase was in third class patronage which rose from 396,634 in 1844 to 764,929 in 1848. Until 1854 passenger revenue exceeded freight revenue, but from 1855 onwards freight produced the major part of the company's revenue.

The E & G had been functioning for only a few months when a group of Edinburgh merchants and bankers sent a memorial to the Lords of the Treasury complaining that mail deliveries in Edinburgh and Glasgow had *deteriorated* since the coming of the railway. This was true, although the deterioration was due to inflexible social custom rather than to railway mismanagement. Hours were long in commercial establishments in those days and the clerks could not have the day's correspondence copied and the originals prepared for dispatch until six or seven o'clock in the evening. It was common practice for clerks to take the letters to their masters' homes to be signed, a process that had to wait until the family had dined. The clerks then took the mail to the post office in time to catch the mail box which closed at ten o'clock. A mail coach left for Glasgow at 10.30 and the letters were delivered first thing next morning.

The E & G doubled its inter-city service a few months after the opening, but even so no train left Edinburgh after seven in the evening. Mail collected in Edinburgh at ten o'clock either had to await the eleven o'clock train next morning or be sent by coach leaving Edinburgh at 4.45 in the morning. In either case the first delivery in Glasgow was missed. If the GPO had called for a mail train at 10.30 it would have had to pay the whole cost, which it declined to do on the grounds that costs had to be kept down to meet the penny post. Public opinion reacted violently when it was suggested that the last collection might be advanced so that the Glasgow bags could catch the seven o'clock train. As one observer put it such a procedure would 'interrupt some very pleasant dinner parties and certainly occasionally the full flow of claret'. The GPO introduced a horse gig which carried the inter-city mail, unguarded, during the night hours.

Second and third class passengers on the E & G travelled in spartan conditions. Third class passengers stood throughout the journey in all weathers in what were virtually crude open trucks. The second class traveller had a roof over his head, but he had to use his ingenuity to escape the blasts that swept through the unglazed windows. Appealing for sitting boards for the third class and windows for the second class, a traveller of 1843 described the rigours of an Edinburgh–Glasgow journey.

> In a second class carriage a few weeks ago the cold draught not only pierced me to the very bone, but I was literally covered with clouds of dust swept through and through by the force of the wind, and the misery of this miserable conveyance was completed by a smart shower effectually battering in the dust upon me, and indeed it would be punishment enough to compel the directors to take a similar trip and thus most effectively have them to consider the sufferings of others.

The coach proprietors, severely hit by the railway, claimed that their conveyances were more comfortable than the trains. Croall put on his *Luck's All* coach in opposition to the railway and ran it via Hamilton in 4 hours at fares of 7s (35p), 5s 6d (27½p) and 4s (20p). 'The First Class or inside of the coach', he explained, 'is handsomely fitted up with Divisions and Arm Rests similar to the First Class Railway Carriages. It must be admitted that no mode of travelling can equal that of a well-appointed four horse coach.' *Luck's All*, on its first return trip from Glasgow was welcomed by large crowds at the West End and cheered all the way along Princes Street.

The pomp and personal attention which saw the departure of the stagecoach had no echo at Queen Street station if the first hand account of a traveller of the period is to be believed. The station booking office was approached by a narrow, dark passage and when he eventually got there the traveller found one man issuing second, third and fourth class tickets.

> Often when the man at the first class table is standing looking on with his hands in his pockets the place is in a state little better than the Black Hole of Calcutta. Among the crowd you may see respectable females often with little children on their hands hemmed in by huge Irish shearers or other characters much less respectable. Of course, the stronger force their way first through the tortuous passage, apparently for no other purpose than to increase the confusion, while the weak and helpless are obliged to submit to positive suffering till the way is cleared.

The scene inside the station was even more chaotic. The second and third-class carriages were well up the tunnel, and the passengers had to squeeze through the narrow space between the sooty tunnel wall and the carriages to reach their seats.

> We got away, however, and were soon enveloped in smoke and steam. But that dreadful tunnel! I thought we were to be in it all night. The engine hissed and snorted and the whole went round, but we were long, long in getting into daylight. When we got there I looked out and found we were merely crawling along; indeed, sometimes we stopped altogether. A good many got out of the carriages, and a proposal was made that all should get out and shove it along.

A passenger who returned to Edinburgh in a forty-carriage excursion train on 7 July 1847 was also involved in an alarming ascent of Cowlairs incline.

> The immense weight on the engine caused certain hooks or chains by which the train was attached to the tender and engine to break. At this time the consternation was very great particularly when it was seen that the engine had left the train. We were ultimately got out of the tunnel, but other two efforts were unsuccessfully made and each time more were brought out more dead than alive with terror and suffocation; and when we did at last get to the top of the incline it was found that many of the females had fainted. There were at least 1,200 to 1,400 persons stowed into somewhere about forty carriages.

A feeling persisted throughout the 1840s that railway travel was not quite safe. That particular excursion did not reach Edinburgh until three o'clock in the morning, by which time the station was besieged by the anxious relatives of the excursionists. Yet official accident figures did not support the popular view of railway safety. In the geographical area covered by this book 2,509,902 passenger journeys were made in the six months ending 30 June 1847. In that time seven people were killed on the railways and five injured. Of the killed, six were railway servants, and the only passenger fatality occurred when a man tried to change compartments while the train was in motion. Of the injured, two were railway servants, one was a contractor who was run down when walking on the line, one was a deaf trespasser, and the last was a passenger who was slightly injured in a minor collision. The following is an analysis of accident returns for the six months in question.

Railway	Passengers carried	Killed	Injured
Ardrossan	39,500		
M & K, Ballochney and Slamannan	122,190	2	
Edinburgh Leith & Granton	258,570		1
Edinburgh & Glasgow	518,155	1	1
Glasgow Paisley & Greenock	395,932		
Glasgow Paisley Kilmarnock & Ayr	467,400	1	3
North British	366,500	1	
Stirlingshire Midland Junct	13,065	1	
Wilsontown Morningside & Coltness	17,938		
Wishaw & Coltness	109,639		
Glasgow Garnkirk & Coatbridge	202,063	1	

The new railways made the people of Central Scotland travel minded; they journeyed in their thousands to see the places that hitherto had only been names to them. For the first time in history the masses got on the move. Hundreds of excursionists from Edinburgh were introduced to the magic of the Firth of Clyde or the Burns country. The advertisements for such excursions gave the impression that the companies were doing the public a great favour in allowing them to enter their trains. The notice of an excursion run from Edinburgh to Ayr in August 1842 began, 'The Directors of the Railway Company, having agreed to allow the subscribers . . .' The excursion was ostensibly for the pupils of the School of Art 'and those friendly to the Institution'. In plain words, anybody who paid for a ticket could go. Institutions and bodies who chartered trains announced that they were operating their excursions 'to take advantage of the generosity of the Railway Directors'.

Industry received a strong impetus from the new railway. In Falkirk, for instance, a rapid expansion of the foundry trade followed the arrival of the railway. Between 1842 and 1872 five new foundries were established. In 1875 three new ironworks were built, and two were brought into operation in 1876 and

1877. In all thirteen new foundries were added between 1854 and 1877.

Troubles assailed the E & G proprietors from various directions. By virtue of certain ancient charters and Acts of Parliament Linlithgow was permitted to levy a local customs duty on carriages and wagons crossing Linlithgow bridge and passing into or through the town. On 4 February 1842 the provost, bailies and council of Linlithgow intimated to the E & G that they intended to levy duty on carriages and wagons crossing the railway bridge and passing through the station. The E & G refused to pay and Linlithgow took the railway company to court. The case began in January 1843 and progressed through various courts with the town winning all the way until in 1853, the House of Lords found in favour of the railway.

The E & G directors included two Sunday trains in their first timetable, and in so doing sparked off a row that locally overshadowed the most important contemporary national events including the momentous debates on the repeal of the Corn Laws. Sunday travel was offensive to a large section of Scottish public opinion and a fierce campaign was mounted against E & G policy. Noisy public meetings took place across the country, traders and travellers were urged to boycott the railway and Sunday travellers arriving at Edinburgh were harangued by a minister preaching a fire-and-brimstone sermon on the station platform. The railway bowed to public opinion and withdrew the trains, but not before its chairman Leadbetter, a Sabbatarian, had resigned.

The E & G was obliged to provide kirk roads at various points along the route. These were paths used by the inhabitants of isolated farms and cottages to get to church on Sundays. Where the railway intersected them the company had to provide stiles in the boundary walls and allow pedestrians to cross the line at these points, but only for the purpose of attending public worship.

When the E & G was extended from Haymarket under the West End of Edinburgh and through Princes Street Gardens to Waverley Bridge the kirk session of the West Kirk 'solemnly resolved to accept no remuneration however large for the passing of the extended railway through their churchyard unless absolute security can be given against railway travelling on the Lord's Day'. The extension was opened on 1 August 1846. It gave the E & G a centrally placed station adjoining and connected with the North British station which had been opened on 22 June 1846 and from which trains ran to Berwick with connections to England.

THE LANCASHIRE PROPRIETORS

A feature of the first two decades of inter-city railway service was the determination of the powerful Lancashire shareholders to play a decisive part in shaping Scottish railway policy. The English shareholders did not see eye to eye with the Scottish management. A Lancashire shareholder reported to a meeting of his fellows in Liverpool, 'I have often in my journeys to Scotland been struck with one fact. I have never seen congregated together a board of directors so utterly inefficient as that of the Edinburgh & Glasgow railway. Mr Learmonth and his co-directors may all be very honourable men in their private capacity, but viewing them as a government I must say that in my humble opinion a more inefficient government never constituted a board of directors.'

The first major clash between the Lancashire proprietors and the E & G board occurred in 1846 over the railway company's policy towards the competing canals. The railway had virtually killed the passenger traffic on the canals, but the canals still retained a worthwhile amount of mineral traffic. The E & G board was haunted by the fear that the Caledonian then under construction from Carlisle to Edinburgh and Glasgow would attempt to seize the Union and Forth & Clyde canals and operate them in opposition to the railway, or even use their beds for the construction of a rival railway. To forestall such a move the railway directors opened negotiations with the canals with a view to acquiring them. The Lancashire proprietors considered it sheer folly to seek amalgamation with parallel canals and so be liable to provide two lots of plant and staff to service one route. They favoured a policy of attrition that would result in the collapse of the canals, and they employed a local firm of solicitors in an effort to thwart board room policy. The letters which passed between Messrs Rowley and Taylor of Manchester and Bannatyne and Kirkwood of Glasgow, the

E

E & G solicitors, throw an interesting light on the relationship between the Lancashire proprietors and the railway management. The following letter was sent from Manchester to Glasgow on 6 August 1846.

Dear Sir,

We beg to inform you that we have received instructions from several influential shareholders to take such measures as we deem desirable in order to prevent the Directors from carrying into effect the various Agreements entered into with the Forth and Clyde and other Canal and Railway Companies and which agreements have not received the sanction of Parliament.

We have obtained the opinion of eminent counsel and which is *very positive* as to the illegality of these Agreements in question; but before proceeding to extremities and in the hope of avoiding expensive litigation we wish to know from you, as the legal advisers to the Company whether the Directors under present circumstances will persist in their endeavours to carry these Agreements into effect. We shall be glad to be informed in the course of the posts whether this is their intention, in which case our instructions are positive. We trust however that legal proceedings may be avoided.

Bannatyne and Kirkwood sent this cautious reply by return of post.

Dear Sirs,

We are favoured with your letter of the 6th current; we shall of course lay this before the first meeting of the Board of Directors, and take their instructions upon it.

But we submit to you, would it not be desirable for you to send us up the case and opinion to which you refer so that we could inform our Directors not only of the precise Agreements to which is referred, but also the grounds they are conceived to be illegal? It would also be desirable that the Directors be informed of the names of your clients.

Rowley and Taylor's reply was dispatched on 10 August.

Dear Sirs,

We beg to acknowledge receipt of your favour of the 8th inst; As we took the opinion of Counsel as alluded to in our last for our own guidance, we can hardly we think be expected to furnish a copy for perusal by the Board, nor do we think that under the circumstances to be called on to furnish a list of our clients. The Chairman of the Board and several other Directors from the various interviews we had when in town must be well aware of the names of some of them. We merely wrote you to know the determination of the Directors in the hope of avoiding further litigation and with the usual courtesy of professional men before proceeding to extremities. We shall await your reply after the meeting of Tuesday next. May we request you to ask the Secretary to furnish us with a full list of the Shareholders, and the number of shares held by each. Our clients have requested us to apply for a complete list up to the present.

The E & G directors agreed to send a list of shareholders to the Lancashire solicitors, but refused to give the individual holdings. In a letter to Rowley and Taylor from Bannatyne and Kirkwood dated 18 August the Glasgow solicitors called their English colleagues' bluff.

Dear Sirs,

The Board directed us to express to you their regret that you should have refused to give them the names of your clients or even to afford them information of the particular Agreements you think illegal, and the grounds on which the supposed illegality rests.

The Board are not aware that you are acquainted with all the Agreements they have entered into with the coterminous Railway Companies, and as you cannot have copies of them may have imperfectly stated the contents of those you are cognisant with in the case laid before Counsel.

Had you furnished the Board with the papers asked, we are directed to state they would have been carefully considered, with reference to the course the Company should pursue, but in absence of these documents the Board can only regret if the concern which they have been placed in charge is plunged into confusion by the adoption of legal steps which are the most unnecessary with the near approach of the Half Yearly Meeting where wishes of the Shareholders can be ascertained.

The Lancashire proprietors won the day in that they forced the E & G to employ J. B. Gregson, an up and coming Lancashire railway administrator, as a consultant. It was said that several English railway companies had offered Gregson the then very generous salary of £2,000 a year for his services. The E & G had to pay him £3,000. Gregson devised a scheme for a unified rail and waterway transport system in the Forth–Clyde valley involving the amalgamation of the Edinburgh & Glasgow, Monkland, Wishaw & Coltness, and Scottish Central railways and the Forth & Clyde, Union and Monkland canals. The plan was not carried out, but Gregson had a hand in shaping the amalgamation of the three Monkland lines.

In 1849 the E & G bought the Union Canal for £209,000. The Lancashire proprietors protested that it was madness to squander money acquiring a beaten rival; they could not appreciate the fear which possible Caledonian intervention inspired in the local management.

ALTERNATIVE ROUTES

On 15 February 1848 the Caledonian was opened from Carlisle to Carstairs with forks from that point to Edinburgh and Glasgow. The forks gave the Caledonian possession of a route between the cities. It was a poor route compared with the E & G; not only was it 8 miles longer, but it was steeply graded in places and the approach to Glasgow through the Monklands was not conducive to high speed. Nevertheless, the Caledonian announced that it would operate an express inter-city service via Carstairs. At the first meeting of the E & G shareholders after the opening of the Caledonian the directors declared that there would be no dividend for the current half year. Instead, the cash available for disbursement would be used to fight the Caledonian. 'We must be prepared to defend our right if invaded.'

The Caledonian service began on 1 April 1848, but it was a poor affair and caused the E & G little concern. There were only four trains a day each way with the best time 2 hours 40 minutes and the worst time 3 hours 6 minutes. Fares were the same as on the E & G. But on 10 July 1848 the Caledonian, relying on the superior performance of its new locomotives, added four non-stop two-hour trains to its Edinburgh and Glasgow timetable. Departures from Glasgow were at 8 and 11 am and 4.15 and 8.30 pm, and from Edinburgh at 8 and 11 am and 4.30 and 8 pm. The E & G countered with four expresses leaving the respective terminals at the same times, one of them doing the journey in 1½ hours.

Then began fare cutting. By the end of July the E & G had reduced its first, second and third class fares to 4s (20p), 3s (15p) and 2s 6d (12½p) and the Caledonian followed suit. The cut fares applied only to through journeys between the cities; passengers joining at intermediate stations had to pay full fares. Thus passengers from Falkirk or Linlithgow to Edinburgh by the E & G or from Lanark to Edinburgh by the Caledonian were charged one third more than through passengers for half the distance. A correspondent in a Glasgow paper likened the contest to 'a skirmish between boys on the street with this difference (not to libel the latter) that there is neither reason, pluck, honesty or honour connected with it.'

The summer was ruinous for both railways. Although the E & G carried an average number of passengers, receipts were nearly halved; dividends were exactly halved—£12 to £6 per cent. The Lancashire shareholders who had interests in both companies suffered a double misfortune. For their mutual protection the rivals made a truce. By 1 September 1848 the E & G first class through fare was up to 10s (50p)—2s (10p) more than it had been on opening day.

Between 1849 and 1870 the E & G (and its successor the North British) established a secondary route between Edinburgh and Glasgow. The first stage, the Edinburgh & Bathgate Railway was opened on 12 November 1849 from a point on the main line near Ratho to the market and manufacturing town of Bathgate which was already served by a branch of the Slamannan Railway from Blackston Junction and by the Wilsontown, Morningside & Coltness Railway from the west and south-west respectively. The second phase came into operation with the opening of the Bathgate & Coatbridge Railway on 11 August 1862. Finally, an extension from Coatbridge (virtually a revival of the Glasgow, Airdrie & Monklands Junction) took the line into the College station in Glasgow. Through services between Edinburgh and Glasgow (College) via Bathgate began on 1 April 1871. Sharp curves and steep gradients prevented the new route from being a real rival, as far as speed was concerned, to the main line, but it passed through rich mineral fields all the way and traffic from that source was very valuable.

Meanwhile, the Caledonian had built a cut-off to eliminate the Carstairs detour. The direct Edinburgh–Glasgow line via Cleland and Midcalder was opened on 9 July 1869 providing a route 46¼ miles long between the cities. The Caledonian was now in a strong position to challenge the former E & G (now North British) supremacy. By 1870 the Caledonian and NB between them were running fifty-four trains a day each way between the cities, many of them nearly empty. The unbridled competition soon gave way to a standard Caledonian pattern of about ten daily stopping trains and five expresses taking 65 minutes for the journey.

The Caledonian line and the North British Bathgate line enclosed a rich mineral belt and the rivals pushed branches into the territory, the Caledonian from the south, the North British from the north. Competition was particularly fierce for the large coal mines with which the area was dotted. The major North British incursion into Caledonian territory was the branch from Polkemmet Junction east of Bathgate to Morningside—the original WM & C. This line passed under the Caledonian line east of Fauldhouse station. A branch off this line took the North British across the Caledonian and into Levenseat Quarry. Farther west on the Bathgate line, at Westcraigs Junction, a North British mineral line climbed up to the Caledonian line at Shotts.

The Caledonian sent a complex system of mineral branches into the area. From Woodmuir Junction east of Breich branches fanned out to serve various collieries, while round Addiewell a separate system served the shale mines. Further east Limefield Junction was another starting point of mineral branches. The lines in this area closely resembled the Monkland lines both for proliferation and profitability. They also were to suffer the same fate; as the minerals became worked out the railways ceased to operate and eventually disappeared. The lines were basically mineral, although the Bathgate–Morningside line carried a passenger service.

A branch line of unusual origin left the Bathgate line $\frac{1}{2}$ mile west of Uphall station. Authorised as a private railway by the Edinburgh District Lunacy Board Act of 30 July 1900 it was opened on 19 June 1905 to serve Bangour Mental Hospital. It was staffed and worked by the North British. The traffic to Bangour consisted entirely of passengers (visitors, patients and staff), coal and freight for the hospital. The North British could book passengers from its station to Bangour, the tickets being marked 'Bangour (Private)'. There was an intermediate station at Dechmont village where many members of the hospital staff lived. The North British had a siding at Dechmont where public traffic was handled. Improved road access led to the abandonment of the Bangour Railway shortly after World War I.

THE STRUGGLE FOR CONTROL

The northern extension of the Caledonian passed under the
E & G main line at Castlecary, swung round to continue on a
course almost parallel with the E & G as far as Greenhill, where
it joined end to end with the Scottish Central. The Scottish
Central continued from Greenhill to Stirling and Perth where
railways already built or promoted extended the line of communication to Dundee and Aberdeen. All traffic coming from
the north and east had to come down the Scottish Central, and
since the traffic fed directly on to the Caledonian that system
was in a fortunate position. But the Edinburgh & Glasgow
proprietors were determined to claim a share of the Scottish
Central traffic. They put in a junction between their line and
the Scottish Central at Greenhill and provided through running
for Scottish Central trains to and from Glasgow Queen Street.
To give Edinburgh a share of the north traffic the Stirlingshire
Midland Junction was authorised on 16 July 1846 to build a line
from Polmont on the E & G through Grahamston (Falkirk) and
across the Forth & Clyde Canal to a junction with the Scottish
Central near Larbert.

The strategic value of the Scottish Central gave rise to much
of the strife between the Caledonian and the Edinburgh &
Glasgow for control of the Forth–Clyde valley. A bewildering
succession of agreements (uneasily observed and frequently
broken), purse-sharing arrangements and proposed amalgamations governed the relationship of the three railways. A proposal
to amalgamate all three was three times turned down by Parliament. The Caledonian tried, unsuccessfully, to get hold of the
E & G. In 1864 the Caledonian sent envoys to the North Eastern
and Great Northern railways suggesting that these lines take
over the E & G in return for giving the Caledonian a free hand
in an attempt to take over the Scottish Central. The climax of
the farce was reached when in 1864 all three Scottish companies went to London (of all places) to negotiate between
themselves. The committees lodged at separate hotels and sent
notes to each other by messengers like the plenipotentiaries of
European powers observing diplomatic niceties before a formal
declaration of war.

The crisis broke when the E & G (which for the moment had a price-fixing agreement with the Caledonian) announced a unilateral reduction of fares and rates. The position was that the North British, unable to forward its traffic from the south over the E & G to the west because of E & G–Caledonian restrictions, had backed a newly promoted independent line between Edinburgh and Glasgow, the Great North British Railway. The new company promised greatly reduced fares, and the E & G simply had to reduce its rates if the Bill for the new line was to be defeated.

In the upshot the North British took over the E & G in 1865 and the Caledonian took over the Scottish Central. The result was that the North British gained entry to Glasgow and became the dominating railway in the Forth–Clyde valley. At the same time the Caledonian was relegated to playing a minor role in Edinburgh.

THE FORTH PORTS

The eastern half of the Edinburgh & Glasgow main line is nowhere far from the Forth and the railway promoters showed great zeal in taking lines down to the ports. Stirling was of little importance as a port at the dawn of the railway age, but Alloa the first port to the east was thriving. Alloa is on the north bank, but on 12 September 1850 the Scottish Central opened a branch from Alloa Junction on its main line north of Larbert to the small harbour of South Alloa from which point passengers and goods were ferried across to Alloa. This arrangement continued until 1 October 1885 when the Alloa Railway provided an extension including a 1,600ft, twenty-span swing bridge, across the river and into Alloa. North British traffic had running powers over this route.

Grangemouth, at the junction of the Forth & Clyde Canal and the Forth, was by far the most important port on the upper reaches. It had been established and developed by the canal company and had built up a large coastal and foreign trade. Most of the traffic from the inland manufacturing areas (as well as export coal) moved along the canal. Grangemouth was only 3 miles from the point where the Stirlingshire Midland Junction line crossed the canal and was an inviting target for

railway promoters. But the canal company, jealous of its preserves, built its own railway from a point 28 chains east of
Grahamston down to the docks. A single line at first, it was
opened for goods in 1860 and for passengers a year later. It was
worked by the E & G and later by the NB.

By the Forth & Clyde Navigation Act of 1887 the Caledonian purchased the canal and all its auxiliaries; the Monkland and Forth & Cart canals, the Drumpellier Railway in the
Monklands *and* the Grangemouth Railway. The Caledonian
thus gained access to territory which the NB had regarded as its
own, and increased its stake in the Forth–Clyde valley. The
Caledonian triumph was neutralised to some extent by con-
cessions which the Caledonian had to grant to the North
British. The NB was given running powers over the Grangemouth branch railway, and access to the entire canal network.
Both companies ran passenger services from Glasgow to
Grangemouth relying on reciprocal running powers.

The net result of the canal take-over was an improvement in
service to manufacturers and traders in the Forth–Clyde valley.
The Caledonian set out to improve the canal and make it pay
its way. It reduced tolls, and abolished tolls for any part of a
passage completed during the night hours. It organised an
efficient cartage service from factories remote from the canal
(some of them served by the North British) and put into service
a fourteen-horse icebreaker to ensure uninterrupted service
during the winter.

Grangemouth prospered under Caledonian management and
in time a second line from the Falkirk area to the docks was
required. This line by-passed Grahamston by leaving the main
line west of the station at Swing Bridge Junction and cutting
across by Bainsford to join the original Grangemouth Railway
at Fouldubs Junction, on the way crossing the canal at Orchard-
hall. The cut-off was built outwards from Grangemouth by the
Caledonian and from Swing Bridge Junction by the North
British. The two sections met and were opened in 1908.

The rise of Grangemouth resulted in the falling into decline
of the ancient port of Borrowstounness (Bo'ness) some three miles
to the east. In the late eighteenth century Defoe described
Bo'ness as second only to Leith for volume of trade with
France and Holland. It was recognised as a head port by the

Customs. The opening of the canal robbed Bo'ness of almost all its trade. In 1810 the Customs withdrew recognition from the port and made Grangemouth the head port; and when the railway age came it was 'a kind of small creek' consisting of two piers enclosing a scouring basin.

The Slamannan & Borrowstounness Railway Act of 1846 gave the Slamannan Railway authority to extend its line from Causewayend to Bo'ness harbour, and to lease the harbour. The town authorities were jubilant; they saw the railway doing for them what the canal had done for Grangemouth. The railway was built, but the harbour was not leased and railborne traffic through the port remained very modest.

In spite of the proximity of Grangemouth the ratepayers of Bo'ness empowered the Harbour Trustees to raise loans to improve the port, offering receipts from future traffic as security. Not surprisingly neither the public nor the Public Works Loan Commissioners would contribute. In near desperation Bo'ness appealed to the railway (now the North British) and in 1878 a new body of eight Harbour Commissioners (four from the town and four from the railway) set about constructing a new dock and basin with a railway loan of £180,000. An increase in trade followed the improvements, but the dual control by town and railway was cumbersome and expensive, and in 1895 the town agreed to transfer the harbour with its considerable liabilities to the North British in exchange for an annuity of £500. But the Caledonian, not content with its conquest of Grangemouth, was determined to thwart the North British in Bo'ness. The Caledonian successfully opposed the NB move and obliged the NB to grant it running powers into the port. The NB had no intention of spending money on a harbour just to have it exploited by its rival, and it withdrew from the scheme.

The people of Bo'ness, rejected by their railway godfather, now supported a Bill to grant the Caledonian running powers into the port on the understanding that it would develop the harbour. To the chagrin of the NB this Bill was granted, and a Caledonian passenger service from Glasgow (Buchanan Street) to Bo'ness began on 1 February 1899. The Caledonian trains left the main line at Carmuirs West Junction, traversed the original Stirlingshire Midland Junction to Polmont, and then followed the Edinburgh and Glasgow main line to Bo'ness

Junction. However, Caledonian intervention proved to be nothing more than a demonstration; it had no more intention of developing the harbour than had the North British. The short-lived passenger service was withdrawn on 1 July 1899. In the end the NB bought the harbour for £282,182 and turned it into a thriving 7-acre wet dock, a 6-acre tidal basin and 2,400ft of quays.

North of Edinburgh the key to communications was the Queensferry Passage, and it was not surprising that early railway promoters had their eyes on this short crossing of the Forth with its well-established ferries. The E & G obtained authority to make a branch from Ratho to South Queensferry in 1845, but the powers lapsed. Revised powers obtained in 1853 allowed the company to build a railway and acquire and work the ferries. The line was opened from Ratho through Kirkliston to Dalmeny on 1 March 1866, to South Queensferry on 1 June 1868, and extended to Port Edgar on 1 October 1878. When the Forth Bridge was opened in March 1890 new connections were made between Winchburgh and Dalmeny for the Glasgow traffic, and between Saughton and Dalmeny for the Edinburgh traffic.

The most important of the Forth ports were Leith, Granton and Newhaven; these are dealt with fully in Chapter IX.

BRANCH LINES

The branches which left the Edinburgh & Glasgow main line on the south side for the most part formed links with the Bathgate line or with the Monkland lines. From Broxburn, the first junction west of Bathgate Junction, a mineral branch was run through the village of Broxburn to join the Bathgate line at Drumshoreland. Further west, opposite Bo'ness Junction, a 1 mile link connected the main line with the Slamannan line at Almond Valley Junction. From that point to Croy the ground rose towards the moorlands to the south of the main line and inhibited the construction of branches in that direction. The next junction was on the down side at Waterside, west of Croy, where direct access was provided to the Monkland lines for traffic to and from the east. Garngaber High Junction, 1¾ miles further on, linked the main line with the Monkland lines giving through running for traffic to and from the west.

On 5 July 1858 the E & G opened its Campsie branch. This left the main line on the up side at Lenzie Junction (near the original Kirkintilloch) dropped down into the Kelvin valley and passed through Kirkintilloch and Milton of Campsie to Lennoxtown at the east end of the Blane Valley and at the foot of the Campsie Fells. The branch, $5\frac{1}{2}$ miles long, was much publicised as a 'picnic' branch. It became a great favourite with Glaswegians. Many thousands of Glasgow children had their first train ride and their first real day in the country by virtue of a Campsie branch excursion. The branch also derived freight from the modest industries, notably print-works, in the small communities it served.

Several lines were built in association with the Campsie branch to exploit the rural valleys between the Campsie Fells and the main line. These little lines were promoted by the valley inhabitants themselves with great gusto, to be worked and eventually taken over by the North British. The Blane Valley Railway, an extension of the Campsie branch through the Blane Valley from Lennoxtown to Killearn (later Dumgoyne) was 8 miles and 29 chains long and was opened for goods on 5 November 1866 and for passengers on 1 July 1867. The rural communities which the line served numbered only a few hundred people and traffic always was sparse. The optimistic local promoters had hoped that the exceptional beauty of the Blane Valley and its proximity to Glasgow would induce the Glasgow merchant community to build large houses in the valley and produce first class traffic. They did just that, but by that time the railway was moribund and the Blane Valley residents swept into Glasgow by car.

The Strathendrick Railway took the line of communication on from Killearn to Aberfoyle making use of the metals of the Forth & Clyde Junction Railway (Stirling to Balloch) between Gartness Junction and Buchlyvie Junction. This line was opened on 1 August 1882 and a through service was offered from Glasgow Queen Street to all stations on the North British, Blane Valley and Strathendrick as well as to two stations, Balfron and Buchlyvie, on the Forth & Clyde Junction. One train serving four railway companies in a 34 mile journey must have led to some intricate behind-the-scenes accountancy. Aberfoyle, a bridgehead for the Trossachs, became a key point for a programme of combined rail and road circular tours organised by the North British.

The River Kelvin rises in the Kilsyth hills and flows westwards for 14 miles to enter the Clyde 2 miles downstream from the city centre of Glasgow. The promoters of the Kelvin Valley Railway were interested in building a line along the $11\frac{1}{4}$ miles of the valley between Kilsyth and Maryhill on the Helensburgh branch of the North British. The line was to cross the Campsie branch just north of Kirkintilloch and $3\frac{1}{2}$ miles west of Kilsyth. The main purpose of the railway was to convey coking coal from the Kelvin Valley pits to the Lanarkshire steelworks via a link with the NB at Birdston Junction near Kirkintilloch, and export coal to the Clyde coal docks via Maryhill. And, like their fellow-promoters of the adjoining 'valley' lines, the KVR proprietors hoped to see established along the route new residential communities.

The promoters were enthusiastic amateurs. The description of the mineral and agricultural resources of their valley in the 1873 KVR prospectus was rather at variance with the sour description of the Kelvin Valley in a current gazetteer. But they were able to whip up local enthusiasm to such an extent that 902 people bought shares and the company was able to announce, 'The North British company are so impressed with the merits of the undertaking, and with the advantages to their own system, that they have entered into an agreement to work the line on favourable terms.' But at the same time, Walker the NB general manager, was reporting to his directors, 'It is simply throwing away money to establish any other stations on the new line than that at Kilsyth, the traffic to and from which would be worked via Lenzie.'

Kilsyth was the only place in the Kelvin Valley worth bothering about, and the NB had paid lip service to the Kelvin Valley because of a Caledonian threat to come into the valley from the east. (A Caledonian branch had already been pushed out from Larbert to Denny in the direction of Kilsyth.) The KVR was authorised on 21 July 1873. The NB built the short eastern section from the Campsie branch (Birdston Junction) to Kilsyth and a passenger and freight service was opened between Kilsyth and Glasgow via Lenzie on 1 June 1878. But having achieved its aim of securing the Kilsyth traffic the major company showed no enthusiasm for completing the 'main' line westwards through the valley to Maryhill. The kv directors complained bitterly about the failure to complete the line and the nb slowly and grudgingly continued with the project. On 4 June 1879 the western section of the kv was opened from Birdston Junction to Maryhill for freight only. There were no fixed signals, the three intermediate stations, Summerston, Balmore and Torrance were without buildings, cranes and weighing machines, and the line was *not* connected with the nb at Maryhill.

The junction at Maryhill was brought into use on 1 October 1879, but no through service was provided between Maryhill and Kilsyth. The nb still continued to route the Glasgow–Kilsyth trains via Lenzie. (One train was run in the morning from Torrance to Maryhill and returned in the evening.) The kv directors, furious because their line was being used as two branches and not as a through route from end to end of the valley, again complained to the nb. The working company agreed to extend the Maryhill–Torrance service to Kilsyth from 29 October 1880. In the first ten days revenue from the extra trains amounted to only a few shillings and the nb, having demonstrated that there was no demand for a service throughout the Kelvin Valley withdrew the trains from the Torrance–Kilsyth section on 31 December 1880.

The Kelvin Valley Railway was amalgamated with the North British on 1 August 1885. The passenger pattern which emerged, and which was maintained for many years, provided a service from Glasgow Queen Street (Low Level) on the Glasgow, City and District line via Maryhill and Torrance to Kilsyth and from Glasgow Queen Street (High Level) via Lenzie to Kilsyth. The expected urban development did not take place and the passenger traffic barely justified the establishment of the intermediate stations. The quiet rural railway enjoyed a brief flurry in May and June each year when on Saturday afternoons long noisy trains full of Sunday School excursionists descended on its little stations.

The railway owed its continuing survival to the fact that the Bairds of Gartsherrie routed their export coal from Gartshore and other collieries over their own private railway system on to the kv and thence to the docks.

The link between Kilsyth and the Caledonian Denny branch

was formed by the Kilsyth & Bonnybridge Railway. This line was first promoted in 1862; revised and extended powers were obtained in 1887 and the line was opened on 2 July 1888 between the Kelvin Valley Railway at Kilsyth and Bonnywater Junction on the Caledonian Denny branch. It was 8½ miles long and single throughout. It ran along the foot of the Kilsyth Hills and parallel with the Forth & Clyde Canal serving the communities of Colzium, Banknock, Dennyloanhead and Bonnybridge. Bonnybridge, an iron-founding town on the canal, had already been given railway communication two years earlier when the Caledonian built a short branch from its main line at Greenhill to Bonnybridge.

The Kilsyth & Bonnybridge was a joint Caledonian and North British enterprise, but it was not a joint railway. It was a 'common' line, with the participants providing their own staffs and trains and sharing expenses. The North British ran trains from Glasgow to Bonnybridge via Kilsyth and the Caledonian undertook to provide reasonable connections to Larbert and the north. The Kelvin Valley and the Kilsyth & Bonnybridge between them provided a secondary route through the Forth–Clyde valley north of the canal.

At Cowlairs Junction the Helensburgh branch (authorised in 1855 as the Glasgow, Dumbarton & Helensburgh Railway) left the main line on the up side, while on the down side the short Sighthill branch authorised in 1853 led round to the E & G company's Sighthill goods depot. This line was also intended to serve as a link between the E & G main line and the Caledonian line out of Glasgow Buchanan Street, but ill-feeling between the companies delayed the completion of the link for several years. The E & G provided accommodation at Sighthill for the Scottish Central to conduct its Glasgow freight business.

ECLIPSE

Falkirk had been a traffic centre in the canal age and the railway age. In the bus age it became the headquarters of Scotland's most enterprising road operator with sad results for the railway network of the Forth–Clyde valley. In the *Falkirk Herald* of 29 March 1919 a bus owner gave the following bus-eye view of the various methods of transport.

On foot   Healthy, but prehistoric.
Cycling   Too much like hard work.
Steamer   Involving train journeys and changes.
Railway   Very costly these days.
Motor touring   The ideal summer pastime.

Study the following table of comparative costs (Railway and Motor) calculated on a party of thirty persons.

Destination	By rail			By motor		
Perth	£15	3s 9d	(£15.19)	£9	2s 6d	(£9.12½)
Grieff	£12	7s 6d	(£12.37½)	£7	2s 6d	(£7.12½)
Dunfermline	£10	2s 6d	(£10.12½)	£6	12s 6d	(£6.62½)

Is there any need for hesitation?

The people of the Forth–Clyde valley did not hesitate; they flocked to the new buses in thousands. The branch lines were first to suffer, and by the 1930s they began to shed their passenger services. Bonnybridge, the last substantial community in the Forth–Clyde valley to be given railway communication, was the first to lose it. The Caledonian branch was closed to passengers on 28 July 1930; the North British service to Bonnybridge ended on 1 February 1935. The Bathgate–Morningside service ended on 1 May 1930.

The Campsie branch and all its associated 'valley' lines lost their passenger services between 1951 and 1964. The rural lines, with their stations often badly sited in relation to the villages they were supposed to serve, were particularly vulnerable to bus competition. Killearn station and Killearn village, for instance, were so far apart that they had separate post offices. The Kelvin Valley service from Maryhill to Kilsyth was withdrawn on 31 March 1951 and from Kirkintilloch to Kilsyth on 4 August 1951. In the following month—29 September 1951 —Aberfoyle saw its last passenger train. The lines were progressively lifted, leaving the once coveted valleys rail-less. The truncated Campsie branch carried a passenger service to Kirkintilloch until 7 September 1964 when it too was withdrawn.

The branches to the River Forth likewise saw the eclipse of their passenger services. The Kirkliston line had its last passenger train on 22 September 1930, the Bo'ness branch closed on 7 May 1956. The Kirkliston line (Queensferry Junction–Dalmeny) was closed entirely on 7 February 1966, but the Bo'ness line has been retained for freight. Passenger services to Grange-mouth and Alloa ceased on 29 January and 16 March 1968 respectively. The Bo'ness branch remains open to Kinniel for mineral traffic.

Pruned of its branch lines and most of its intermediate stations the original main line of the Edinburgh & Glasgow remains vigorous and efficient. By 1971 the stations served were Bishopbriggs, Lenzie (no longer a junction), Croy, Falkirk (High), Polmont, Linlithgow and Haymarket. In steam days the disposal of engines and rolling stock at each end of the short inter-city journey involved much unproductive mileage, with the result that the locomotives spent some three hours on shed for every hour on the road. From 1958 intensively-used DMUS gave a fast, reliable and economic half-hourly service between the cities.

On 3 May 1971 the inter-city service was revolutionised by the replacement of the DMLI's by locomotive-hauled trains (a locomotive at each end) taking only 43 minutes for the journey. Trains departing from Edinburgh and Glasgow on the hour stop only at Haymarket, those leaving at the half-hour stop additionally at Falkirk (High).

The former Caledonian line via Shotts still carries a passenger service, but the passenger service on the Bathgate route ended on 8 January 1956.

F

CHAPTER IV

The South-east Triangle

By February 1842 Edinburgh was in railway communication with Glasgow via the Edinburgh & Glasgow; with Greenock via the Glasgow Paisley & Greenock; and with Ayr via the Glasgow, Paisley Kilmarnock & Ayr railways. But all the territory east and south of the Scottish capital was still without railways—except for the local, horse-operated Edinburgh & Dalkeith, to be described in Chapter IX.

On 8 January 1842 a group of Edinburgh businessmen met in the office of the Edinburgh & Glasgow Railway, under the chairmanship of John Learmonth to discuss the possibility of building railways into the virgin territory. The country the meeting had in mind included 60 miles of coastline between Edinburgh and Berwick on Tweed, and the rich grain producing counties of Haddington and East Lothian. It was decided to start with a modest 30 mile line from Edinburgh to the coastal town of Dunbar, and the North British Railway was formed to construct the line.

The North British failed to attract financial support either in Scotland or England. English capitalists who had given substantial, indeed crucial, support to the Edinburgh & Glasgow saw no merit in what to them was a local Scottish line. The same capitalists indicated that they might be interested in the North British if the line was taken from Edinburgh to Berwick to link with a potential railway that might be built northwards from Newcastle towards the Border.

Edinburgh, with its position at the northern end of the Great North Road, had for generations been a key point in Anglo-Scottish transport. Stagecoaches and carriers used the road, and there was a steady steamer trade between Edinburgh's port of Leith and London. Only the bolder minds accepted the possibility that the railway would become the prime carrier between

Scotland and England. Local railways like the Edinburgh & Glasgow and Glasgow, Paisley Kilmarnock & Ayr had demonstrated that a railway *generated* traffic. Before the railway age people travelled mainly because they had to; when the railways came they travelled because they wanted to. What was not appreciated was that an Anglo-Scottish railway likewise would create new traffic. A census of traffic on the Great North Road and on the Leith–London shipping lane was no more an indication of the potential traffic on an Edinburgh–London railway than was a census taken on the Glasgow–Paisley road an indication of traffic on the Glasgow and Paisley railway. The experts who served on the Royal Commission on Anglo-Scottish services in 1841 were no wiser than the rest when they decided that traffic between Scotland and England would at best justify only one railway, and that line would have to come up the middle of the country through Lancaster, and Carlisle.

It was in this discouraging atmosphere that the North British revised its prospectus and announced that Berwick would be the southern terminus of its line. The far-seeing directors were convinced that sooner or later their line would be linked across the Tweed to an English railway not yet built and that Edinburgh would be put in through rail communication with London. The men of the North British set their sights high. In the south were the Border woollen towns and beyond them, the city of Carlisle, a potential railway key point. As early as 1844 the North British committed its resources to the railway conquest of the great triangle of country bounded by Edinburgh, Berwick and Carlisle. What seemed like a pipe dream in 1844 was a reality by 1862.

The North British Railway was authorised on 4 July 1844 to run from Edinburgh to Berwick with a branch from Longniddry to Haddington. The directors had had considerable trouble over choice of route. Haddington was a royal burgh, and royal burghs were apt to stand on their dignity. Where railway promotion was concerned they expected to be placed prominently on the main line, geographical and engineering considerations notwithstanding. The North British wanted to route its line through Haddington if only because there were several wealthy, potential shareholders in the town whose support the directors were anxious to win. But their very experienced engineer reported that to take the line through Haddington would add greatly to the basic cost and to the expense of working the line when eventually it was built. Haddington, of necessity, was relegated to a branch line, but the North British promised that through carriages would be run to Edinburgh and that convenient connections would be provided with trains going south.

The North British opened for public traffic on 22 June 1846. It took an easy course across the county of Haddington and the East Lothian wheatfields to Dunbar. From that point it turned inland and climbed up a spur of the Lammermuir Hills before descending the valley of the Eye Water to emerge on the coast at Burnmouth. Finally it ran along the cliff tops to a station on the high north bank of the Tweed at Berwick. The nearest railway to the south was at Newcastle more than 60 miles distant. Passengers for the south detrained at Berwick and were taken forward by coach to Newcastle, two rail-and-coach services being provided each weekday. On 1 July 1847 the Newcastle & Berwick Railway reached Tweedmouth on the south bank of the Tweed. There was as yet no railway bridge across the Tweed and passengers for the south were ferried between the North British and Newcastle & Berwick trains by omnibus.

First results seemed to indicate that the assessment of the 1841 Royal Commission had been right. On most days one omnibus was sufficient to transport all the 'international' passengers wanting to cross the Tweed. In 1849, when the railway had been in operation for three years, only 5,792 passengers were booked by the North British from Edinburgh to London. In the same period the shipping lines plying between Leith and Granton and London booked 11,584 passengers. The opening on 29 August 1850 of the Royal Border Bridge across the Tweed produced an increase in traffic. That autumn there was a portent of things to come when the Edinburgh papers reported that 600 visitors from England had assembled on Calton Hill to hear a Mr Cook lecture on the attractions of the Capital. Mr Cook, it appeared, had brought his (paying) guests all the way from Leicester by special train. In the following year passengers went by the thousand to London to see the Great Exhibition at £1 11s 6d (£1.57½) per head third class. The age of international travel for all had dawned.

By running market trains the North British enabled farmers

EXCURSION TO ENGLAND.

Arrangements have been made with the DIREC-
TORS of the NORTH BRITISH & BERWICK
& NEWCASTLE RAILWAYS, for a Cheap Plea-
sure Excursion to

BERWICK AND NEWCASTLE.

A Special Train will leave the North Bridge Station at Seven o'clock, on the Morning of

WEDNESDAY, 22D AUGUST,

Calling to take up Passengers at PORTOBELLO,
INVERESK, LONGNIDDERY (for Haddington),
and DUNBAR, reaching Berwick about Nine
o'clock. The Train will here wait for a few minutes
to take in Passengers from BERWICK to NEW-
CASTLE, arriving in Newcastle about half-past
Eleven.

The Parties who have arranged this trip to England announce it with perfect confidence, on account
of the complete nature of the Travelling arrangements, and because the district of country through
which the Party will pass is famed for its varied
and picturesque scenery. Each Passenger, on Purchasing his Ticket, will be furnished with a Card,
which will inform them of all that is to be seen in
Newcastle.

FARES FROM EDINBURGH TO NEWCASTLE AND BACK :
FIRST CLASS, 15s. ; SECOND CLASS, 12s. ;
THIRD CLASS, 9s.

TO BERWICK AND BACK :
8s., 6s., and 4s. 6d.

FROM BERWICK TO NEWCASTLE AND BACK :
FIRST CLASS, 8s. 6d. ; SECOND CLASS, 6s. 6d. ;
THIRD CLASS, 5s.

Parties from EDINBURGH to NEWCASTLE will
have the privilege of Returning on the 23d or 24th,
by any of the ordinary Trains ; those from Edinburgh to Berwick only, will return by the Half-past
Four o'Clock Train, same day ; and Passengers
from BERWICK to NEWCASTLE will return the same
day, by the Train which leaves Newcastle at a Quarter to Seven P.M.

Tickets to be had at the following places :—
Johnstone & Hunter, 15 Princes' Street ; A. D
Campbell, 58 South Bridge ; Dr. Gray, 20 Bristo
Street ; Dr Menzies, 8 Spence's Place ; T. Fenton,
66 George Street ; M, Fairgrieve, 99 Princes
Street ; A. Muirhead, bookseller, 29 Nicolson
Street ; R. Murray, confectioner, 2 St Patrick
Square ; E. Shepherd, confectioner, 7 Kirkgate,
Leith.
Any other information may be obtained by apply-
ing to J. D. Bennet, 4 Bank Street ; or D. Bruce,
5 Alison Square.

Edinburgh, 14th Aug. 1849.

Excursions to England. A North British Railway advertisement in *The Scotsman* of 18 August 1849 to get fresh produce to the main markets with greater ease and far quicker than ever before. One such train left Berwick at 4.30 am and delivered farm produce to the Edinburgh market, which immediately adjoined the station, at 7.15. A second market train starting from Haddington ran right through to Glasgow. Haddington, however, did rather badly out of the railway. The burgh had housed the biggest grain market in Scotland, but when the railway came dealers found it more convenient to send their grain direct to the larger centres like Glasgow and Edinburgh. And in spite of the demonstrations of the populace when the railway was projected, Haddington gave little support to the line. The branch, built as double line in anticipation of the promised traffic, was singled on 7 October 1856. Every weekday at noon a Scottish produce train left Edinburgh for London with fresh meat and fish and live cattle and sheep. Sheep were carried for 3s 6d (17½p), lambs for 2s 6d (12½p) and a cattle wagon could be hired for the journey to London for £8 6s (£8.30).

Within a few years of the opening of the main line the North British constructed several feeder lines. One, opened on 15 August 1849, ran from Reston on the main line through the Merse of Berwickshire to Dunse (later Duns). One road coach once a day was all the traffic Dunse sent to Reston, but the North British directors, firm in their belief that the branch would create new traffic, built it substantially with double track. They were wrong. The branch had to be singled in 1857 when it was clear that the expected increase in traffic never would materialise. Further north a short branch was taken from Tranent (later Prestonpans) to the Tranent pits a mile south of the main line. Coal was the company's biggest source of revenue. The North British established one of its three coal weighing stations at Tranent; the others were at Niddrie and Falahill. By 1851 the stations were weighing and dispatching to consumers 249,409 tons of coal annually.

Meanwhile, in the Edinburgh area the North British had consolidated its position by acquiring and reconditioning the Edinburgh & Dalkeith Railway, with its strategic routes and long established access to factories and pits.

THE COASTAL BRANCHES

The Edinburgh–Berwick line between Longniddry and Dunbar cut across the base of the peninsula that terminates at Gullane Point. In 1850 the peninsula contained pleasant agricultural and meadowlands with a few scattered communities. North Berwick on the coast 4½ miles from the main line at Drem was the only place of size. It had a population of 1,643 in 1841, a harbour dry at low tide, and a pier from which there was a cargo sailing once a week to Leith, the outward trade being mainly in potatoes with coal and manure the main imports.

When the North British got powers to run a line from Drem to North Berwick on 16 June 1846 the company had in mind the promotion of the town as a high class residential outer suburb of Edinburgh, providing accommodation for professional men who were obliged to work in the city and who wanted to live quietly beside the sea. The railway company made it known to prospective new residents that they would be eligible for one of their Line of Residence tickets, a special kind of season ticket granted by the board to selected applicants provided that the applicants fulfilled certain conditions. The main condition was that the holder must occupy a house situated within a mile of a North British station, that he must work in Edinburgh and use the trains of the North British Railway to travel to and from his place of business. With this scheme the railway company hoped to foster a prosperous community that would contribute a steady flow of first class traffic over the years.

The branch was opened to Williamstown on 13 August 1849 and extended to North Berwick on 17 June 1850. There was an intermediate station at Dirleton. As an act of faith in the future prosperity of the branch the company made a roadbed to take double line although only single line was laid. But traffic did not develop to anything like the extent expected. By the winter of 1856 results were so discouraging that the steam-hauled service between North Berwick and Drem was withdrawn and replaced by a horse-drawn rail vehicle. The resulting deceleration in service caused a Line of Residence ticket holder to sue the North British in the Court of Session for damages of £5,000. The company had no difficulty in proving that the passenger had procured his ticket by presenting false information to the directors; he was merely a summer visitor to North Berwick and did not own a house there. He lost his case.

Regular traffic picked up slowly as the town grew, but it was the summer traffic that made the branch worthwhile. Good beaches and bracing air brought the family holiday-makers flocking to the resort. Scotland, too, was a land of golf, and all the Scottish railways exploited the golf courses on their systems to the full. North Berwick emerged as a first class golfing centre. One course was functioning when the railway came; two more had been added by 1874.

The potential of the peninsula as a golfing enclave was part of the reason for an attempt made in 1893 to reach North Berwick by a second route. The new line was promoted by the Aberlady, Gullane & North Berwick Railway to run from Aberlady Junction near Longniddry on the Edinburgh–Berwick line to a proposed junction with the North Berwick branch near North Berwick, the trains on the new line to use the existing station. The line was opened as far as Gullane on 1 April 1898 and got no further. A railway-owned omnibus filled the gap between Gullane and North Berwick. The Aberlady, Gullane & North Berwick company was absorbed by the North British on 1 August 1890.

More golf courses were opened along the coast. One, Luffness, on the Gullane line, was given a private platform for the exclusive use of its members. The coast branches, before and after World War I, had their own restaurant car named train, the 'Lothian Coast Express'. This train left Glasgow at 3.53 and Edinburgh Waverley at 4.55. It divided at Longniddry, one portion going to Aberlady (5.26 arr) and Gullane (5.32 arr), the other to Drem where it divided again sending portions to North Berwick (5.38 arr) and Dunbar (5.42 arr). The various portions left the following morning from Dunbar (7.55), North Berwick (8.00), Gullane at 8.00, and the train was due to arrive at Edinburgh at 8.43 and Glasgow at 9.46.

Along the 30 miles of rugged, cliff-bound coastline between Dunbar and Berwick there are landing places only at Coldingham Shore, Eyemouth and Burnmouth. Eyemouth stands at the head of a small bay where the Eye Water joins the North

Sea. In 1881 it housed 2,935 people and its business was fishing and fish curing; it was the headquarters of the fishery district extending from St Abbs Head to Amble.

On 13 October 1881 Eyemouth's forty-eight boats left harbour on a routine fishing cruise. On the following day a great storm claimed twenty boats and 129 men leaving Eyemouth with 107 widows and 351 orphans. The stricken village fought to regain its prosperity with such effect that between the date of the disaster and June 1882 the depleted crews landed, among other catches, 1,050 tons of haddock and the processing factories dispatched 67,915 barrels of herrings. Almost all the output was carted to Burnmouth and Berwick for dispatch by rail. The mussel bait used in the industry came from Lincolnshire by train.

It was against this background that a committee consisting of the local Member of Parliament, the chief magistrate and four townsmen met on 11 October 1883 to consider the building of a private railway from Eyemouth to the main line at Burnmouth, a distance of 3 miles. A public meeting held a week later endorsed the idea and a campaign to raise funds was opened. The railway promoters were determined to build the railway on their own, without North British help, although they hoped to come to an agreement with the North British about the working of the line. The scheme suffered from all the defects of an amateur promotion. The would-be railway builders appointed as their solicitor a country lawyer with no experience of railway affairs, and the local bank agent was invited to be secretary 'on the footing that no remuneration can at present be promised'. A local contractor offered to build the line and purchase 300 shares, 'and that he would find a friend who would take up to 600 shares'. He was told he would get the contract if he introduced at least £6,000 of capital and accepted £3,000 of his fee in shares.

The Eyemouth Railway promoters canvassed financial support from fish merchants and salesmen in London, Edinburgh, Glasgow, Birmingham and Manchester. But a year after the first public meeting only 453 shares had been taken up; 338 were purchased outside the village, 82 by townsfolk and only 33 of the 260 by local fishermen. Although insufficient capital had been subscribed to justify the letting of a contract the Eyemouth

Railway was incorporated on 18 August 1884 and a Board of Trade Certificate issued permitting its construction. The engineer urged that construction should begin at once so that advantage could be taken of the prevailing low wages and low cost of materials. Because of these factors it was possible to reduce the capital by £8,000, but even this inducement did not produce the necessary support.

The dispirited board was riven by parochial disputes. One faction wanted to save money by stopping the line short of the village thus obviating the necessity for an expensive bridge over the Eye. Another faction advocated the abandonment of the route as planned and the substitution of an entirely new line that would leave the main line at Reston and enter Eyemouth from the north. The 'new route' faction got the support of Coldingham Shore through which the line was planned to pass. With its fine beach Coldingham thought that a railway would develop the village into a first class resort.

Several years passed with repeated appeals for money falling on deaf ears. Then in 1888 Sir James Miller raised the company out of the financial doldrums by taking 500 shares, a gesture which led the jubilant board into giving him the chairmanship of the company. Construction began in July 1889 and the Eyemouth Railway was opened on 13 April 1891. It had functioned as a private company until 1 August 1890 when it had been taken over by the North British.

With the arrival of the railway Eyemouth developed as a 'family' holiday resort. Fishermen always could find room in their small cottages for a succession of families from Edinburgh or Glasgow and the income from the summer lodgers and the spending money they brought with them played a welcome part in the local economy. Traffic on the branch showed a steady increase. In 1913, 25,593 passengers booked at Eyemouth, while by 1920 the figure was 34,798. The passenger revenue in 1913 was £2,498 and in 1920 £12,102, indicating that individual journeys must have been short—probably most of them were return trips to nearby Berwick for domestic reasons. Goods figures for the same years were £1,628 and £4,278.

THE TWEED TOWNS

The North British attempt to reach Carlisle began with the authorisation of the Edinburgh & Hawick Railway on 31 July 1845. The line ran from the acquired Edinburgh & Dalkeith Railway at Dalhousie up the valley of the South Esk and Gore Water through Gorebridge, Fushiebridge and Tynehead to reach the gap between the Moorfoots and Lammermuirs at Falahill; then it tumbled down the valley of the Gala Water, and passed through the Tweed Valley and by Melrose, St Boswells and Hassendean to Hawick. The opening of the Hawick line on 1 November 1849 put the railway within reach of a group of manufacturing towns.

The River Tweed rises in southern Peeblesshire and, following a winding 94 mile course through the Border hills, enters the sea at Tweedmouth in Northumberland. Tributaries like the Gala, the Teviot, the Leader, the Jed, the Ettrick and the Yarrow pour down side valleys to join the main stream. At the beginning of the railway age the hills that fed the waterways supported great flocks of sheep, the wool from which found its way to the wool towns in the valleys. The pure water of the streams was perfect for the processing of the raw wool, but the streams themselves were useless for transport except for small craft over very short, isolated stretches. Every town had its mills producing superb textiles with the generic name *tweed*. Some of the mills worked on water power because of the difficulty of getting coal along the poor valley roads. North British policy was to see a railway taken to every mill town.

The opening of the Hawick line put the two most important tweed towns in direct communication with the Lothian coalfields—Hawick itself and Galashiels. The effect on Galashiels was immediate and progressive. By 1882 it had four spinning mills and seventeen woollen mills, and its great stone warehouses dispatched fine quality cloths all over the world. Melrose used its talent to convert the raw material of the Tweedside hills into rugs, carpets and hosiery as well as tweeds and tartans. Hitherto little known names—Laidlaw, Pringle and Wilson among others—became synonyms for well designed, top quality textiles.

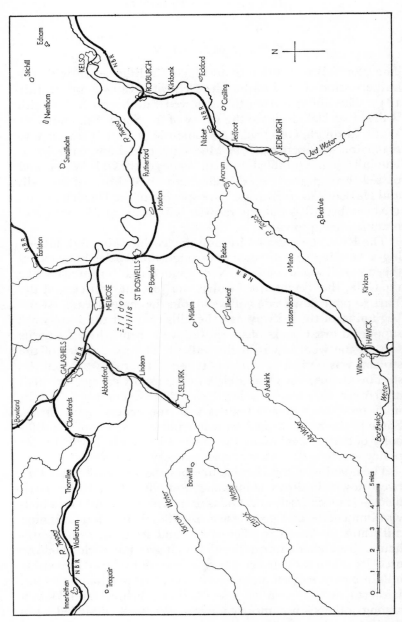

The tweed manufacturing districts

One by one the Tweed towns benefitted from the coming of the railway. In some cases the North British built branches to selected towns, in others communities promoted their own railways to link up with the main stem and eventually to be absorbed by the parent company. The first branch to be constructed ran from St Boswells on the main line to Kelso on the left bank of the Tweed opposite the point where it is joined by the Teviot. The line was first opened to Wallace Nick on the outskirts of Kelso on 17 June 1850 and to Kelso (Maxwellheugh) on 1 June 1851, intermediate stations being provided at Maxton, Rutherford and Roxburgh. The eastern terminus of the branch was only 1½ miles from the western terminus of the York, Newcastle & Berwick railway's line from Tweedmouth. A link was forged between the two systems and a direct route was thus provided between the North of England and the Tweed towns. For a short time through passenger trains were run from Edinburgh to Berwick via Galashiels and Kelso.

A small private company, the Jedburgh Railway Company, promoted a short line to run from Roxburgh on the Kelso branch down to Jedburgh on the left bank of the Jed. It was opened on 17 July 1856 and worked by the North British by which company it was absorbed on 3 July 1860. The stations on the line were Old Ormiston (later Kirkbank), Nisbet and Jedfoot Bridge. The terminal station was ¾ mile from Jedburgh market place, and an omnibus was operated in connection with the trains.

Selkirk on the right bank of the Ettrick Water and 6½ miles from Galashiels got rail communication on 5 April 1856. At the beginning of the nineteenth century Selkirk had been described as 'an ill-built irregular, decaying place fast hastening to extinction'. It was in better fettle when the railway came, and the railway was to ensure its continuing prosperity. Selkirk specialised in Cheviot and Saxony yarns and tweeds and tartans.

On 18 June 1866 a line reached Galashiels from Innerleithen and Peebles. It was, in fact, the continuation of a railway that had been opened by the Peebles Railway Company from Eskbank on the Edinburgh–Hawick line to Peebles on 4 July 1855. With its extension, the Peebles line formed a wide loop between Eskbank and Galashiels embracing Hawthornden, Roslin, Penicuik, and Leadburn as well as Peebles, Cardrona and Innerleithen. Peebles only just qualified as a Tweed town in the manufacturing sense by virtue of its two woollen mills. It functioned mainly as a spa-type resort, a function made possible by the advent of rail connection. In 1881 the Peebles Hydropathic Establishment was built, and the 'hydro' omnibus collecting newly arrived passengers at the station became a familiar feature of the town landscape.

On 4 July 1864 the Leadburn, Linton & Dolphinton Railway opened a railway from Leadburn on the Peebles line to Dolphinton in south-eastern Lanarkshire. The company intended to develop the pleasant country east of Leadburn with stations placed at Lamancha, Coalyburn (later Macbie Hill), West Linton (later Broomlee) and Dolphinton itself. The LL & D was absorbed by the North British on 31 July 1865.

The Berwickshire Railway Company was formed to build a line from Dunse, the terminus of the branch from Reston through Marchmont, Greenlaw, Gordon and Earlston to Ravenswood Junction on the Hawick line just north of St Boswells station. The line was boldly promoted and adequately financed locally, but with a singular lack of vision. What the promoters had in mind was a cross country line providing a direct link between the Edinburgh–Berwick main line and the Edinburgh–Hawick line. The Tweedmouth-Kelso–St Boswells cross country line already provided a similar service and it is difficult to see how the Berwickshire Railway hoped to attract sufficient traffic to justify a second line. Nevertheless, the Berwickshire Railway was built and opened as far as Earlston on 16 November 1863. Between Earlston and St Boswells the railway had to be carried across the gorge of the Tweed at Leaderfoot and the construction of the necessary nineteen-arch masonry viaduct delayed the completion of the line until 2 October 1865.

When the pattern of the Tweed town railways was complete, Galashiels and St Boswells emerged as the key centres. Traffic from Selkirk and Peebles converged on Galashiels, from Kelso and the Berwickshire Railway on St Boswells. The railways served their communities well for many years. In addition to the basic traffic generated by the tweed industry there was brisk business in livestock especially after the autumn cattle fairs. Sir Walter Scott's association with the district—his home at Abbotsford was turned into a literary shrine—gave rise to a thriving trade in tourists eager to see 'the Scott country'.

The peak year for the Tweed town lines was 1920. At Galashiels that year 274,442 passengers bought tickets to the value of £41,781. Goods revenue for the year was £42,376 making the total income of the station £84,157. Hawick booked 127,845 passengers for a revenue of £46,286. With £44,230 added for freight the total income of the station was £90,516. Traffic originating on the Jedburgh branch produced £21,126. The Selkirk branch contributed £34,914. Livestock figures were formidable. St Boswells dispatched 275,771 head during 1920, Hawick 268,780. These were the great local centres of the livestock trade. But almost every station in the area sent cattle to the main markets by train. In 1920 the wayside station at Kirkbank on the Jedburgh branch dispatched 11,748 head. On market days St Boswells and Hawick were like ranch towns, and for days afterwards long livestock trains, many of them bound for destinations south of the Border, followed each other in procession along the lines leading away from the Tweed towns.

THE WAVERLEY ROUTE

When the railway reached Hawick in 1849 it was never the intention of the North British that it would terminate there. Carlisle was the goal. But it was 1862 before North British trains reached Cumbrian soil.

Address : SLOAN & SON,
67 CASTLE STREET AND 49 BROUGHTON. 6954

OPENING OF THE
WAVERLEY ROUTE OF RAILWAY.
THE PRICE OF
ENGLISH COALS GREATLY REDUCED.

PLASHETTS COALS (of the Quality of Newcastle) to be had on application to the SEVERAL STATION-AGENTS of the NORTH BRITISH RAILWAY COMPANY.
September 1862. 502

ROWLANDS' MACASSAR OIL.—

Following the opening of the Waverley route an advertisement in *The Scotsman* of 11 October 1862 offers English coal at reduced rates

The lush plains of Cumberland and the key railway centre of Carlisle were separated from Hawick by barren moorland, daunting to the engineers and holding little prospect of originating traffic. In spite of its uninviting aspect the right of con-

quest of the Border territory was hotly contested by rival promoters. While the North British was planning to extend its
Hawick line to Carlisle the Caledonian showed determination
to build a line out from Carlisle to Hawick.

The North British proposed to take a line from Hawick up
the valley of the Slitrig to Limekilnedge then down Liddesdale
by Newcastleton and Kershopefoot to Scotch Dyke and Carlisle. It was to be a double line trunk route. The Caledonian
line was to follow a route somewhat to the north of the North
British line. It included Langholm in Dumfriesshire, the most
populous town in the area (2,558 in 1861). The Caledonian was
to be a single line; there was no promise that it would become a
trunk line through the Borders. Plainly the Caledonian promoted the railway in an attempt to keep the North British out
of Carlisle.

The Caledonian won the support of Langholm. The Tweed
towns opted wholeheartedly for the North British, thanks
largely to the ebullient North British chairman Richard Hodgson, a Border man himself and Member of Parliament for
Northumberland. Hodgson embarked on a crusade of the
Border towns proclaiming the virtues of the North British line.
His missionary fervour convinced the populace that they had
everything to gain from the North British scheme. Hodgson
became a popular hero. In August 1858 Hawick declared a
public holiday in his honour and a thousand guests (including
the mayor of Carlisle) sat down with him to a grand open-air
dinner in the decorated, beflagged town.

The Border Union (North British) Railway Act received the
royal assent on 21 July 1859. In its final form the line consisted
of a 43 mile main line from Hawick to Carlisle, a branch from
Riddings Junction to Langholm, and another branch from
Longtown to Gretna on the Caledonian main line. The Border
Union Railway was opened throughout on 1 July 1862, and the
route through the Borders from Edinburgh to Carlisle was advertised as the Waverley route, the title being inspired by the
Waverley novels of Sir Walter Scott.

The North British well knew that it would be among enemies
at Carlisle. The Caledonian and London & North Western had
already established an efficient service between Scotland and
England and were to embark on a secret agreement aimed at

Page 101 (*above*) Waverley station, Edinburgh, in 1959; (*below*) cutting the Mound tunnel (north bore), Edinburgh

Page 102 The Lothian Coast Express. This famous North British Railway holiday express, with its well turned out brown locomotive and red carriages, looked very handsome

denying a share of the traffic to the North British. In particular, traffic arriving from the south and destined for Edinburgh was to be sent by the Caledonian unless specifically consigned by the Waverley route. This policy was so effective that North British locomotive stores purchased in the Midlands reached the company's St Margarets works in Edinburgh labelled 'via Caledonian Railway'.

To circumvent the Carlisle blockade the North British leased (and subsequently absorbed) the Carlisle & Silloth Bay Railway & Docks Company's assets in Cumberland. This gave the North British a through route direct from Edinburgh to the port of Silloth on the Cumberland coast. The company was thus in a position to by-pass Carlisle and take freight from any part of its system to Silloth for shipment to Liverpool and other ports in its own or in privately owned steamers. The rates for freight passing through Carlisle were governed by an Anglo-Scottish traffic agreement between the companies concerned. Rates on the North British rail and sea route were not so inhibited. The North British could and did undercut its rivals, and brisk canvassing, especially in Dundee and Leith, won considerable traffic for the Silloth route.

On the day the Border Union Railway was opened there also was opened the associated Border Counties Railway. This line left the Border Union at Riccarton and straggled southward over the hills before crossing the Border to drop down through Bellingham, Reedsmouth and Chollerford to Hexham in the Tyne Gap where it joined the Newcastle–Carlisle line of the North Eastern Railway. To begin with the Border Counties Railway had been an English enterprise. Its promoter, W. H. Charlton of Hesleyside, thought there would be an advantage in taking a railway to the untapped Plashetts coalfield high in the hills on the English side of the Border. But his enthusiasm was not shared by the English capitalists, and the Border Counties made slow progress.

Richard Hodgson and Charlton were friends, and it was not long before direction of the enterprise passed to the North British chairman. He got financial support for the railway from Tweed town manufacturers and other Scottish interests, and the line was brought across the Border and down to the Border Union at Riccarton. The North British got running powers over

G

the North Eastern from Hexham to Newcastle, and a through passenger service was offered from Edinburgh to Newcastle via Galashiels, Riccarton and Hexham. The fastest train on this most circuitous route took 4 hours and 50 minutes. A train stopping at every station, and leaving Edinburgh at 6.40, took 6½ hours.

Great things were expected in the Tweed towns of Plashetts coal. On the very day the railway was opened the new colliery, which had been developed as the railway was under construction, sent samples of coal to merchants in all the Tweed towns. But the coal did not live up to expectations; although it was good house coal, it was not ideal for industrial use. The butchers of Hawick, however, applauded the opening of the line. They found that they could buy beasts at the Newcastle market and have them taken quickly and cheaply to Hawick over the Border Counties. The railway made a modest living from the sheep among which it meandered. At a later stage Armstrong Whitworth established a gun range in the hills and the railway earned revenue from transporting heavy guns between Newcastle and the testing site.

The Waverley route had several offshoots in its first 20 miles out of Edinburgh; these branches are described in the chapter on Edinburgh's railways. On 2 July 1901 a light railway was opened from Fountainhall to Lauder. For many years Lauder had been served by an omnibus (privately operated but subsidised by the North British) which connected with certain trains at Stow. Lauder, situated in Lauderdale on the right bank of the Leader Water, had no other transport except a Monday carrier to Dalkeith and a Galashiels carrier on Saturdays. The light railway made the town much more accessible, especially to trout fishers to whom it was a Mecca.

Waverley route results were disappointing at first, and gave rise to acrimonious discussions in the North British boardroom. Some of the directors had wanted nothing to do with the Border Union and a route to Carlisle. They urged that the whole line south of Hawick be sold to any English company that would buy it—or that it be abandoned. Five million pounds had been sunk in it, and it was earning only branch line revenue. It was not until 1 May 1876 when the Midland reached Carlisle with its own independent Settle–Carlisle line that the Waverley route came into its own. The Midland and the North British put on an express service from Edinburgh to London (St Pancras) with the Glasgow & South Western contributing Glasgow–London traffic. The companies made a point of compensating for the longer time spent on the journey (compared with the East Coast and West Coast routes) by providing superior rolling stock. The Waverley route trains did not make serious inroads into the Edinburgh–London traffic by the East Coast—there were nearly four times the number of through trains on the East Coast route than on the Waverley route—but the people of the Tweed towns were given direct services to London and the industrial towns of the north of England and the Midlands.

The Waverley route was only relatively successful. It was a millstone round the necks of its successive owners. Its steep gradients called for expensive double-heading of trains. Maintenance was costly. There was difficulty in keeping it open in wintertime. And always there was the spectre of the unproductive miles between Hawick and Carlisle. The returns for the intermediate stations on the Border Union for 1920—one of the best years on the route—tell their own story.

	Revenue	
	Passenger	*Goods*
	£	£
Stobs	1,016	247
Shankend	147	419
Riccarton Jct	529	1,177
Steele Road	381	181
Newcastleton	2,250	1,425
Kershopefoot	281	131
Penton	1,029	1,425
Riddings Jct	1,262	1,025
Scotch Dyke	486	271
Longtown	4,550	9,025
Harker	249	646

The eleven stations contributed only £28,152 to North British earnings. If the revenue for Longtown (£13,575) is deducted the ten remaining stations contributed a meagre £14,577. And that was in a good year.

THE SOUTH-EAST TRIANGLE NOW

The triangle of country bounded by Edinburgh, Carlisle and Berwick is almost as bare on the present day railway map as it was on the map of 1846 when the North British advertised its first train. The complex of main, cross-country and branch lines built up from the original Edinburgh–Berwick base line with so much expenditure of capital, enterprise and enthusiasm, has vanished. The railway once so wildly welcomed has been forsaken by a populace that no longer has need of its services.

The prosperity of 1920 was deceptive. In the succeeding years the new motor buses and carriers' trucks made inroads into traffic that had belonged exclusively to the railway. Lauder lost its passenger service on 12 September 1932, and on the same day trains ceased calling at Gullane. Passenger service was withdrawn from Dolphinton on 1 April 1933. The Border rivers, which had played their part in bringing the railways into existence, were to deal them a heavy blow. On 12 August 1948 6·28in of rain fell in the area making the rainfall for the week 10·46in. The rivers became raging, destroying torrents! By nightfall the Berwickshire Railway between Dunse (now Duns) and Earlston and the Jedburgh branch were so badly damaged that it was decided to close them to passengers there and then. The Duns and Selkirk branches were closed to passengers on 10 September 1951. The last passenger train ran on the Border Counties line on 15 October 1956. The services to Galashiels via Peebles and from Eyemouth to Burnmouth ended on 5 February 1962. The end of the passenger service was followed in most cases by the withdrawal of freight and the lifting of the lines. By 1968, of all the North British branches in the triangle, only the North Berwick branch remained.

By 1968 the Waverley route itself was in jeopardy. The trains still carried a reasonable number of passengers from Edinburgh to Leeds and Sheffield, but few passengers travelled beyond Sheffield. The trains which left Edinburgh as Anglo-Scottish expresses functioned in their last hundred miles or so as English local trains. A survey taken between Kettering and St Pancras on board an Edinburgh-London express on a peak Saturday in July 1963 showed that fewer than forty people were being carried, and not all of them from Scotland, although the train had been full and standing as far as Leeds. The writing was on the wall for the Waverley route. The Midland route trains could be sent over the old Caledonian line from Edinburgh to Carlisle. The Tweed towns would be deprived of rail communication, but the ravages of the motorcar had already reduced patronage of the rail facilities. Only over the lonely stretch of line between Hawick and Carlisle were the people as dependent on the railway in 1968 as they had been when it was opened in 1862. Roads were few, and road transport so inadequate that any person in Newcastleton who had to visit a Carlisle hospital for out-patient treatment could not have got back to his home on the same day had he depended on the bus. The railway was essential to the few. But their interests were sacrificed in the cause of economy. The Waverley route was closed on 6 January 1969.

The last up train over the route was the night sleeper that left Edinburgh on the night of Sunday, 5 January 1969. When it reached Newcastleton in the early hours of the winter morning the level-crossing gates were padlocked against it and the people of the village were massed to meet it. They barred the passage of the important London train, the last they would see, for more than an hour. It was a stirring if futile episode in the story of the Border railways, but a far cry from that summer evening in Hawick so long ago when the whole town cheered Richard Hodgson for bringing the railway to the Borders.

CHAPTER V

The South-west Triangle

THE AYRSHIRE RAILWAY

Some six years before the gentlemen in Edinburgh sat pondering over the rail conquest of the south-east triangle, a like-minded group of Glasgow men met to consider the feasibility of spreading a railway network over the corresponding south-west triangle. The base line of the triangle was envisaged as stretching from Portpatrick on the extreme west coast of Wigtownshire, along the Scottish side of the Solway to terminate at Carlisle. The sides were to be lines drawn from Glasgow to Carlisle and Glasgow to Portpatrick. The triangle would thus enclose the counties of Renfrew, Dumfries, Ayr, Kirkcudbright and Wigtown.

The south-west and south-east triangles had certain common characteristics. Like its eastern counterpart the south-west triangle had a long coastline with ports capable of exploitation. There were market and manufacturing towns like Paisley, Kilmarnock and Dumfries. There were mineral fields and farmlands. There were river valleys and passes through which a route might be taken into England. The Scott country of the south-east triangle had a literary parallel in the Burns country of the south-west. In the end one company was to develop and dominate the south-west as the North British did the south-east.

A major transportation scheme for the area was introduced on 20 June 1806 with the authorisation of the Glasgow, Paisley & Ardrossan Canal. This boldly planned waterway was intended to link Glasgow through Paisley, Johnstone and the Garnock Valley with the port of Ardrossan on the Ayrshire coast. Cargoes from Glasgow, instead of having to make the difficult passage down the shallow River Clyde and through the

Firth of Clyde with its contrary winds, would be dispatched cross-country by barge for a swift journey to Ardrossan unimpeded by navigational difficulties. Ardrossan was seen as a coming, major deep-sea port.

The canal was opened from Glasgow to Johnstone on 4 November 1813. All on one level it was easily operated, and although it was some twenty miles short of its objective it generated a gratifying traffic in passengers and freight. Nevertheless, the promoters had to call a long pause for money-raising purposes, and during the pause the transport scene changed radically. A deepened Clyde was no longer a hazard to vessels trading from the heart of Glasgow and contrary winds were no obstacle to the new steamboats navigating the Firth. Most significant of all the railway age had dawned. The canal proprietors, bowing to progress, decided to continue their project westwards as a railway. The Ardrossan & Johnstone Railway was authorised on 14 June 1827.

Meanwhile, pioneer railway promoters were examining the possibility of a modest but potentially profitable line from Paisley to Glasgow. In 1829 and again in 1830 a census of pedestrians was taken on the Glasgow and Paisley road. The results, reported for one week of each year, were as follows.

	1829	1830
Monday	538	589
Tuesday	441	461
Wednesday	593	466
Thursday	434	397
Friday	541	483
Saturday	1,223	1,065
Sunday		1,154

But the major movement between the two centres took place by canal. The canal had made mass transport cheap and convenient for the first time and increasing patronage of its services acted as a spur to the railway promoters. Statistics of traffic on the canal between 1831 and 1836 gave a convincing picture of the growing trade. (See table on p 111.)

If any further inducement was needed the promoters found it in the rapidly rising population figures in the counties west and south of Glasgow. Between 1821 and 1831 the population

THE
FOUNDATION STONE OF THIS VIADUCT,
on the Line of the
Cumnock Branch of the Glasgow, Paisley, Kilmarnock & Ayr Railway,
was laid according to the ancient usages of Masonry,
ON THE FIFTH DAY OF SEPTEMBER,
IN THE YEAR OF OUR LORD ONE THOUSAND, EIGHT HUNDRED & FORTY SIX,
IN THE TENTH YEAR OF THE REIGN OF
HER MAJESTY QUEEN VICTORIA;
AND IN THE YEAR OF MASONRY FIVE THOUSAND, EIGHT HUNDRED AND FORTY SIX.

Officers of Mother Kilwinning Lodge.

George Fullarton Esqr. of Fullarton, M.W. G.M & P.G.M.
George Johnstone Esqr. of Redburn, M.W.D.M.
John Wyllie Esqr. Kilwinning, Senior Grand Warden.
James Small Esqr. Kilwinning, Junior Grand Warden.
James Blair Esqr. Kilwinning, Secretary.
Robert Dickie Esqr. Kilwinning, Treasurer.
Revd. Dr. Archd. Campbell, Chaplain.
Bryce Conn, Tyler.

Railway Directors.

JAMES McCALL ESQR. *CHAIRMAN.*

JAMES CAMPBELL ESQR.	W. G. MITCHELL ESQR.
JOHN HENDERSON ESQR.	JOHN MILLER ESQR.
GEORGE STIRLING ESQR.	R. DOUGLAS ALSTON ESQR.
ARCHD. SMITH ESQR.	HUGH MILLER ESQR.
THOMAS D. DOUGLAS ESQR.	WILLIAM BROOKS ESQR.

Secretary.	Manager.
J. F. SMITH ESQR.	WILLIAM JOHNSTONE ESQR.
Engineer.	Resident Engineer.
JOHN MILLER ESQR.	WILLIAM McCANDLISH ESQR.
Contractors.	Manager of Works.
MESSRS. ROSS & MITCHELL.	MR. JOHN FULTON.

ENGD. BY ALLAN & FERGUSON,
GLASGOW.

A reproduction of an original engraving presented to a guest at the opening of the Ballochmyle Viaduct. The ceremony was more a Masonic than a railway occasion of Ayr had risen from 86,541 to 145,055, Dumfries from 62,960 to 73,770, Kirkcudbright from 33,684 to 40,590, and Renfrew from 93,172 to 133,443. The increase in twenty years over the whole area was 125,808.

	Passengers	Goods (Tons)
1831	29,455	48,191
1832	148,516	51,198
1833	240,062	53,194
1834	307,275	57,853
1835	373,290	60,510
1836	423,186	67,305

By 1836 there were two serious contenders in the field, one group aiming at building a railway from Glasgow to Paisley and Ayr, the other a line from Glasgow to Paisley and Greenock. After some preliminary skirmishing for ground between Glasgow and Paisley, the rival promoters decided to build a joint line between the two points. The Greenock company's line diverged at Paisley, and its affairs will be discussed in a later chapter. The Ayrshire company intended to follow the route proposed for the canal through the Garnock Valley and then along the coast to a terminus at Ayr 40 miles from Glasgow. There was to be a branch from Dalry to Kilmarnock. This plan pleased everybody except the people of Kilmarnock who objected to being relegated to a branch line, and they produced a scheme of their own which would put Kilmarnock on the main line. The Kilmarnock line was to climb directly over the Renfrewshire uplands from Glasgow to Kilmarnock thence by Troon and Monkton to Ayr. Kilmarnock was to the Ayrshire company what Haddington had been to the North British. It was an important place with merchants and manufacturers who were potential shareholders and customers, and whom the railway wished to placate. But the price of pleasing Kilmarnock was a steeply-graded main line which would be expensive to operate. The Ayrshire promoters wisely asked George Stephenson to adjudicate and his verdict was for the easy way round through the Garnock Valley. This route was remarkably attractive to the engineers. The stations at Glasgow and Ayr were respectively 35 and 24ft above sea level and the highest point of the line at Kilbirnie Loch was only 95ft above sea level. Apart from

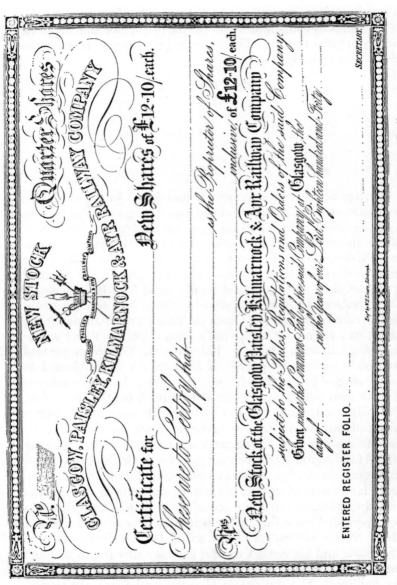

A share certificate of the Glasgow, Paisley, Kilmarnock & Ayr Railway

some earth cutting near Johnstone and a 224yd tunnel on the joint line at Arkleston there were no heavy works. The Glasgow, Paisley Kilmarnock & Ayr Railway was authorised on 15 July 1837.

The Act allowed seven years for the completion of the line. In fact, revenue earning trains were running throughout twenty-six months after the cutting of the first sod. The commendable speed of construction was due in part to the fact that the building of the line was entrusted to sixteen local contractors in lengths ranging from 2,000 to 12,520yd. All the contractors had men and plant immediately at hand. For instance a 2,000yd stretch at the west end of Kilbirnie Loch was built by Harvey and Spence of nearby Dalry while the Prestwick–Ayr section was the work of Parker and Robb of Ayr.

The first stretch of line—that from Ayr to Prestwick—was opened only fourteen months after the commencement of the contract. According to a contemporary GPK & A report to shareholders the section was opened far in advance of the rest of the line in order to provide training for the inexperienced crews. But a passenger service was offered too. The line was extended to Kilwinning on 23 March 1840 and to Beith on 1 July. On the thirteenth of the same month the Joint Line was opened from Glasgow to Paisley and extended to Howwood ten days later. The final link between Howwood and Beith came into operation on 12 August 1840. The line was double throughout, but during the construction period passenger trains worked single line on one line only while the other line was used to move constructional materials.

Long before the official opening day GPK & A directors saw that the success of the railway would far exceed their most sanguine expectations. The estimate of revenue for a full year had been £1,407 5s 6d (£1,407.27½). Between 5 August 1839 and 5 August 1840, with the line incomplete, the actual revenue was £5,084 6s 2d (£5,084.31). The number of passengers carried was 137,117 compared with an estimated 21,350. The company had planned to cater for 23,980 local passengers between Glasgow and Paisley between 14 July and 14 August 1840; in fact, 52,696 passengers were carried for an income of £1,835 19s 7d (£1,835.98), instead of the expected £891 14s (£891.70). Glaswegians flocked to the Ayrshire beaches, and coast and country folk packed the city-bound trains which for the first time in history enabled them to make a quick, cheap trip to Glasgow. Passenger capacity was limited only by the shortage of rolling stock and locomotives. As each new locomotive arrived from the maker it was put straight into traffic without trial, a procedure which, according to the engineer of the line, led to 'irregularities'.

The haste of the railway's construction was only too evident to the passengers. The stations listed in the timetable scarcely existed on the ground. At best they were crude ash platforms with rudimentary buildings. Even the Glasgow station was not ready for more than a year after the opening of the line. The trains swirled along in clouds of dust raised from the sand or ash ballast. Third class passengers required considerable endurance. The early third class carriages were delivered with seats but they were removed by order of the directors. The entirely open vehicles were divided into four sections by waist-high wooden partitions. The carriages quickly became known to their patrons as *bughts*—sheep pens. (Are ye gaun on the bughts, Jock?) A passenger described a carriage as 'something like a sheep pen mounted on wheels with a bar running from end to end under which you must creep if you wish to lie on the opposite side of the carriage'. The passenger was most tolerant about the clouds of sand with which he was deluged. 'This I do not find fault with as it may be a consequence of the newness of the road. But why is it that there is not even a bare plank on which the third class may sit?' First class passengers took a different view of the journey to the coast. One gentleman commented, 'From here [Barassie] you have scarcely time to give a pinch of snuff to the gentleman seated next to you and make a remark on the prospect around till the belching monster whose locomotive powers, although he has drawn you above thirty miles, are as fresh and vigorous as when he commenced his journey, brings you to the station house at Troon.'

Kilmarnock had to make do with a connecting coach service from Irvine (five trips per day) until the branch from Dalry was opened on 4 April 1843. At first the Kilmarnock & Troon played no part in the new railway system. It continued to function independently as a horse-operated waggonway until 16 July 1846 when it was leased to the GPK & A and regauged and equipped to take locomotives. The line was purchased by the parent system on 16 July 1899.

The advent of the railway in Ayrshire resulted in the quantity of coal shipped from Ardrossan and Troon rising from 169,000 tons in 1836 to 470,000 tons in 1855. Of this 120,000 tons were exported direct to foreign ports and a further 30,000 tons were sent coastwise for transhipment to overseas destinations. The traffic through the ports, however, was one way; imports totalled only 6,000 tons per annum, an imbalance that resulted in much empty stock working on the railways.

An important and immediate effect of the coming of the railway was the opening of the Glengarnock steelworks which became the largest establishment of its kind in Ayrshire. Later, the Nobel explosives factory, hidden for safety among the sand dunes between Irvine and Stevenston, brought lucrative business to the railway.

The effect on the coastal resorts was enormous. The population figures, to the nearest hundred, tell their story more eloquently than words.

	1811	1851	1891	1931	1941
Ardrossan	400	2,100	5,300	6,900	8,600
Saltcoats	3,000	4,300	5,900	10,200	12,500
Largs	700	2,800	3,200	6,100	7,400
Irvine	4,000	7,500	9,100	12,000	14,400
Ayr	5,000	17,600	24,000	36,800	44,500
Prestwick	300	800	1,500	8,500	11,700
Troon	200	2,400	3,300	8,500	10,300

The simple, unspoiled resorts with their glorious beaches and ample accommodation for people who did not mind overcrowding—and Glasgow families of ten or more were used to sleeping in two-roomed houses—attracted a prodigious holiday trade. Day trippers swelled the throng. The resorts never lost their popularity over the years. In 1938 the LMS reported that it was taking between 40,000 and 50,000 passengers to the Ayrshire resorts on a Saturday afternoon. In the same year the company carried 397,600 people to the coast in 'evening breather' trains which left Glasgow and other places when the factories and offices closed and gave their patrons a few hours on the beaches for fares as low as 1s 3d (6p) return.

In the first year of the GPK & A, the competing Glasgow, Paisley & Johnstone Canal carried 400,000 passengers and 76,000 tons of goods. Moreover the canal carried its third class passengers in 'swift' boats offering them seats, and roofs over their heads. As a first step to winning the canal traffic for the railway the Joint Line and the GPK & A reduced their fares between Glasgow and Johnstone. The canal proprietors in turn cut their fares. The fare war lasted for a year, by the end of which time it was clear that the canal age was all but over. In return for a guaranteed annual payment by the railway of £1,358 the canal company agreed to sell its swifts, omnibuses and parcel vans, to convey passengers at a speed of not more than 4 miles an hour and to pay the railway a toll of 2d for every passenger booked by canal boat. Three days after the signing of the agreement the railway put up its third class fare from Glasgow to Paisley by 100 per cent and three months later by 200 per cent.

NEW ROUTE TO ENGLAND

The GPK & A directors lost no time in exploiting the canal company's valuable assets in the Ardrossan area. By an Incorporation Act of 23 July 1840 the Ardrossan & Johnstone Railway was separated from the canal interests and renamed the Ardrossan Railway. The same Act authorised its regauging and improvement to take locomotives. The permanent way works were implemented in less than a week; on 27 July the locomotive *Firefly* appeared on the Ardrossan Railway which virtually became a branch of the GPK & A from Kilwinning to the new harbour at Ardrossan. On 20 August 1840 the Ayrshire company started a steamer service between Ardrossan and Liverpool in connection with trains from Glasgow.

The new service was inaugurated by *Fire King*, a vessel with a peculiar history. The GPK & A described her in its advertisements as 'a very fast sailing steamship'. She was, in fact, a wooden pleasure yacht, the outcome of a conversation between Assheton Smith, the yachtsman, and Robert Napier, the Clyde engineer. Smith designed the vessel with what he called hollow water lines—moulded concave sections under the bow. Napier engined her, and her owner boldly wagered £5,000 that she would beat anything afloat in a race from Dover round the Eddystone lighthouse. Such was the peculiar craft the railway bought for £23,000 when a brand new orthodox packet steamer could have been had for £16,000.

Somewhat rashly the GPK & A announced that its new service brought London within 24 hours of Glasgow for the first time. The boat train left Glasgow at 2 pm. *Fire King* was due out of Ardrossan at 4 pm and took 13 hours on the voyage. The connecting train from Liverpool was allowed 9 hours to get to London. In theory, with good timekeeping and smart transfer of passengers at Liverpool, the Ayrshire company could fulfil its boast with minutes to spare. In practice the vessel often was late at Liverpool and passengers missed the booked connection. Nevertheless, the railway-operated service caused a flutter in shipping circles. Old-established operators in the Glasgow–Liverpool trade reduced their fares for the single passage from 20s (£1.0) to 15s (75p), the fare charged on the railway boat.

The service failed to attract paying loads. Scottish travellers preferred the traditional route to the south—mail coach to Leith, and steamer from Leith to Hull or London. It was ironical that while the GPK & A was trying to attract freight to the new route, Crouch, the London-based carrier, through agents in Ayr, Kilmarnock and Paisley was getting substantial local freight for transit to London via the East Coast route. By October the Ayrshire company was forced to raise the fare for the Ardrossan–Liverpool passage to 20s (£1.00). A month later the company sold *Fire King* to the experienced operators, George and James Burns, stipulating that the vessel must be employed on the Ardrossan–Liverpool run for at least a year. But after a further month of poor trade the railway released Burns from the terms of the contract and on 15 December 1840 *Fire King* was withdrawn.

When the ship re-emerged on 30 April 1841 as 'the celebrated steamer' it traded between Ardrossan and Fleetwood offering 'steam communication between Glasgow, Manchester, Birmingham and London'. The new service had resulted from the enterprise of the Preston & Wyre Railway which was anxious to exploit its new harbour at Fleetwood. A special boat train left Glasgow on Wednesdays and Fridays to connect with the steamer departure from Ardrossan. The fares were 17s 6d (87½p) cabin and 5s 6d (27½p) steerage. The journey from Fleetwood to London was made over the Preston & Wyre, Grand Junction and London & Birmingham railways. The return services were on Tuesdays and Thursdays, the 9.45 am from Euston connecting with the 9 pm departure of *Fire King* from Fleetwood. In spite of the shortened sea journey the service was not a success. Fleetwood harbour was still unfinished, and berthing difficulties resulted in missed connections with the passengers having to spend a whole day in the town. Once again the sailing was abandoned.

By 1843 the Preston & Wyre had Fleetwood operating smoothly with regular services to the Isle of Man and Ireland, and the English company renewed its attempt to establish a sea link with the GPK & A. A representative visited Glasgow to canvass support from local business men, and on 27 February he was invited to state his case at a meeting of Ayrshire shareholders. He was at pains to point out that Fleetwood harbour was now accessible at all states of the tide. The outcome of the talks was that two vessels, *Her Majesty* and *Royal Consort* were put on the run and operated a thrice weekly service. The response was such that the GPK & A was able to supplement its boat train with a freight only boat train. However, by the end of the decade shippers had the choice of three direct railway routes to England and the importance of the Ardrossan–Fleetwood service diminished.

TRUNK ROUTE TO THE SOUTH

With Ayr and the associated coastal ports secure, the GPK & A turned its attention to finding a rail route to England. The company came to an arrangement with the Glasgow, Dumfries & Carlisle Railway whereby the Ayrshire line would extend its system from Kilmarnock south to Horsecleuch near Old Cumnock while the Dumfries company would build a line north from Carlisle to meet it. The GPK & A extension by itself was an innocuous branch from Kilmarnock and as such did not attract much opposition. But the Glasgow, Dumfries & Carlisle if successful would convert, as was the intention, the harmless branch line into part of an Anglo-Scottish trunk route. The

Page 119 (above) A Caledonian Railway poster of 1915; (below) a typical 'local view' postcard which passed through the mail in 1913. The sender, obviously proud of her local station, says on the reverse, 'The event of the day is the arrival and departure of those stolid looking milk cans'

Page 120 (*above*) Carstairs Junction on 25 April 1913. The overall roof
was demolished the following day; (*below*) Peebles station, North British
Railway

result was that the Dumfries company found itself in the thick of a fierce controversy that raged over the question of whether the Annandale route favoured by the Caledonian or the Nithsdale route of the Dumfries company should be built. At one point the Glasgow, Dumfries & Carlisle considered taking its line across the Solway on a long viaduct to link with railways in Cumberland thus by-passing Carlisle. The Caledonian chairman on the other hand, concerned by public fears expressed at the thought of the railway climbing to Beattock summit, suggested to his board that they abandon their proposed route south of Crawford, and instead take the line through the Dalveen Pass to reach Sanquhar, from which point it could follow the Nithsdale route earmarked by the Dumfries company.

The GPK & A and the GD & C took their bills to Parliament in the spring of 1845. The Ayrshire company's extension was authorised on 28 July, but the Caledonian secured the defeat of the Dumfries bill. An amended bill which provided for the GD & C joining the Caledonian main line at Gretna and its trains running over Caledonian metals into Carlisle received the royal assent on 16 July 1846. The GPK & A extension was opened from Kilmarnock to Auchinleck on 9 August 1848, and to Closeburn on 15 October 1849. The line linked up with the GD & C on 28 October 1850. On that day the Ayrshire and Dumfries companies, with 171 miles of line between them, amalgamated to form the Glasgow & South Western Railway.

The G & SW main line from Glasgow to the south ran via Paisley, Dalry, Kilmarnock, Dumfries and Annan. The section from Glasgow to Kilmarnock was easy but roundabout. The direct line between Glasgow and Kilmarnock which the original directors had favoured and which George Stephenson had vetoed became feasible with the increase in locomotive power, and on 2 June 1865 the South Western got powers to build a cut-off between Glasgow and Kilmarnock via Cathcart, Netherlee and Stewarton.

The Caledonian had reason to be aggrieved at the South Western move. On 27 September 1848 a Caledonian protegé, the Glasgow, Barrhead & Neilston Direct Railway, had been opened as far as Barrhead and on 5 October 1855 was extended to Crofthead. The line, operated as a Glasgow outer suburban route, was nevertheless a Caledonian arrow pointing in the

H

direction of Kilmarnock. For twenty years it remained a threat to the South Western. When the G & SW announced its intention to build its new line to Kilmarnock, the first part of which would run parallel to the long-established Caledonian Barrhead line, the Caledonian sought and obtained an Act to extend its Barrhead line to Kilmarnock. The rival companies then embarked on the folly of building two parallel lines between the two points. The South Western had built a section out from Kilmarnock before the boards reached the sensible conclusion to extend the Caledonian line—which was half-way to Kilmarnock already—to that town as a joint venture. The railway was opened throughout, and with a branch to Beith, on 26 June 1863 as the Glasgow, Barrhead & Kilmarnock Joint Line. The G & SW had acquired a new, improved route to the south at a minimum cost, and the Caledonian had won access to Kilmarnock. The Anglo-Scottish route came fully into its own on 1 May 1876 with the opening of the Midland Railway Settle–Carlisle line and the establishment of through express trains between St Enoch and St Pancras.

THE LURE OF IRELAND

The country south of Ayr and west of Dumfries had less to offer the railway promoters than Ayrshire itself. There were minerals and rich agricultural areas it is true, but there were also high, bare moorlands, and miles of empty coastline, and the few small towns were widely scattered. But beyond the western coast lay Ireland, and it was Ireland that lured the railway speculators. The titles of the early companies showed how men's minds worked; the *Glasgow & Belfast Union Railway*, the *British & Irish Grand Junction Railway*, the *Girvan, Stranraer & North of Ireland Junction Railway*.

To get to Ireland the railway builders first had to get to Portpatrick on the west coast of the Rhinns of Galloway. Building westwards from the railhead at Dumfries meant crossing successively Annandale, the Urr, the Dee, the Fleet, the Cree, the Badenoch and the Luce, all within a space of 70 miles, only to be met by a formidable drop down to Portpatrick village and an awkward entry to the harbour. The approach from the north entailed a long climb over the bleak, brown tableland of South Ayrshire and a corresponding descent to the Wigtownshire coast.

Legend has it that Portpatrick was the place where St Patrick placed his foot when he crossed from Ireland to Scotland in one bound. It was to put a curse on railway builders who tried to reach it. It was a terrible place for both trains and ships to get into. The harbour was a triangular inlet in the cliffs with the sea forming the base of the triangle. It was open to the prevailing south-west winds and the rolling swell that came in from the sea. But it commanded the short sea route to Ireland—Donaghadee faced it only 21 miles away in County Down—and that was a prime consideration in the days of sail. It was through Portpatrick that the Government sent troops to Ireland. The passage was used by 20,000 head of cattle a year, and 10,000 letters passed through Donaghadee every week. In spite of its geographical limitations and successive adverse reports on its operation by experts, the Government refused to relinquish Portpatrick. In 1770 Captain Smeaton CE had reported that Portpatrick could not be made a safe, all-weather harbour, but the Government insisted on spending money on it. Another adverse report by Captain Evans in 1846 was followed by a further expenditure of public money. By then steam had supplanted sail and robbed the short sea route of some of its significance. The Irish mail had been transferred to the Holyhead–Dublin route. The sad little port was in decline economically when the railway builders came along with their ambitious plans. Rigby Wason, the Ayrshire railway promoter who stood to benefit if a railway went through to Portpatrick said, 'I have always denounced the public expenditure at Portpatrick as little short of a swindling transaction, and I cannot be a party to any act which shall compromise such opinion however beneficial it may be to my property.' The grand railways of the 1840s never reached fruition. Instead a series of little railways struggled into existence with local support and, after many vicissitudes, were forged into the two routes which were to become the highways to Ireland.

The approach to Portpatrick through Galloway began with the opening of the Castle Douglas & Dumfries Railway on 7 November 1859. Meanwhile, on 10 August 1857 another company had been authorised to continue the line of communica-

tion from Castle Douglas to Portpatrick and the line was opened
from Castle Douglas to Stranraer on 12 March 1861. The line—
the Portpatrick Railway—reached Portpatrick village on 28
August 1862, and the branch to the harbour was opened on
1 October 1862. Portpatrick was now in direct rail communication with London and a new steamboat service between the
port and Donaghadee provided the much sought after short sea
route to Ireland. Work on improving the unsatisfactory harbour
continued until 1865, some of the money being contributed by
the London & North Western Railway, the English company
with the greatest interest in the route. But the £500,000 spent
on it, as any local fisherman could have forecast, was thrown
away. Portpatrick was abandoned as a packet station in 1874,
and a new packet station was established at Stranraer on the
sheltered waters of Loch Ryan, with Larne now the railway
port in Ireland.

The working of the railway presented problems. The G & SW
worked the Castle Douglas & Dumfries Railway, and it was
expected that that company would take over the whole route.
But by offering the Portpatrick company more favourable rates
the Caledonian got possession, an arrangement that was to last
for nearly twenty years. On 9 July 1877 another small local
company, the Wigtownshire Railway, opened a line from Newton Stewart to Wigtown, Millisle and Whithorn with a branch
from Millisle to the small tidal harbour at Garlieston. By 1885
both the Portpatrick and the Wigtownshire were in dire straits
and the system was saved from collapse by the amalgamation
of the two railways into the Portpatrick & Wigtownshire Joint
Railway under the somewhat ponderous auspices of the London
& North Western, the Midland, the Caledonian and the Glasgow & South Western. Subsequently the trains were worked in
turn by the Caledonian and South Western. Meanwhile, the
Castle Douglas & Dumfries had been vested in the G & SW along
with the Kirkcudbright Railway which had opened from Castle
Douglas to Kirkcudbright on 17 February 1864.

So the Stranraer–Portpatrick section lost its main line status
early in its career and became a branch serving a small coastal
village. The line through Galloway functioned over the years as
a transit medium for people travelling to or from Ireland. The
most important passengers traversed the line at night and never

saw the country through which they passed. In spite of the effort and enthusiasm that went into its construction, the railway's impact on the local community was slight.

The drive south from Ayr began with the opening of the Ayr & Maybole Railway on 15 September 1856 for goods and on 13 October 1856 for passengers. The line was continued to Girvan by the Maybole & Girvan Railway opened on 24 May 1860. The country between Ayr and Girvan was good agricultural land, the potato crop alone offering valuable potential traffic. The promoters had pointed to the untilled fields around Girvan—untilled because there were no adequate means of transporting their products—as an argument in favour of the railway.

Girvan had a small harbour, and there was talk of developing it as packet station for Ireland. But Portpatrick remained the desirable goal in the minds of the railway promoters. However, several years passed before a group of promoters could be found who were courageous (or foolhardy) enough to tackle the unpromising country south of Girvan. The Girvan & Portpatrick Junction Railway, 32 miles long, was built to connect Girvan with Challoch on the Portpatrick Railway and by use of running powers to reach Portpatrick. The building and operation of the line were beset by disasters including the collapse of a major viaduct over the Stinchar and a subsequent costly court case, amateurish management and a chronic shortage of money.

Opened on 5 October 1870 the G & PJ straggled over the moors serving isolated communities whose populations were numbered in hundreds. It depended for its success on transit passengers from Glasgow to Ireland, but the Irish traffic was firmly wedded to the cheap direct sailings from the Clyde and showed scant interest in the short sea route. The G & SW which worked the line found itself operating trains which earned shillings and pence rather than pounds. The G & P J coffers were drained to such an extent that the company had no money with which to pay the tolls demanded by the Portpatrick Railway for use of its metals between Challoch Junction and Portpatrick. On 7 February 1882 the Portpatrick Railway barred the entry of G & PJ trains to its territory, and a through service was not resumed until 3 August 1884. In the spring of 1886 the railway closed down entirely for two months and in the following year

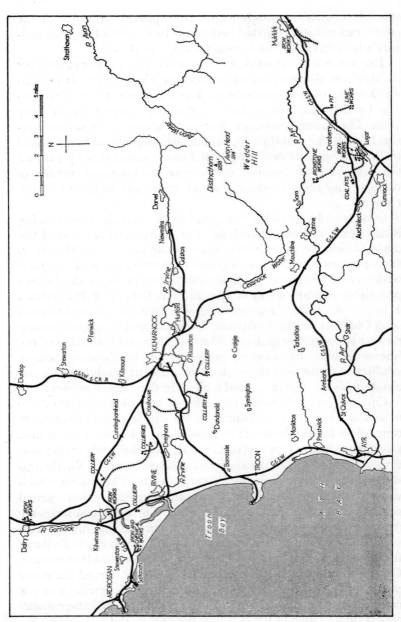

The mineral districts of Ayrshire in 1882

it was reorganised as the Ayrshire & Wigtownshire Railway by a syndicate of London financiers. The line was vested in the G & SW on 26 June 1892.

Ballantrae, the fishing port on the Ayrshire coast 13 miles south of Girvan was the objective of several railway schemes. 'There is at our doors', a local writer commented, 'a vast fishing field waiting for a railway for its full development. A railway to Ballantrae would pay better than any other branch line in the West of Scotland.' A branch could have been taken along the shore from Girvan or down the Stinchar Valley from Pinwherry on the G & PJ; but Ballantrae never got its railway. Nevertheless, during the herring season the port was the scene of lively competition between the Caledonian and the G & SW. The Caledonian carted the fish down the coast road to Stranraer for shipment to Billingsgate via the PP & W. The G & SW used a hundred horses to cart its share of the fish to Girvan. By then the Midland route was open and it was natural that the London-bound fish should be routed G & SW–Midland. But the L & NW found it worth while to have a representative at Girvan to canvass merchants to send their fish by the West Coast route. In March 1877 the LNW agent at Girvan found a Midland man in a fish wagon changing the 'Via LNWR' labels on the herring barrels to 'Via MR'. On complaining to the stationmaster the Euston man was denounced as 'an LNWR prig' and ejected from the station. The affair ended in the local police court.

BRANCHES AND CROSS-COUNTRY LINES

The G & SW served the area between the Kilmarnock–Dumfries main line and the Ayrshire coast line by a system which criss-crossed the mining and agricultural districts of mid-Ayrshire. A line running east from Ayr joined the coast line to the Kilmarnock–Dumfries line at Mauchline. Further north another short cross-country line—the original Kilmarnock & Troon—joined the main line at Barassie. Further north again a line from Closeburn on the Dalry–Kilmarnock line ran to Irvine giving a through connection from Kilmarnock to Ardrossan and Largs.

On 18 March 1854 a branch was taken from Ayr up the Doon Valley to Dalmellington mainly to suit the requirements

of the Dalmellington Iron Company. From Holehouse Junction
on the Dalmellington branch a line was taken east to Cronberry
on the branch from Auchinleck to Muirkirk which had been
opened on 9 August 1848. At Muirkirk the G & SW met head on
with the Caledonian branch from Lanark. A fourth line left the
Rankinston line at Belston Junction to join the Ayr–Mauchline
line at Annbank.

Branches off the Kilmarnock–Dumfries line were Kilmarnock
to Galston (9 August 1848) and Newmilns (20 May 1850), and
the Catrine branch from Brackenhill Junction (1 March 1903).
On 3 January 1905 a light railway was opened between Dumfries and Moniaive to serve the villages of the Cairn Valley.

On 3 January 1905 a new route was opened between Girvan
and Ayr to serve the small villages on the coast. It was a light
railway which left the main line at Alloway Junction and re-
joined it just north of Girvan. Its main function was to serve the
golf course and the large hotel which the G & SW established at
Turnberry in an attempt to create a high class tourist amenity.

NORTH AYRSHIRE DEVELOPMENTS

In the 1880s no fewer than eighty-four pits in the Hamilton
area of Lanarkshire were sending export coal to Ardrossan.
Much of this traffic originated on the Caledonian and was
worked via Rutherglen and Gushetfaulds to continue its
journey to the port over G & SW metals. This fact so irked the
Caledonian that independent rail access to Ardrossan became
a keystone of company policy.

The Glasgow, Barrhead & Kilmarnock, half Caledonian
owned, ran over the hills of North Ayrshire while down in the
valley immediately to the north was the main line of the G & SW.
At one point the two railways were barely 6 miles apart. The
Caledonian saw that by building a short strategic link line between the GB & K and the South Western it could cut out much
G & SW mileage. The result was the authorisation of the Barrmill
& Kilwinning Railway on 20 August 1883. This line, 6½ miles
long, dropped steeply down the hill from Barrmill on the Beith
branch of the GB & K to join the South Western at Kilwinning.
With this line complete the Caledonian would be in a position
to send the Lanarkshire coal over the GB & K to Barrmill thence

by its subsidiary to Kilwinning, thus greatly reducing its dependence on the G & SW.

Even more promising things were in the offing. The Earl of Eglinton, always interested in any scheme which would enhance the value of Ardrossan harbour, gave his support to the Barrmill & Kilwinning. The company was reconstituted as the Lanarkshire & Ayrshire Railway with Eglinton as its chairman, and on 28 August 1884 was authorised to extend $6\frac{1}{4}$ miles from Killwinning to Ardrossan. This meant that the Caledonian now had command of a route from Glasgow to Ardrossan 29 miles 65 chains long compared with the South Western's existing route of 32 miles 33 chains. And that was not all. The 1884 Act empowered the L & A to make branch lines into sensitive G & SW territory. One was from Kilwinning to Irvine and the other from Giffen to Glengarnock steelworks and Kilbirnie, hitherto the preserve of the South Western. The new railway received excellent local support, all but £15,000 of the £375,000 capital required being subscribed without Caledonian help.

The G & SW, alarmed at the imminent invasion of its heartland, on 11 August 1884 invoked running powers which it held over North British lines in Lanarkshire. This enabled the company to reach twenty-eight pits in the Hamilton and Bothwell districts with its own locomotives and crews. It offered to take coal from Lanarkshire to Ardrossan for 9s (45p) a ton less than the rate quoted via Greenock. But the experiment was not a success and was discontinued after six months.

The L & A took its line from Kilwinning to Ardrossan through Stevenston and Saltcoats on a route parallel to the South Western but to the east of it, so that the L & A stations were sited somewhat inconveniently at the backs of the towns. The line was opened from Barrmill to Ardrossan on 4 September 1888, the L & A being allowed to make a temporary connection with the G & SW to give its traffic access to Ardrossan harbour pending the completion of its own harbour facilities. A two platform station was constructed at Montgomerie Pier at the north side of the harbour and a 29 chain extension to it from the town station was brought into use on 2 June 1890. The Kilbirnie branch was opened for goods on 1 November 1889 and for passengers on 2 December 1889. The Irvine branch was opened on 2 June 1890, through carriages being run from Glasgow.

Up to this time privately-owned steamers had sailed from Ardrossan to Ireland, Arran and other destinations in connection with G & SW trains. The Caledonian offered a staggering challenge to its long-established rival. The South Western passengers for Arran were conveyed on a small vessel the *Scotia*. The vessel that met the bright new Arran expresses of the Caledonian Railway at Montgomerie Pier was a large fast paddle steamer, *Duchess of Hamilton*, specially built for the Arran trade and operated by the Caledonian's subsidiary, the Caledonian Steam Packet Company. With the Caledonian paying special attention to timekeeping and comfort three out of every four of *Scotia*'s passengers defected, and the South Western had to subsidise its proprietor to induce him to sail at all. The L & A was equally successful with a 'daylight' service to Belfast and back organised in co-operation with G. & J. Burns using the large steamer *Adder*. So satisfactory was the traffic through Montgomerie Pier that the L & A put in hand the doubling of the single line extension from Ardrossan town and the installation of improved passenger handling facilities at the pier.

Faced with the destruction of its Arran traffic the G & SW fought a bitter and costly legal battle with the Clyde steamer operators for the right to run its own steamers. This right the company won on 2 August 1892. Six and a half months later there was launched from the yard of J. & G. Thomson of Clydebank the vessel that was to retrieve the South Western's fortunes. She was the large two-funnelled paddle steamer *Glen Sannox*. Built regardless of expense she was the fastest vessel on the Clyde. When she inaugurated the G & SW service on 6 June 1892 she berthed at a pier that had been extended and modernised to compare favourably with the Caledonian pier. The scene was now set for a keen contest.

The South Western was in a position to offer a service from Glasgow to Brodick in the remarkable time of 80 minutes. (The best time for the same journey in 1970 was 119 minutes.) The Caledonian at once produced an 80 minute timing which called for smart work on the rail link, for the Caledonian route, although shorter than the South Western, was heavily graded. The Caledonian Arran boat express which left Glasgow Central at 8.45 am was in Ardrossan at 9.30 having stopped only at Eglinton Street (Glasgow). This train was followed by a similarly-timed Belfast boat express at 9.5, the day return fare from Glasgow to Belfast being 6s (30p). The competition led to extremely fast rail timings. In 1897 the G & SW found itself running the fastest train in Britain; this was an up morning boat train which covered the 24½ miles from Ardrossan to Paisley in 25 minutes at an average speed of 58·2 miles an hour. Increases in speed were matched by decreases in fares. The *Commercial Traveller* advised its readers that they could make 'an artistic use of tickets' on the Ayrshire coast lines.

The Saturday afternoon services by the rival routes in 1892 were as follows.

	Caledonian	*G & SW*
Glasgow dep	1.40	1.55
Ardrossan arr	2.25	2.40
Brodick	3.5	3.20
Lamlash	3.25	3.40
King's Cross	3.35	3.50
Whiting Bay	3.45	4.0

It was typical of the age that this concentration of transport expertise—express trains, fast steamers and harbour improvements—was mounted to serve a mountainous, feudal island with its population of 4,637 souls for the most part spread thinly in coastal villages. Except for a few peak Saturdays in high summer the service was not used to full capacity. The spectacle of the two large steamers, one of them a voracious coal eater, chasing each other round the little Arran piers illustrated Victorian railway extravagance at its worst. The vainglorious denizens of the board rooms knew it was madness, but they would not unbend until sheer economic necessity forced them to see reason. The companies came to an agreement whereby their respective vessels, instead of following each other, sailed direct from Ardrossan to either Brodick or Whiting Bay before calling at the Arran piers from north to south and south to north. The Saturday afternoon pattern in 1905 was as follows.

	Caledonian	*G & SW*
Glasgow	1.40	1.55
Ardrossan arr	2.25	2.38
Whiting Bay	3.20	4.0
Lamlash	3.45	3.40
Brodick	4.10	3.20

Even this scheme proved to be too generous and the companies agreed that only one steamer would service both piers at Ardrossan.

The Caledonian must have been surprised at the warmth of the welcome it received from the travelling public and commercial community of Ayrshire. When the L & A first opened the Caledonian put canvassers into the area to cajole business away from the South Western. The response was favourable. A Caledonian representative reported that the Ayrshire Foundry Company of Stevenston 'were very urgent to have a connection'. The Caledonian somewhat boldly offered to build a branch into the works for a guaranteed two-thirds of the traffic, but settled for a branch costing £1,086 9s 3d (£1,086.46), and a guarantee of half the traffic. Nobel's explosives factory at Stevenston, which gave the South Western 2,000 tons of traffic a month, promised to patronise the L & A if its rates compared favourably with those of the G & SW. Wm Hudson & Co of Irvine, chemical manufacturers, asked for a connection as did other manufacturers in the area. The success of the L & A is best seen in the reports to the shareholders. In the year ending 31 January 1893 passenger trains ran 11,048 miles and goods trains 175,599 miles. A year later the corresponding figures were 116,287 and 194,354.

The strongest reaction to the presence of the Caledonian in the county came from the town of Ayr. Disenchanted with the South Western's fifty year monopoly 677 traders, merchants and industrialists of Ayr signed, within one week in August 1889, a memorial asking the Caledonian 'to take forthwith such measures as might be necessary for the extension of their railway to the town and harbour of Ayr'. The petitioners were at pains to stress that no 'ordinary residents' had signed the memorial, only citizens who were potential consignors of goods. When the Caledonian was slow to reply Provost Ferguson and the town clerk led a deputation of magistrates to the railway company's headquarters and presented a written guarantee from 560 traders that they would give half their traffic to the L & A for a minimum of ten years after the opening of the line. A site for the Caledonian station in the High Street was part of the deal. On the same day fifty traders from Maybole offered support, and promises of financial help came from Monkton, Prestwick, New Prestwick and Wallacetown.

Strain, the engineer of the L & A, reported on the scheme which involved the doubling of the Irvine branch and its extension for 12¼ miles to Ayr. There was to be a branch to Troon harbour and connections to the G & SW Mauchline and Ayr lines so that Caledonian trains would have access to Muirkirk in either direction. The cost of the new lines, totalling 15¼ miles, was estimated at £440,000. The Caledonian route from Glasgow to Ayr would be 39 miles against the South Western's 40½ miles.

At the time of the Ayr proposal the Caledonian was more concerned with taking the L & A east rather than west and south. The company resented paying tolls for use of the GB & K and was determined to have a Caledonian-controlled route throughout from Glasgow to Ardrossan. The L & A got authority to extend eastward on 1 July 1897 and the first sod was cut at Lugton on 6 June 1898. The new line ran parallel to the Beith branch as far as Giffen Junction, then paralleled the GB & K to Lugton from which point it dropped through Uplawmoor, Neilston and Whitecraigs to the outer suburbs of Glasgow. At Cathcart it made contact with the Caledonian Cathcart Circle and through it gained direct access to Glasgow Central. The L & A main line still continuing eastward skirted the southern fringe of the city to Newton where it joined the main south line of the Caledonian. The line was opened from Giffen to Cathcart for goods on 1 April 1903 and passengers on 1 May, giving the Caledonian its own through route from Glasgow to Ardrossan 31 miles 67 chains long. With the opening of the section from Cathcart to Newton on 6 January 1904, coal from Lanarkshire and beyond could be taken direct to Ardrossan on Caledonian-controlled metals.

Although the port of Ardrossan dominated the North Ayrshire scene the G & SW exploited the coast north of Ardrossan to its profit. The township of Largs looked promising. It had a pier at which steamers called on the way to Millport on the Great Cumbrae and other resorts further afield. The South Western gave thought to building a line from Kilmacolm on the Greenock line through the hills to Largs, but the plan was abandoned in favour of an extension of the Ardrossan branch up the coast through West Kilbride and Fairlie. By an Act of 26 May 1873 the line was extended from Holm Junction, Ardrossan, to Fairlie with a fork from Parkhouse Junction on the new line, to Castlehill Junction on the original Ardrossan line. The branch was opened to West Kilbride on 1 May 1878, to Fairlie on 1 June 1880 and to Fairlie Pier on 1 July 1882. The final stretch from Fairlie Pier Junction to Largs was opened on 1 June 1885. Fairlie Pier was splendidly placed for serving Millport and it also offered the shortest sea crossing from the mainland to Campbeltown. A brisk traffic was generated with fast trains running direct from Glasgow to Fairlie Pier.

The traffic flow on the main line to the coast increased to such an extent that the G & SW sought a relief line between Paisley and Kilbirnie where the traffic was densest. A solution was found in the provision of a loop line leaving the Greenock line at Cart Junction and running along the north shore of Kilbirnie Loch to join the main line at Brownhill Junction, Dalry. The loop was opened on 1 June 1905.

THE YEARS OF DECLINE

The south-west triangle came out of the railway recession rather better than did the south-east triangle. Both sides of the triangle survive; only the base has vanished. The main line from Glasgow to Gretna is intact together with the line from Glasgow to Ayr, Girvan and Stranraer. Services between Dumfries and Challoch Junction and Castle Douglas and Kirkcudbright ceased on 14 June 1965, and the 'Port Road', which long since had been shorn of its branches, disappeared from the map. From the date of closure the Euston–Stranraer boat trains were routed via Mauchline and Ayr. The line between Stranraer Harbour Junction and Stranraer Town was closed on 7 March 1966. The ferries on the short sea crossing carry a heavy traffic in private cars, and road vehicles including milk tankers, but all of it moves to the pierhead by road.

The decline of the former Lanarkshire & Ayrshire system began with the opening of Rothesay Dock at Clydebank in 1907. This dock, designed with all the latest appliances for handling minerals, was only 9 miles from Glasgow and within 20 miles of most of the Lanarkshire coalfields. Much of the coal traffic that formerly had gone to Ardrossan now went to Clydebank. But the Caledonian made stout efforts to attract custom to what was an expensive and relatively new line. Even offal traffic from the Glasgow markets was acceptable. Fish offal was carried in open wagons, and some annoyance was caused to local residents when the offal trains were stabled at wayside stations at weekends.

After the first war the fortunes of the L & A declined rapidly. In 1920 the mileage run by all traffic totalled 535,734. In 1922 the mileage was down to 308,776 and in 1923 to 293,054. The grouping of 1923, which put all the Ayrshire railways under the common ownership of the LMS, and so eliminated competition, accelerated the decline. The Irvine branch lost its passenger service on 28 July 1930, and was closed completely on 30 December 1939. A note in the Third Statistical Account of Scotland says, 'The train on this line towards the end of its existence consisted of an engine and a single carriage, and rejoiced in the colloquial name of The Riviera Express.' Local passenger services on the main stem of the L & A ceased west of Uplawmoor on 4 July 1932, but through excursion trains and boat trains continued to use the route to Ardrossan until 1939. On 16 June 1947 a 34 chain spur was put in between the G & SW and L & A at Ardeer allowing boat trains to run direct from the G & SW line to Montgomerie Pier. This line, from Stevenston No 1 to Montgomerie Pier, was closed completely on 18 April 1966. The last boat train had run on 10 September 1965. All the L & A track east of Giffen had been removed by 1955. Giffen has been retained to serve a Government establishment.

The closure of branches, cross-country lines and wayside stations followed the familiar pattern. The Maidens line, never well patronised, was closed between Alloway Junction and Maidens on 1 December 1930, but was re-opened from 4 July 1932 to 31 May 1933. The southern half of the line from Girvan to Maidens remained open until 2 March 1942 mainly to service Turnberry Hotel. After the Second World War the line was re-opened from Alloway Junction to Heads of Ayr for traffic to and from a holiday camp. The Catrine branch and the Cairn Valley line were closed on 3 May 1943, the Dalmellington branch on 6 April 1964. Passenger services between Kilmarnock and Ardrossan ceased on 6 April 1964 and the Crosshouse–Irvine line which carried these trains was closed on 11 October 1965. Regular passenger services were withdrawn between Cart Junction and Brownhill Junction on 27 June 1966, although the line still proves useful in emergencies when the main line is out of use.

CHAPTER VI

The Central Trunk

'THE NATIONAL LINE'

By 1836 a trunk railway was being forged from London north-wards through the Midlands towards the north of England. The London & Birmingham Railway was open, the Grand Junction was under construction from Birmingham to Warrington and the North Union was projected as far as Preston. At this point the directors of the Grand Junction conceived the bold idea of carrying the line on to Carlisle and for a hundred miles into Scotland to tap the cities of Edinburgh and Glasgow. With this object in view they instructed their engineer, Joseph Locke, to survey a route.

The direct route from Carlisle to Glasgow was by Telford's coach road up Annandale and down Clydesdale. Locke followed the road for some 40 miles north of Carlisle and found the ter-rain to his liking. But at Moffat the road began a 10 mile climb into the hills on a gradient so steep that Locke decided no loco-motive could surmount it. The engineer retraced his steps to Gretna and began the exploration of gentler Nithsdale some-what to the west. The route was longer but feasible. And there were other advantages in using it. In Glasgow the GPK & A was in the process of formation and this line would form the northern section of the international trunk route. The Edinburgh & Glas-gow too was being talked about and it would form a continua-tion of the route to Edinburgh. The distance from London to Glasgow would be 417 miles and to Edinburgh 463 miles.

This scheme would have gone forward had not it been for the intervention of John James Hope Johnstone. Hope Johnstone was a Member of Parliament, a banker, a chief magistrate and the proprietor of the Annandale estates. He was determined that the railway would not by-pass Annandale. Convinced that

Locke had taken too hasty a look at the gradients involved he dispatched his factor, Charles Stewart, to Liverpool to persuade Locke to re-survey the Annandale route. This Locke duly did, and he accepted the view that the route was practicable after all. Its special merit was that it was much shorter, the journey to Glasgow involving a saving of some 20 miles and to Edinburgh 50 miles.

The new survey was not complete until 1837 and by that time the GPK & A promoters had got their Act. At that time it was believed that there could be only one Anglo-Scottish line, and there developed a contest to see who would build it. The Glasgow-promoted line was largely locally financed and was engineered by Scotland's leading railway engineer, John Miller. The Glasgow men felt they had been betrayed by the English engineer and his English masters.

The Annandale supporters were greatly heartened when the 1841 Royal Commission reported that 'so far as regards the interest of the traveller, both with respect to the economy of his time and of his purse, the preferable route for the railway communication to Edinburgh and Glasgow would be by the proposed Carlisle and Lockerbie line with a branch from Symington'. The promoters, however, were given a stern warning that they must get their line built in reasonable time otherwise an alternative route might be considered.

The impetus for the promotion of the Annandale line came from England and the potential proprietors were too busy with schemes in the north of England to give immediate attention to Scottish transport. It was 1844 before active promotion was undertaken and by then the Glasgow, Dumfries & Carlisle was in prospect and the North British had floated a line that was to be the embryo East Coast route.

The Annandale line, in spite of its English parentage, appeared in the prospectus as the Caledonian Railway. It was an aggressively Scottish line which did not scruple to annex the arms of Scotland and the motto *Nemo me impune lacessit* as its own emblem and blatantly call itself the National Line. The Caledonian had its roots in Carlisle, a long trunk stretching up through the lateral valleys of the Annan and Clyde, a branch from Carstairs to Edinburgh and, eventually, a matted foliage spread over the infinitely rich Lanarkshire coalfields. The

Caledonian Railway was authorised on 31 July 1845 and opened throughout from Carlisle to Edinburgh and Glasgow on 15 February 1848. It was extended to meet the Scottish Central Railway at Castlecary on 7 August 1848.

The Caledonian was the first railway to provide a direct service from Scotland to England 'without change of carriage' as the company's advertisements put it. The East Coast route from Edinburgh to London had been in operation for nearly a year but its passengers had to change trains at the Tweed and the Tyne. No express trains were run on the Caledonian for more than two months, the company explaining that it was waiting 'until the line is a little more consolidated'. But on 10 March 1848 the Post Office expressed its confidence in the new route when it transferred the London–Edinburgh mails from the East Coast to the West Coast route. The day mail train left London at 8.30 am arriving in Glasgow at 1.40 am and Edinburgh at 1.30 am next day. The night mail left London at 8.45 pm and was due in Glasgow at 1.55 pm and in Edinburgh at 1.45 pm the following day. The first express train between Glasgow, Edinburgh and London ran on 1 May 1848. It carried first class passengers only at a fare of £3 17s 6d (£3.87½) single and took 12½ hours for the journey. In the same month an express service was opened between Edinburgh and Glasgow and Manchester, Liverpool and Birmingham, the times being 8 hours to Manchester and Liverpool and 9½ hours to Birmingham.

The Caledonian took full advantage of the Great Exhibition of 1851 to popularise Anglo-Scottish travel. A single ticket from Glasgow or Edinburgh to London at £1 10s (£1.50) was offered on the night mail on Wednesdays and Saturdays, and on two day mail trains every week-day. On Friday nights seven or fourteen day-return tickets were issued at £4, £3 and £2 first, second, and third class respectively. Special trains were chartered to clubs, societies and other organisations, the members of which got further reductions. A Mr Marcus who described himself as 'manager and conductor of excursion trains' considered it his duty 'to give the public every advantage of participating in the liberality of the railway companies'. The proprietors of Murray's Time Tables announced that they had 'arranged to run a train from Glasgow to London at 30s [£1.50] return, but the first

200 tickets will be sold at 27s [£1.35]. Every arrangement has been made along the lines for the safe conveyance of this train and we expect it will reach London early on the Thursday afternoon.' Not all the excursionists were satisfied with their first experience of international travel. Travellers who left Edinburgh with the 9 pm train found that their carriages were not attached to the southbound mail train at Carlisle as promised. 'The truth is that at every station where other trains were arriving from branch railways we had the mortification to see our train sided off until all others were in turn dispatched.' The excursionists were 22 hours on the journey.

The Exhibition year saw the eclipse of the passenger service between the Clyde and the Thames. The last remaining vessel in the trade, the *European*, had been specially fitted out with extra bunks for the Exhibition trade and a round voyage was offered at £3 5s (£3.25) inclusive of meals. During the summer the fare was reduced to £3, and at the end of the Exhibition the service was finally withdrawn.

The Caledonian's ability to convey traffic from any place in Scotland served by rail to any place in England without transshipment was of special interest to the farming community. Hitherto, prime cattle for Smithfield had been driven south on the roads or carried in cumbersome floats. Either process was prolonged and costly in terms of feeding stuffs and drovers' wages. Animals died on the journey and the survivors reached the London market in poor condition. The Caledonian started a livestock service from Scotland to London on 16 June 1848. The company offered to carry from 8 to 10 fat cattle for £8 7s (£8.35), and sheep 'new out of the wool' at 2s 3d (11p) per head. Caledonian agents toured the cattle markets pointing out the advantages of sending cattle by rail. The farmers were told that the duration of the journey was so short that the beasts need not be watered and fed in transit, nor would it be necessary to employ drovers. Dealers at Doune market, for instance, were reminded that there was a station only 4 miles away at Dunblane on the newly-opened Scottish Central Railway.

Tradition dies hard, and farmers insisted on sending drovers with the first Caledonian cattle train. The company provided a third-class carriage for them. The train crossed the Border with seventeen wagons, two of which had been picked up at Lockerbie, and the journey to London took 25 hours. On the following day a cattle train was run from Glasgow and Edinburgh to Liverpool, the animals being delivered at the market on the day of dispatch. The company intended to run its cattle trains once a week. By 21 October the London train was crossing the Border every night from Monday to Friday. Separate sections of the train were dispatched from Glasgow and Edinburgh and these sections were joined at Carstairs by a section off the Scottish Central. The potential was great; 100,000 sheep were transferred from the feeding grounds in north-east Scotland to England annually. The Caledonian provided double-decked wagons for sheep.

The service flourished, although it had its teething troubles. A Scottish farmer, beguiled by the Caledonian advertisements but knowing nothing about the new mode of conveyance arrived at a station with 100 sheep for consignment to Kent. He did not have the money to pay for them, but the Caledonian conveyed them on credit. When the bill was presented in Kent the consignee complained bitterly that he was charged 4s 6d (22½p) instead of the promised 2s 3d (11p) per head. The railway company replied that his sheep, far from being newly clipped were 'more like llamas than sheep' and had taken up a lot of room on the train.

GRETNA

The Caledonian station at Gretna was situated immediately south of the Border. With the completion of the Glasgow, Dumfries & Carlisle Railway in 1850, and its emergence with the GPK & A as the Glasgow & South Western Railway, Gretna Junction was formed just north of Gretna station, and on Scottish soil. Then by 1862 the North British line from Longtown on the Waverley route was opened to Gretna South Junction. The G & SW, of course, had running powers from Gretna Junction over Caledonian metals to Carlisle, and the North British operated a local service from Longtown to Gretna Green, the first station on the G & SW line. There was, therefore, the intriguing Border situation where trains of all three companies—the Caledonian, the North British and the Glasgow & South Western—all used the 24 chains of Cale-

donian track between Gretna South Junction and Gretna
Junction. The North British had its own station at Gretna
within sight of the Caledonian station. The North British local
trains stopped first at the NB station and then at the Caledonian
station, but only to set down passengers proceeding with
Caledonian main line trains. On the return journey the North
British trains stopped at Gretna (Caledonian) unconditionally.
The North British and G & SW interchanged goods traffic at
Gretna Green, a small yard being established there for the
purpose.

The coming of the railway had social implications for the
Border people. Local folks complained that the railway had
resulted in a large increase in the notorious Gretna Green
'anvil' marriages. No longer had the English runaways to face
the expense of a post-chaise; the new trains whisked them
across the Border and delivered them at the blacksmith's shop
for a few shillings.

Then there was trouble with the Customs. Among the com-
modities that the railway carried were casks of Scotch whisky.
The law of the time decreed that whisky could not be imported
into England in quantities of less than 20 gallons, and each
consignment had to be accompanied by a certificate stating
that duty had been paid.

The railway provided a heaven-sent medium for persons who
were minded to transport whisky across the Border in quantities
less than the legal minimum and without benefit of Customs
clearance. Smuggling was rife, and railway employees joined
in the sport. After several passengers and staff had found themselves in court the Caledonian displayed at all its stations a
large poster boldly worded as follows.

> The Caledonian Railway Company refuse to undertake the Con-
> veyance of Spirits, except when conditions of the Excise Regulations
> have been complied with, and when they are supplied with the name
> and address of the party sending and the party to receive the Consign-
> ment. All Packages containing Liquids of any description are liable to
> detention on suspicion to avoid which it is desirable their contents
> should be stated at the time of booking.

When the Midland reached Carlisle in 1876 and the G & SW
and the English company embarked on their fruitful partner-

ship the Border people once more found cause for complaint. There were no facilities at Carlisle for the handling of exchange freight and the wagons had to be taken across the Border to Gretna Green and marshalled in the small yard which hitherto had accommodated North British interchange traffic. The yard was entirely inadequate for the new traffic, with the result that the G & SW had to conduct its shunting operations on Sundays. The clink of buffers on the unlawful day drove the local Sabbatarians into a frenzy. The G & SW promised to suspend operations during the hours of public worship, but that did not placate the offended churchgoers. The General Assembly of the Church of Scotland was about to open in Edinburgh and the complaint was incorporated in a ponderous memorial presented to the Assembly by the Presbytery of Annan.

> Whereas it is of great importance in the interests of religion and the welfare of the people the Sabbath Day be duly observed; And whereas the Presbytery of Annan have had their attention called to the fact of a serious desecration of the Sabbath at the Gretna Parish by the Glasgow & South Western Railway making up and arranging goods trains on the Lord's Day; And whereas the Presbytery have memorialised the directors of the railway without effect, except as regard the hours of public worship; And whereas the Presbytery deem the matter of great importance to the Church in general as well as to this particular parish; It is humbly overtured by the Presbytery of Annan that the coming General Assembly shall take these premises into their consideration and adopt such best measures as they may deem for the suppression of the evil complained of.

The G & SW undertook to transfer their Sunday shunting operations to English soil as soon as the technical facilities were available.

THE BRANCHES

The Caledonian had hoped to complement its main south to north trunk line with a west to east line running from Ayr to Berwick-on-Tweed. Promoted as the Caledonian Extension Railway the route was by Muirkirk, Biggar, Stobo, Peebles, Innerleithen, Galashiels, Melrose and Kelso. This line, 104 miles long, together with the main line would have quartered southern Scotland and given the Caledonian control of the region. But finance was not forthcoming, and the scheme lapsed. Eventually it was possible to travel from Ayr to Berwick more or less by the route proposed by the Caledonian Extension Railway. But the line was neither planned nor operated as a cross-country line. It was built in pieces, the work of many hands, and it was purely fortuitous that a coast to coast route was the final result.

The southernmost of the branches off the Caledonian main line (other than the North British Gretna–Longtown branch), began as a bold scheme for an alternative route to England. In the 1860s the West Cumberland iron ore mines suddenly stepped up their production. In 1857 the district produced 22,000 tons of hematite; by 1863 the annual output had risen to 150,000 tons. Two thirds of this tonnage was moved by rail and the little railways of Cumberland experienced a boom. The Whitehaven Junction paid a dividend of 15 per cent, the Maryport & Carlisle 10 per cent and the Whitehaven, Cleator & Egremont 13 per cent. By this time the Monkland iron mines had been denuded of their best ores, and much of the Cumberland ore was going to the Lanarkshire steelworks. The route taken by the iron ore trains was via Carlisle and was of necessity circuitous. There were men in Cumberland and in Dumfriesshire who thought a fortune was to be made by providing a new railway that would cross the Solway and strike diagonally across the south-east corner of Dumfriesshire to join the Caledonian main line at Kirtlebridge. Such a railway would by-pass Carlisle and shorten the route to the Lanarkshire steelworks by 20 miles. The planners saw no reason to believe that their iron ore railway would be less prosperous than the existing West Cumberland lines.

In 1864 two schemes were put forward, the Annandale & Solway Junction and the Dumfries & Cumberland Junction. Both schemes demanded a long bridge over the Solway, an estuary notorious for its shifting sands and treacherous tides. The *Railway Times* poured scorn on the promoters whom it called *adventurers*. A sarcastic editorial pictured the surveyors out with divining rods among the sandbanks looking for foundations for the great new bridge—'that noble arch of Baron Munchausen'.

But the two enthusiastic gentlemen from Dumfries and their two colleagues from Cumberland who made up the railway committee were not to be put off by the opinion of a mere London journal. They successfully promoted the Solway Junction Railway with a capital of £315,000 with the object of building a 20½ mile line from Kirtlebridge on the Caledonian to Brayton on the Maryport & Carlisle. The line was begun in 1865 and opened for goods and minerals in 1869 and for passengers in 1870. The Solway viaduct, 1,940yd long was carried on 193 cast-iron piers. Anticipating trouble from the scouring tides and shifting sands the engineer protected the piers with timber buttresses. The line was single throughout but like many of their contemporary promoters, the Solway Junction men acquired enough land for double line and all bridges—including the Solway viaduct—were built to support two tracks.

Traffic at first seemed to justify the promoters' faith in the venture. The Caledonian had a strong financial interest in the line, and the Lanarkshire ore trains were now routed via the Solway viaduct, although worked by Solway Junction engines and staff. In 1873 the Caledonian bought the Scottish section of the line outright and agreed to work the English part. The whole railway passed into Caledonian hands in 1895.

The expected trouble with the viaduct began early. In the winter of 1875–6 ice formed inside the cast-iron columns and produced cracks. Then in 1881 ice floes in the Solway demolished 45 piers and caused £30,000 worth of damage. The costly maintenance of the viaduct perhaps was justified while the railway was earning worthwhile revenue, but by the end of the nineteenth century the best of the Cumberland hematite had been worked out, and the Lanarkshire steel mills had turned to Spanish ore which could be shipped direct to the Clyde. During World War I the line from Annan to Brayton (including the Solway viaduct) was completely closed. In 1920 traffic was resumed throughout, but the neglect of the war years had had a bad effect on the viaduct. The meagre traffic now using the route did not justify heavy repairs, and the structure was condemned in September 1921. It stood derelict for a decade, used only by pedestrians making clandestine crossings especially on Sunday nights when, their own public houses dark and shuttered, the Scots were lured across the water by the lights of the English hostelries. The viaduct was demolished between 1933 and 1935.

On 1 September 1863 a Caledonian subsidiary, the Dumfries, Lochmaben & Lockerbie Railway, established a link between the G & SW and Caledonian main lines. The line was part of the Caledonian policy of forcing a way westward into rival territory. The company wanted a station of its own in Dumfries, but had to settle for a bay platform in the existing G & SW station. When the Caledonian started a direct service from Dumfries to Edinburgh via Lockerbie the G & SW retaliated with a service to Edinburgh via Gretna and the Waverley route.

At the time of the Caledonian's advent in Dumfries, the Portpatrick Railway was trying to make a success of its long, straggling line to Stranraer and Portpatrick and the G & SW was expecting to be invited to take over from the smaller company. However, the Portpatrick gladly accepted a generous offer of Caledonian equipment and expertise. The Portpatrick, of course, was isolated from the Caledonian by the Dumfries–Castle Douglas line, but the Caledonian had no difficulty in getting running powers over that G & SW preserve. The result was that the Caledonian not only shared in the Irish trade by the short sea route, but had control of passenger journeys and freight consignments originating in the south-west of Scotland. A passenger booking from say Newton Stewart to Carlisle found that his ticket, unless he specified otherwise, was routed via Dumfries and Lockerbie (Caledonian all the way) instead of by the shorter and more direct G & SW route via Annan. The Caledonian remained the working company until the formation of the Portpatrick and Wigtownshire Joint Railway on 6 August 1885.

The Caledonian main line passed 2 miles to the west of Moffat, a fashionable spa town nestling in the shade of the Lowther Hills. Moffat was described as 'an exceedingly Scotch and respectable Baden Baden'. Its shops were said to sell luxuries as well as necessities. In 1878 local interests built a large hydropathic establishment in order to exploit the three mineral wells then enjoying a vogue. All the spa needed for success was a railway, and in 1881 the Moffat Railway was promoted locally, and opened between Beattock on the main line and the town on 2 April 1883. The resident population of Moffat was then 2,161. There were visitors all the year round to the hydropathic establishment, and the railway stimulated summer holiday traffic. For a time Moffat had its own train to Glasgow, the Tinto Express.

From Beattock the main line going north climbs for 10 miles to Beattock Summit before beginning a descent of the Clyde Valley through Crawford and Elvanfoot. From Elvanfoot westwards ran a line very different from the Moffat branch. It was built as a light railway to give communication to the isolated villages of Leadhills (reached in 1901) and Wanlockhead where it terminated in 1902. The railway climbed up the bare hillside above the Elvan Water, and the trains stopped anywhere to pick up or set down passengers and parcels. It was a pleasantly informal railway, but profitless to its owners. In ordinary times one carriage and a van were all that were needed to cater for demand. A hope that the railway would lead to a revival of the lead mining industry in the area was not fulfilled.

On 5 November 1860 the Caledonian-sponsored Symington, Biggar & Broughton Railway opened a line from Symington on the main line into Tweeddale. It had reached Peebles by 1864. The Caledonian station at Peebles was on the opposite side of the Tweed from the North British station and although a single line connecting bridge was built across the river it was used only sparingly for the interchange of freight traffic. A feature of the Peebles branch were the dead meat trains which were dispatched to the London market.

Carstairs was one of the most notable railway junctions in Scotland from the first coming of the Caledonian. There the Glasgow and Edinburgh lines forked. There was much topping and tailing of trains as traffic was sorted out for the two great Scottish cities and for the line north to Stirling, Perth and Aberdeen. The junction grew in importance as new routes were added. In 1867 a branch was built from Carstairs to Dolphinton, already served by the North British from the east. On 5 January 1855, the Lanark Railway, a private company, had built a line from Cleghorn on the main line north of Carstairs to Lanark. Suitable spurs at Cleghorn made possible the running of trains to Lanark direct from Glasgow or from Edinburgh via Carstairs. The Lanark Railway was acquired by the Caledonian on 23 July 1860.

Since 1848 Muirkirk had been served from the west by a G & SW branch, but the gap between Muirkirk and the Cale-

donian main line, across the Douglas Moors, had remained un-
filled. It was a sore point with the people of Ayr that whereas in
stage coach days they had had a direct cross-country service to
Edinburgh, there was no such service in the railway age. Public
meetings had urged the G & sw to extend its line from Muirkirk
all the way to Edinburgh, but the company had shown no
interest in taking so formidable a leap. There was open talk in
Ayr of asking the Caledonian to build a line out from Carstairs
to Ayr.

Before the days of the Truck Acts Muirkirk had been a 'company town' run by the Baird Iron and Coal Company. Almost
everybody in the town was employed by 'the company' and the
company store supplied all their needs. The arrival of the railway stimulated the iron and coal industry. In 1848 there were
two local pits; half a century later there were eight. The industry flourished and the population was still rising when in
the early 1860s the Caledonian first thought about taking a line
west in the direction of Muirkirk. The line was opened from
Lanark to Douglas on 1 April 1864. It was extended to Muirkirk on 1 January 1873 for freight only. A passenger service was
started on 1 June 1874, but it was June 1878 before the company
yielded to pressure from Ayr and provided through trains
from Ayr to Edinburgh via Muirkirk and Carstairs. The first
two trains left without a single passenger and the Caledonian
agent reported that 'not half a dozen' passengers used the first
six trains. The local press complained that the trains were badly
timed and inadequately advertised. In fact, the Caledonian
route from Ayr to Edinburgh, which looked so direct on the
map, was beset by operating difficulties which tended to make
the journey dreary and long. It was quicker and no more costly
to travel via Glasgow and the North British using express trains
all the way. But if the passenger traffic was desultory the
mineral traffic made the construction of the railway well worth
while for the Caledonian. Output of pits and ironworks increased until the end of the century, Muirkirk's prosperity being
indicated by a rise in population from 3,253 in 1870 to a peak of
5,670 in 1901. A steady decline followed until 1923 when the
furnaces were doused during a trade dispute, never to reopen.
As the ironworks closed so did the ancillary industries and some
of the pits. Muirkirk took on a look of desolation. Population

dropped as the displaced workers sought jobs elsewhere. By 1934 only the Kames Pit was working but the railway still maintained fifteen engines at Muirkirk to handle the traffic in 1939. By 1947 the number was down to five, and the railway, once an important source of employment, was providing jobs for only thirty people. Today the railway has vanished completely from Muirkirk and the moors around it.

THE LANARKSHIRE EL DORADO

Lanarkshire was an El Dorado for the railways. Scotland's largest coalfield, its greatest manufacturing city and its most concentrated conurbation of industrial towns were contained within its boundaries. Raw materials and manufactures in abundance poured on to the rails enriching those whose business it was to carry them. Some 250 pits poured 17 million tons of coal on to the county's railways annually. The Caledonian Motherwell accounts office alone invoiced 12 million tons. Processions of long coal trains, and vast sidings holding row after row of coal wagons, were features of the Lanarkshire landscape. Ross and Strathavan Junction sorting sidings each handled 4,000 wagons per day, and the Bothwell (North British) yard dealt with sixty trains per day in round-the-clock shifts, six days per week.

The original Caledonian main line terminated at Garriongill 12 miles north of Carstairs at which point it joined the Wishaw & Coltness Railway to gain access to Glasgow over that company's lines and those of the Glasgow, Garnkirk & Coatbridge. A second and more direct route to Glasgow from Motherwell was created by the opening of the Clydesdale Junction Railway on 1 June 1849. This line linked the Polloc & Govan Railway (a short line which had evolved from a tramway used mainly to convey the products of Dixon's ironworks to the Clyde) with the Wishaw & Coltness at Motherwell. The terminus in Glasgow, South Side, was remote from the city centre and was used only by local trains. It was not until the Central station was opened that the main line trains abandoned the north-about route into Glasgow.

The Caledonian and North British vied with each other to gain access to the growing Lanarkshire towns. Both companies

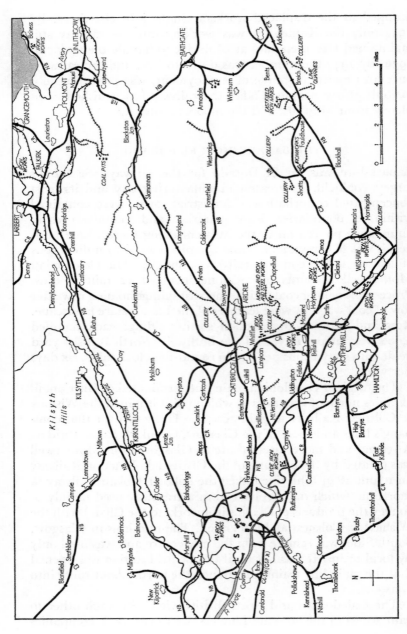

The mineral districts of Lanarkshire and Linlithgowshire

had inherited routes from the early Monkland lines. The North British had reached Coatbridge via the Monkland & Kirkintilloch, the Caledonian by the Glasgow, Garnkirk & Coatbridge. The pattern of future development involved the consolidating and improving of existing assets and extending the network to other towns. Certain key lines were established. One was the Rutherglen–Coatbridge line of the Caledonian opened from Rutherglen on the main Glasgow–Carlisle line to Coatbridge on the Carlisle–Stirling line on 20 September 1865 for goods and 8 January 1866 for passengers. This line allowed traffic to be taken from industrial Lanarkshire and the docks of the Clyde direct to the north. Another useful line opened on 1 June 1880 joined the main line at Law Junction with the Glasgow–Edinburgh line at Carfin (later Holytown) passing through Wishaw on the way. A spur to the main line at Shieldmuir junction created a loop through Wishaw Central that was to prove very helpful in relieving traffic on the main line. The Caledonian first reached Hamilton by means of a branch from Newton opened on 17 September 1849, and the North British gained access to the town with a branch from Shettleston on the Bathgate line opened on 1 April 1878. The North British trains on the Edinburgh–Glasgow route via Bathgate served Coatbridge and Airdrie. The Caledonian reached Airdrie with a branch from its Coatbridge line through Langloan on 1 June 1886, and an extension to Calderbank and Newhouse was opened on 2 July 1888.

Competition between the two companies gave rise to much duplication of services. Hamilton, for instance had four stations, two on each railway. The 1907 timetable showed 10 Caledonian trains from Glasgow to Hamilton, 11 by the North British. Uddington was served by 21 Caledonian trains, and 10 North British, while Airdrie had 19 Caledonian trains against 25 of the North British.

The Lesmahagow Railway was promoted jointly by that company and the Caledonian to run from Motherwell to Coalburn on the Douglas Moors. The attraction was the famous cannel coal of the area—a highly volatile mineral much in demand by the gas industry—and it was as a mineral line that the railway was opened on 1 December 1856, as far as Lesmahagow (later renamed Brocketsbrae). Passenger services were started

on 1 January 1868. The line eventually was extended to Coalburn, but a further extension to Muirkirk was partly built but
never opened. However, a link was put in between the Coalburn
line at Alton Heights and the Muirkirk line at Poniel Junction.
On 14 July 1876 a branch was opened from the Lesmahagow
line at Ross Junction to Hamilton. Various minor branches and
spurs were built in the area up to 1905; these included the line
from Hamilton to Strathaven via Quarter and Glassford, the
Strathaven and Darvel worked jointly by the Caledonian and
Glasgow and South Western and the Mid-Lanark line which
provided a link between Coalburn and Stathaven. The lines in
the rural west of Lanarkshire were not successful. The Strathaven–Darvel section was abandoned on 9 September 1939. The
line to Strathaven via Quarter survived until 29 September
1945.

The Clyde basin was favoured by nature as a site for heavy
industry, but both the raw materials and the finished products
of heavy industry require sophisticated transport. Before the
coming of the railways the heaviest loads were dragged to the
Monkland Canal for shipment to Glasgow and beyond. But
there was a limit to the loads that could be dealt with by this
method. The railways set off an industrial revolution in
Lanarkshire. Motherwell, which had a population of only 726
in 1841, grew into a town of 12,904 people in forty years. In
1881 of the 3,671 people classed as industrial workers 2,470
were engaged in the mineral industry. Wishaw, described as a
small village in 1841, had quadrupled its population by 1881 to
become the centre of a vast mineral trade. Coatbridge which
had received its industrial impetus from the Monkland lines
expanded enormously in the era of the new railways. Its population of 1,509 in 1841 had become 18,425 in 1881.

Steelworks and factories were built almost cheek by jowl
along the railways. In Motherwell the Glasgow Iron Company
with fifty furnaces and eight rolling mills operated the largest
ironworks complex in Scotland. In 1871 David Colville opened
a steelworks that became the largest under one owner in the
United Kingdom. Bridge building, tube making and other
heavy engineering ventures were possible only because the
railway could handle the finished products.

TRUNK WITHOUT BRANCHES

The 73 miles of the original central trunk between Carlisle and Carstairs stands as sturdy as ever, but shorn of all its branches and all its intermediate stations except two—Lockerbie and Beattock. Put another way, any place south of Carstairs is inaccessible from Glasgow by rail. Buses travelling between Glasgow and London and other English destinations pass through communities that once had a railway station but, with a few exceptions, they do not set down local passengers. Local bus services are sparse. An inquirer at a main Glasgow bus station in 1967 wanted to know how to get to Wanlockhead, and was told that the place was not even in the timetable. A helpful inspector found a letter giving details of a bus service from Abington on the former Caledonian line to Sanquhar on the old G & SW via Wanlockhead, but the information was four years out of date. A telephone call to Sanquhar produced the information that the bus indeed ran from Sanquhar to Abington early in the morning and returned late in the afternoon, *but not on school holidays*. And the inquirer wanted to travel on a school holiday. It was impossible to obtain in the great city of Glasgow public transport to a village some sixty miles away. It was no comfort to the frustrated traveller to know that had he called at an airline office a few blocks away he could have had a ticket for Bangkok at the touch of a computerised button.

As elsewhere intensive bus services destroyed most of the Lanarkshire lines. But the main towns are served today by a circular diesel multiple unit service from Glasgow, the frequency and speed of which would astonish the general managers of the great railway companies of old who thought their competitive zeal was producing the last word in service. Motherwell is also served by electric trains from Glasgow via Kirkhill. And the heavy industries are only marginally less dependent on the railways than they were fifty years ago. The main movement of ore now is from the ore terminal at General Terminus on the Clyde to the great Ravenscraig steelworks at Motherwell.

K

CHAPTER VII

The River Clyde and Loch Lomond

In April 1802 Hugh Crawford, senior magistrate of Greenock, wrote to the lord provost of Glasgow asking the city's support for a railway between Greenock and Glasgow. The Town Council met to consider the matter and had no hesitation in concluding that such a railway was 'of no interest or concern to Glasgow'.

From Glasgow to the Tail o' the Bank, where the River Clyde merges into the Firth, is a distance of 25 miles. In 1802 Greenock and neighbouring Port Glasgow, guarding the entrance to the river, were nursing a sense of insecurity. Until Golborne canalised the Clyde in the closing years of the eighteenth century almost all the overseas trade of Glasgow and its hinterland had passed through Greenock or Port Glasgow. Cotton and tobacco from the Americas had piled up on the quays along with Scottish manufactures bound for countries right round the globe. Imports and exports alike had been carted over the narrow rough road between Greenock and Glasgow or taken slowly up the river in small vessels. With improved navigation more and more ships by-passed Greenock and sailed direct to Glasgow. Land transport languished, and it was little wonder that the Glasgow magistrates had no enthusiasm for Greenock's proposed railway. Glasgow was river-orientated. The city's faith in the river seemed justified when in 1812 Henry Bell put his *Comet*, the first commercial steamboat to ply on European waters, on the Clyde. The pioneer vessel was followed quickly by a fleet of small steamboats which served Glasgow and the river ports, and drove most of the remaining carters off the Greenock road.

Between 1801 and 1831 Greenock, in spite of its fears, prospered. Increasing international trade led to a demand for ships and the town's speciality, the building and equipping of wooden sailing ships, kept up to nine yards busy. The population increased in thirty years from 17,190 to 27,082. Paisley saw a similar increase in population and prosperity. In 1801 the population was 25,058, in 1831 it was 46,272. In 1812 J. and J. Clark started the manufacture of cotton thread in the town and in 1826 John Coats established a similar factory. Between them Coats and Clark were to make Paisley the world centre for cotton thread. The town's weaving industry was growing fast; it employed 6,000 operatives in 1817. Presently, two of the weaving families, the Browns and the Polsons, built a factory for scouring and starching their muslins, and in so doing founded a food industry.

THE GLASGOW, PAISLEY & GREENOCK

The success of the Garnkirk & Glasgow Railway and the Paisley Canal had demonstrated that there was a market for mass transportation. The railway promoters who, in the thirties, began to investigate the possibility of building a line from Glasgow through Paisley to Port Glasgow and Greenock sought to exploit the growing trade of the south bank towns and attract to their line a share of the vigorous passenger traffic generated by the river boats.

The Glasgow, Paisley & Greenock got its Act on 15 July 1837, the day on which the GPK & A also got its Act. The two companies shared a common route to Paisley, but the GP & G did not open until March 1841, seven months after the Ayrshire line, due to engineering difficulties at Bishopton. The railway ran from Paisley to Bishopton on a straight and level course before burrowing through a hard whinstone ridge to reach the river bank which it followed closely to its terminus in Greenock.

The imminent opening of the GP & G was viewed with trepidation by the Clyde steamboat operators. Some saw the railway driving the boats off the river as ruthlessly as the boats had driven the coaches off the Greenock road. The most pessimistic among them put their vessels up for sale, but the more astute explored the possibility of operating between Greenock and the resorts of the lower Firth in connection with the trains. Meanwhile, in February 1841, a month before the railway opened, the GP & G bought shares in the Rothesay Steam Packet Company and acquired an interest in two paddle vessels, *Maid of*

Bute and *Isle of Bute*. The company advertised for 'respectable shopkeepers' to act as its agents in the principal resorts. The result was that on the opening of the line the GP & G was in a position to offer through rail and steamer connections via Greenock to eight Clyde resorts. There were six sailings to Gourock, six to Helensburgh, two to Rosneath, two to Gare-lochhead and two each to Rothesay, Largs and Millport. The railway steamers left from Custom House Quay, Greenock which was approached from the railway station in Cathcart Street by the unsavoury East Quay Lane. Free transhipment of luggage was provided and a conveyance was run for women and children. Men had to walk—or run, for the company urged passengers to use 'all expedition' in their passage from station to pier.

The steamboats took from 2½ to 3½ hours to sail from Glasgow to Greenock depending on the state of the tide and the density of traffic. The trains did the journey in less than an hour and cut the overall journey time to the lower Firth resorts, making day trips with ample time ashore possible for the first time. The railway terminus in Bridge Street was a short walk from Glasgow Bridge, unlike the inconvenient steamboat berths which were then a mile downstream from the city. Again, the Clyde in its upper reaches was no sylvan stream. It carried Glasgow's raw sewage and the effluent of numerous chemical works to the sea. Paddle wheels churning through this turgid broth on hot days produced an effect which, the guide book tells us, 'offended the olfactory organ'. The trains were a godsend to the fastidious.

In the Glasgow Fair Week in July 1841 the GP & G carried 21,890 passengers for a revenue of £1,332. On one day of the Paisley annual summer holiday in the following month the company ran twenty-five trains each way and would have run more had it not run short of engines. 'Thousands were disappointed,' reported the *Paisley Advertiser*. 'The pressure of passengers was tremendous; hats and still more, ladies' bonnets and other articles of dress were terribly crushed, and one woman had her leg broken.' The GP & G carried 8,200 passengers that day.

One of the Glasgow–Liverpool steamboat operators, who hitherto had terminated his sailings at Greenock and transferred his passengers to river boats for the rest of the voyage to Glasgow, announced in April 1841 that in future this practice would cease and passengers were directed to the trains. All the Liverpool and Irish operators included in their notices the information that passengers could save time on their journeys by using the railway. One of the steamboat owners on the Lochgoilhead station found that, instead of making one daily return sailing to Glasgow he could make two to Greenock. His advertisement rather quaintly advised his patrons that the vessel would leave Lochgoilhead at 'half past six o'clock to overtake the half past eight train for Glasgow'.

The year in which the railway came to Greenock was one of crisis for the shipbuilding industry. In the first year of the railway's operation six shipyards in the town building timber vessels closed. The iron age had struck shipbuilding suddenly. The industry quickly adapted itself to the new conditions; yards were equipped and men trained to build iron ships, and the attendant engineering shops expanded as the demand for marine machinery increased. The change was fortuitous for the railway. Timber for the wooden ships had been imported by sea. The new yards got their raw materials from the Scottish industrial belt and brought revenue to the railway.

The GP & G ran two goods trains from Glasgow to Greenock daily; the outward services were at 6.50 am and 3.30 pm and the return services left Greenock at 12.45 and 6.30 pm. Goods handling facilities were available at Bridge Street, but shippers were instructed to deliver their consignments at the company's nearby Port Eglinton goods depot. Goods for dispatch by passenger train had to be delivered an hour before departure of the train. The practice was for consignments to be loaded in a wagon which was propelled to Bridge Street by shunting engine and attached to the passenger train just before departure. The company also operated a parcels service; parcels handed in at the town office were dispatched by the first available train. A considerable traffic developed of goods for onward dispatch by steamer from Greenock. Soon the volume was such that the steamers could not wait until all the freight had been transshipped, and customers were instructed to send their goods by the train previous to the advertised steamer connection. The GP & G proprietors had reason to be pleased with their first season in business.

The river steam boat operators fought back. In the ten years following the opening of the railway they were to place forty-two new steamers on the river. They persuaded the Clyde Trustees to give them a wharf at the Broomielaw adjoining Glasgow Bridge and even more convenient than Bridge Street station. And they cut their fares to 1s (5p) cabin and 6d (2½p) steerage for the Glasgow–Greenock passage compared with 2s 6d (12½p) and 1s 6d (7½p) on the trains.

The railway replied by cutting fares and increasing services. The result was an enormous upsurge of traffic which in turn caused serious overcrowding on trains. 'Instead of putting only so many passengers as there was room for into the compartment in which I happened to be seated some half dozen were *pushed* in by the manager himself,' complained a passenger. But a contemporary journal gave a happy picture of the Glasgow crowds liberated from the city by the magic of the Greenock Railway and its Ayrshire neighbour.

> It is now that the Clyde bears on its bright bosom thousands of joyous tourists bound to the various charming localities which stud the lochs of this noble Scottish stream. And now it is that various railways whirl along their living cargoes to the land of Burns. Monster trains during this charming weather lose all their horrors or rather like monsters on the stage are gazed at as mirth-provoking personages.

The article went to approve of low fares for trippers, but cautioned the railways against 'any capricious or thoughtless lowering of fares for people travelling on business'.

How well merited the warning was became apparent when the GP & G accountant made up the balance sheet for the apparently successful year 1842. In the Glasgow Fair Week of 1842 the railway carried 33,887 passengers—11,997 more than had been carried in the corresponding week of 1841. But, thanks to fare-cutting, the extra revenue was only £72. The railway's average fare was 10d (4p) compared with the 1s 7d (8p) estimated average in the parliamentary report. Shareholders complained bitterly about mismanagement of the steamboat operation, maintaining that the steamboat portion of a through journey was being financed out of the average fare, and that the steamer passengers were being carried for nothing. On 1 September 1842 the directors put on sackcloth and ashes and cut their salaries by half. On the same day the wages of every employee were reduced.

The Caledonian took an early interest in the Greenock line with the intention of taking it over in due course. In 1847, six months before the opening of the Caledonian, an amalgamation was sanctioned between the CR and GP & G, although the actual union did not take place until 1851. Errington, of Locke and Errington who engineered the Caledonian, managed the Greenock line for a time, and he was followed by Locke and Errington's agent, Robert Sinclair, who was to become manager and locomotive superintendent of the Caledonian. The GP & G workshops in Greenock came under Caledonian control and Sinclair developed them to serve the major company. With the opening of the Caledonian in 1848, and the Clydesdale Junction in 1849 a direct route was provided between Greenock and Edinburgh. Three through trains were included in the 1859 timetable.

But all was not well with the Greenock Railway in the late forties. The *Glasgow Advertiser* in September 1850 put down the company's malaise to 'a set of vampires of the most insatiable appetite secretly devouring the substance of their property'. A shareholders' committee of inquiry named the company secretary as the leading vampire; he had embezzled £4,000 of the company's money. Directors were found to have awarded each other generous fees and raised the wages of favoured officials willy-nilly. Errington, during his term of office as manager had a salary of £400, but a mysterious entry against his name showed that he had been paid £1,286 8s (£1,286.40) for 'extra time'. Even Sinclair's locomotive department did not escape censure; the shareholders wanted to know why the books showed the purchase price of coke at 25s (£1.25) a ton when the highest price in Glasgow was 21s (£1.05).

The truth behind the vexed question of unprofitable steamer operation was brought to light. The committee found that the steamboat companies associated with the railways had no capital other than that contributed by the railway; £9,613 13s 11d (£9,613.69½) of GP & G money had been lost in steamboat ventures. 'In short the steamboat company was nothing else than steamboats purchased with the money of some of the shareholders, worked under the direction of the directors with

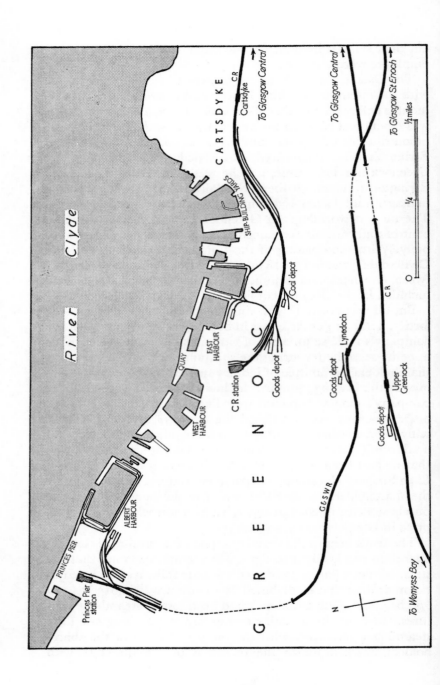

River Clyde

CARTSDYKE

CR

Cartsdyke

To Glasgow Central

SHIP-BUILDING YARDS

Coal depot

EAST HARBOUR

Goods depot

QUAY

CR station

WEST HARBOUR

G R E E N O C K

ALBERT HARBOUR

PRINCES PIER

Princes Pier station

G & S W R

Goods depot

Lynedoch

Goods depot

Upper Greenock

C R

To Glasgow Central

To Glasgow St Enoch

0   ¼   ½ miles

N

To Wemyss Bay

Tasker's (deputy chairman) brother-in-law as manager, and all this at the risk and expense of the company by whom the loss was ultimately borne, all of which was most carefully concealed from the shareholders in the printed statements.'

There were no mass sackings—just a shuffle round of jobs resulting in a reconstituted board that promised to be more businesslike in future. The new board functioned for less than a year. From 1851 Caledonian money and managerial skills brought sound prosperity to the Greenock line. A key point of Caledonian policy was to work in close co-operation with the steamers but to leave their management in the hands of the steamboat operators. By 1866 the *Glasgow Herald* was able to report:

> For some time past the goods and mineral traffic on the Greenock branch of the Caledonian has been so great that it has been found impossible to meet the pressure. At the Greenock terminus the main line and sidings are invariably blocked up for miles with goods and mineral wagons. In consequence of this the passenger traffic has been considerably impeded, scarcely a train arriving or departing without requiring to be stopped or shunted. In order to relieve the pressure relays of men and engines are engaged night and day, Sundays included, loading and discharging. No perceptible relief, however, is yet observable.

THE WEMYSS BAY RAILWAY

In 1862 a group of Greenock men got an Act to build a line between Port Glasgow and Wemyss Bay. The idea behind the project was sound. Steamers plying from Greenock to Rothesay and resorts on the lower Firth first had to make their way round the great elbow bend at Gourock, whereas a pier at Wemyss Bay would be almost opposite Rothesay and half an hour sailing distance from the Bute resort. The new railway was to leave the Greenock line a short distance west of Port Glasgow station, rise up the hill face behind Greenock and drop down by Inverkip to Wemyss Bay, a total distance of 10 miles. Again, Greenock was hemmed in between hills and the river, and the sponsors of the Greenock & Wemyss Bay reasoned that the town must expand *upwards* towards their railway; an Upper Greenock station was in their plans.

The line was opened on 13 May 1865, the Caledonian work-

ing it for the owners for 45 per cent of the receipts. The Caledonian provided through trains from Bridge Street station,
Glasgow and three new steamers were put on the Wemyss Bay–
Millport–Rothesay routes. But the railway that was to provide
a short cut to Rothesay almost at once earned a reputation for
unreliability. The staff was inexperienced in single line working
and operational delays were frequent. A rockfall and a tunnel
collapse added to the difficulties. Passengers kept to the
Greenock trains and the new Wemyss Bay boats were withdrawn. Thereafter the pier was served by steamers plying between Glasgow, Greenock, Millport and Rothesay, but there
were no guaranteed connections. If a train was about due when
a steamer called it would await the arrival of the train; if there
was no train the steamer sailed on. Passengers arriving by rail
had to wait up to three hours for a steamer connection. Nor did
Greenock expand upwards, and the company had to sell the
ground they had bought for factory sidings at Upper Greenock.
What had promised to be an imaginative and useful line of
communication degenerated into a fiasco in a few years.

The turning point came in 1869 when Captain Alexander
Campbell left the Anchor Line to take up the management of
the Wemyss Bay Steamboat Company. Campbell was a skipper
with a flair for management, and he brought with him hand-
picked assistants of outstanding ability. David Jackson, also
from the Anchor Line, was appointed chief steward and raised
the catering on the Wemyss Bay boats to a new high standard.
Engineer Walter Templeton, brought home from service with
the Turkish navy, took care of the mechanical side. First class
service was accompanied by extremely low fares; the return
fare from Glasgow to Rothesay by the shortest and fastest route
was only 2s 6d (12½p). This policy was dictated by the Caledonian in the face of bitter opposition from the owning company.
'The Caledonian Railway Company and Captain Campbell
have begun to run the traffic from Wemyss Bay to the various
places on the coast without even asking the sanction of this
Company and at rates which this Company expressly dis-
approved,' complained the G & WB chairman. But the 'half-
crown fare' made Wemyss Bay. The sum collected in pier dues
in 1870–1 was £47 10s (£47.50); in 1880–1 it was £624 9s 4d
(£624.46½). In 1870–1 407,985 passengers were carried on the

route; in 1880–1 the figure was 770,632. The company paid its first dividend—5½ per cent—in 1878.

The Greenock and Wemyss Bay remained nominally independent until it was amalgamated with the Caledonian on 1 August 1893.

THE GREENOCK & AYRSHIRE

The Greenock & Wemyss Bay scarcely had started to function when Greenock promoted another railway. The Greenock & Ayrshire was to have its own pier a short distance west of Custom House Quay, and from there it was to strike up over the hills behind Port Glasgow and then drop down the valley of the Gryffe Water to make an end-on connection with the G & SW branch at Bridge of Weir. By establishing this line the Greenock merchants hoped to attract coal and mineral traffic direct from Ayrshire and so enhance the importance of the town as a seaport. Imports, it was hoped, would flow over the line through Ayrshire to destinations in England thus breaking the Caledonian monopoly of traffic out of Greenock. Again, the City of Glasgow Union Railway, then being constructed to link the G & SW and the NB would provide a through route from the new Greenock pier to destinations in the east of Scotland. The Greenock & Ayrshire was to be worked by the G & SW and stand much in the same relationship to the parent company as the Wemyss Bay to the Caledonian.

The Caledonian had long feared an assault on its Greenock stronghold, and now it had materialised. The G & A prospectus emphasised the Ayrshire link, but it was all too clear that the most important outcome of the new railway would be the creation of an entirely new route between Glasgow and Greenock; especially since the G & SW was planning to link its Bridge of Weir branch and the main Paisley–Ayr line with a spur between Cart Junction and Elderslie. With the G & A in its hands the G & SW would be in Greenock in full cry. Every day for one week G & SW booking clerks all over the system had been instructed to ask passengers booking for Paisley if they were travelling on to Greenock! The Caledonian opposed the Bill on the grounds that it provided an adequate service to Greenock and the coast at cheap fares. But the G & A got its Act on 5 July

1865 and opened for mineral traffic on 1 September 1869, for goods on 1 October and passengers on 23 December.

The Caledonian adopted a policy of appeasement by offering the new railway a share of its traffic, but when the peace offering was spurned a full-scale commercial war developed between the CR and the G & SW. Fares were cut until it was possible to travel from Glasgow to Greenock by either route for 6d (2½p). The trains of both companies converged on Bridge Street via the Glasgow and Paisley Joint line and delays while awaiting platform accommodation became endemic.

The real fireworks took place in the struggle for the coast traffic. The G & A's Princes Pier provided easy access between the trains and steamers whereas Caledonian passengers still had to walk from the station to Custom House Quay. But the G & A was not in a position to exploit its physical advantages. The Caledonian, long entrenched in Greenock, had the ears of the steamboat operators and used all its guile to persuade them to boycott the new pier. But one morning the renowned Captain Williamson, inward bound with his popular *Sultana*, took her into Princes Pier and the passengers flocked to the Glasgow & Ayrshire trains.

The steamboat men came to an arrangement whereby they creamed the traffic from both railways. The steamers picked up passengers from the Caledonian train at Custom House Quay and a few minutes later called at Princes Pier to embark passengers from the G & A train. The Caledonian deliberately slowed down its trains so that steamer departures from Customs House Quay were delayed and G & A passengers were kept waiting on Princes Pier. The Caledonian hoped that a policy of attrition would sicken the passengers into returning to its trains, but it had quite the opposite effect. If the public could be trifled with the Post Office could not. The Caledonian lost its mail contract which was transferred to the G & SW. More and more vessels deserted Custom House Quay for Princes Pier and soon only a handful of passengers trudged down East Quay Lane to make the Caledonian connection. Two years after its opening the G & A was carrying 200,000 passengers annually and established as *the* route to the coast. It was this turn of events that induced the Caledonian to concentrate on improving the Wemyss Bay route.

Freight traffic was disappointing; the expected flow of coal and minerals from Ayrshire did not materialise, the shippers preferring the established routes. Greenock Harbour Trustees halved the charges on vessels coming to the port in ballast to load minerals, but this inducement had no substantial effect. The passenger traffic although brisk was unremunerative. There were far too many trains chasing too few passengers, and the fiercely competitive fares were uneconomic. 'The railway is an utter failure,' admitted Provost Morton of Greenock, who had much to do with its promotion.

After two ruinous years the rival companies entered on a joint purse agreement whereby the Caledonian took 57⅔ of the Greenock revenue and the G & SW 42⅓. With the removal of unbridled competition, services were cut and fares fixed at a realistic level.

The G & A was amalgamated with the G & SW on 1 August 1872.

THE VALE OF LEVEN

The north bank of the Clyde lagged ten years behind the south bank in railway development. Helensburgh, the north bank equivalent of Greenock, was a sedate residential town of some 2,100 people with no commercial ambitions. 'It has no productive industry beyond what is required to meet its own wants and those of the summer visitors,' said the gazetteer. In the 24 miles between Helensburgh and Glasgow there was only one town of any importance, Dumbarton. And in 1840 a long-established chemical and glass industry in the town was dying and the shipyard that was to make its name had not yet been established. There was little on the north bank to attract railway promoters.

The 5 miles long valley down which the River Leven ran from Loch Lomond to the Clyde at Dumbarton was a different proposition. In the Vale of Leven were bleaching, printing and dyeing works with world-wide markets. The Glasgow, Paisley & Greenock had hoped to establish a ferry station on its line at Langbank, and run wagon ferries across the river to Dumbarton from where the traffic would be taken by rail to Balloch on Loch Lomond, but it was refused permission to proceed with the plan.

Loch Lomond was attractive to railway promoters. It was the largest sheet of inland water in the country, and it only awaited easy accessibility to make it famous. In 1803 Dorothy Wordsworth had arrived on its banks rather in the fashion of David Livingstone discovering a central African lake, and had written of its glories. 'Steamers of any power or tonnage could ply if only people could be got to the loch in sufficient numbers to fill them,' observed a traveller in 1840.

Loch Lomond was a link in the coach and steamer route from Glasgow to Inverness. Travellers from Glasgow changed to steamers at Balloch and were taken to Inverarnan 2 miles up the canalised River Falloch at the head of the loch, and conveyed from there by coaches to Oban, Fort William and Inverness. The loch also generated some useful freight traffic. Slate was quarried at Balmaha and in the hinterland of the village were the quarries producing 'Kilmaronock pavement'. Urban development in Glasgow and other towns had created a steady demand for these materials. Slate and stone were ferried across Loch Lomond from Aber pier on the east shore to Balloch where the cargoes were transferred to small 'Leven lighters' for passage down the Leven to the Clyde, thence to Glasgow, Paisley and Greenock. Some of the stone was carted to Glasgow from Balloch. The heavy carts joined the slow convoys of vehicles carrying calico from the printing works to the city markets, and the road through the Vale of Leven often was blocked with traffic. In 1840, James Thomson, civil engineer of Glasgow, expressed surprise that the fruitful vale had not been given communications more in keeping with its requirements. He was then surveying a canal from Bowling on the Clyde to Balloch, and he estimated that such a canal would attract 35,000 tons of freight a year. A provisional committee had produced detailed plans for a canal when the Caledonian & Dumbartonshire Railway appeared on the scene.

THE CALEDONIAN & DUMBARTONSHIRE

The first proposal for a railway on the north bank of the Clyde came in 1844 when a group of local proprietors, among them Colquhoun of Luss and Smollett, the MP for Dumbarton, produced their Caledonian & Dumbartonshire scheme. The line was to start at a junction with the Edinburgh & Glasgow near Cowlairs, and circle the north-west of Glasgow before striking down the Clyde to Dumbarton. From there one fork was to go up the Vale of Leven to Balloch and the other down the Clyde to Helensburgh. A lease of the line was offered to the Edinburgh & Glasgow and refused, but the Glasgow, Garnkirk & Coatbridge promptly offered to lease the c & d for seven years, and the route was altered to link with the GG & C. The E & G promoted a rival line over more or less the same ground, but its Bill was defeated. Then, in 1847, the Caledonian, as successors to the GG & C, guaranteed a dividend of 5 per cent to the c & d as the price of gaining a foothold on the north bank. But Caledonian ambitions received a setback when the rural proprietors announced that they preferred to build the c & d without outside help.

The promoters decided to use their limited resources to develop the most profitable part of their route, and they started on the construction of an $8\frac{1}{2}$ mile L-shaped line linking Bowling with Dumbarton and Balloch. Bowling was a good choice of terminus, for the line stood a chance of picking up traffic both from the canal and the river. The line of communication visualised was Glasgow to Bowling by steamer, Bowling to Balloch by train, thence steamer on Loch Lomond.

The railway was soon in trouble. Its future was too uncertain to attract the mass capital that had made the south bank schemes a success. Local subscribers defaulted on a distressing scale; after repeated calls only £36,000 of the £72,000 needed for completion of the railway had been subscribed. The directors had just called for a year's pause in construction when the ship-owning brothers George and James Burns took a lease of the line. It was an apt sponsorship. The railway was two-thirds a waterborne operation, and the Burns brothers were famous for their cheap and efficient steamer services. They had a large pier built at Balloch and a separate railway pier, Frisky Wharf, constructed at Bowling for the rapid handling of passengers and freight.

'The Dumbartonshire Railway, Railway to Loch Lomond and the Highlands' was opened for passenger traffic on 15 July 1850. Eight sailings a day from Glasgow from 7 am to 6 pm connected with trains at Bowling. The river passage took approximately 1 hour and the railway journey 30 minutes. The 8.45 and 4.15 departures from Glasgow gave through steamer connections to Inverarnan. Passengers by the morning service could be in Oban the same evening. Fares from Glasgow to Balloch were 1s 6d (7½p) first and cabin, 1s 2d (6p) first and steerage, and 11d (4½p) third and steerage, while through tickets to Invernarnan cost 3s (15p) first and cabin and 2s (10p) second and steerage. Two vessels owned by the Loch Lomond Steamboat Company operated between Balloch and Inverarnan. Burns put their own *Pilot* exclusively on short distance excursion work from Balloch in an effort to develop the tourist trade.

First class passengers who joined C & D trains at Bowling found themselves in a saloon somewhat pretentious for the size of the railway. 'It is a square apartment seated all round and with a couch in the centre, and so lofty that a tall person may walk up and down at his leisure.' Neilson supplied two engines 'constructed on the principle of having no tender', and with a large iron water tank 'under the floor'. They were, in fact, Adams light tanks, a species then enjoying a vogue.

The little railway did reasonably well. Because of it many thousands of people saw Loch Lomond for the first time. In one day 600 excursionists travelled from Edinburgh to Balloch by the E & G, Clyde steamers and C & D. Cargo and parcels were carried from Glasgow to Bowling by special steamers. An extension of the canal basin at Bowling enabled the railway, on 29 December 1850, to accept its first canal-borne mineral traffic, mainly Monkland coal. On 1 February 1851 the connecting cargo service on the Clyde was replaced by cargo vessels operating on the canal between Port Dundas and Bowling.

THE FORTH & CLYDE JUNCTION

In 1851 a railway assault on the Clyde and Loch Lomond was made from the east. At that time the Edinburgh & Glasgow Railway had no direct access to the harbour of Glasgow; all attempts to take a line to the north bank of the river or across the river by bridge had been defeated. The Forth & Clyde Junction Railway was promoted in Stirling with the object of

Page 169 (*above*) An experimental diesel multiple unit built by ACV Sales in 1952, on test at Ayr on an Ayr–Dalmellington service; (*below*) a Sentinel steam rail car arriving at Blanefield from Aberfoyle in 1932

Page 170 (*above*) Steamers at Balloch Pier, Loch Lomond;
(*below*) *Glen Sannox* in Brodick Bay, Arran, in winter

building a line from that town through the rural country north of the Campsie Fells to join the Caledonian & Dumbartonshire in the Vale of Leven. Coal from central Scotland would then pass direct to the wharves at Bowling. The railway was first mooted in 1845 when the promoters announced, 'Few railways have been projected with greater prospect of success than this. The traffic will be very great—connecting by the best and shortest line the two great rivers of east and west.' The scheme collapsed in the aftermath of the Mania.

On its revival six years later the scheme looked just as attractive to the promoters. Stirling had become an important railway centre with lines radiating from it to north, east and south. The Forth & Clyde got running powers over the Stirling & Dunfermline Railway, and over the Caledonian & Dumbartonshire to Bowling. The proprietors had visions of their trains carrying Fife export coal all the way to the Clyde, to say nothing of pig iron from Oakley. Finished textiles from the Vale of Leven factories for export to Europe from Forth ports would make up the freight on the return trip.

The building of the 30 miles and 56 chains of line across the flat, pastoral country produced no great engineering difficulties. There was a friendly, family atmosphere about the whole operation. Most of the directors lived on the route or within sight of it, among them Robert Cunninghame Graham, William Leckie Ewing, Robert Bruce and Thomas Auchterlonie. When the contractor ran into temporary difficulties eight of the directors raised a loan on his behalf. Most of the landowners gave the ground for nothing—enough for a double line although only a single line was laid. Alexander Smollett of Bonhill in the Vale of Leven struck one of the few discordant notes. He owned a bridge over the Leven and he complained that the income derived from the pontage was placed in jeopardy by the railway. He was guaranteed £100 a year in compensation. In February 1856 the *Stirling Journal* reported, 'Our ears were startled last week with the neighing of the iron horse in shape of a locomotive coming rattling along the Forth & Clyde Railway.' On 18 March 1856 the line was opened from Stirling to Buchlyvie (15½ miles) and on 26 May was opened throughout.

The Forth & Clyde never became the trunk route its opti-

L

mistic promoters envisaged. It was a typical cross-country rural line, a farmer's line. It served a scattered and static population and there was little originating traffic other than the agricultural products of the district. Farmers found that they could get their milk to town markets with greater speed than hitherto, and a small but regular milk traffic developed. The company established a dung depot at Stirling, and the harvest of the urban streets found a ready sale at stations along the line. The through traffic was more lucrative, but the export coal trains from Fife did not materialise.

The Forth & Clyde provided the first through rail link between Edinburgh and Glasgow and Loch Lomond. At an early stage the company minutes reported that a Mr Cooke [sic] had inspected the line and had included it in his Grand Scottish Tour. Through the years the summer traffic from east and central districts formed the major item in the line's passenger revenue. The subsequent opening of the Strathendrick Railway enabled F & C passengers to reach Aberfoyle and the Trossachs by changing trains at Buchlyvie.

As originally planned the F & C was to join the C & D with a junction facing Dumbarton, but the junction as built faced Balloch. This meant that traffic coming off the F & C ran toward Loch Lomond and not the Clyde. This significant alteration seems to have been made without parliamentary permission. A letter has survived written by Young, manager of the C & D, expressing his directors' approval of the plan to link up near Balloch 'the same as if the junction were made in the direction of Alexandria'.

The F & C directors were enterprising in their quest for traffic. The Dalmonach print works near Jamestown offered custom—coal and raw materials in, finished goods out, and on 1 August 1861 the company got an Act to make a siding into the works. The local authority was most apprehensive about the siding crossing the public highway to reach the works, and stringent safeguards were demanded to protect pedestrians and vehicles on the road. The company was prohibited from using the siding during the morning and evening hours when the factory employees were going to and from work. The prohibited hours incorporated in the Act throw an interesting light on working conditions of the period; 5 to 6 am and 6 to 7 pm.

The Forth & Clyde managed its own affairs from its Stirling office, but the Scottish Central provided engines and crews, and rented space to the F & C at its Stirling station. At the end of the first year the rural proprietors decided that the Scottish Central was overcharging for its services and that the F & C would not get on its feet until it owned and managed its locomotives and stock. The directors terminated their contract with the Scottish Central on 7 February 1860, and as soon as their decision became known salesmen from locomotive and carriage builders deluged the little office with plans and drawings. While the directors were pondering over their choice of engine, Thomas Yarrow, writing from the Arbroath headquarters of the Scottish North Eastern Railway offered to supply locomotives and men and to act as visiting superintendent to the F & C. The F & C directors rejected his proposal, but accepted the offer of an SNE engine on loan. Thomas Wood was appointed locomotive superintendent at £150 per annum and for this sum he was expected to function also as Inspector of the Line. The Canada Works, Birkenhead won the F & C contract for four engines and when they were delivered early in 1861 Wood assumed the title of Manager of Locomotives.

The stock ordered by the company shows the traffic pattern they hoped would develop. There were ten passenger vehicles (three first class, two composites and five third class) and 272 goods vehicles. Of these 10 were cattle trucks, 2 covered vans, 2 brake vans and 255 'platform wagons'. Two passenger luggage vans and 1 milk truck were added shortly afterwards.

The great amalgamations of 1865 brought the North British to the north bank of the Clyde and the Vale of Leven and the Caledonian to Stirling. The Caledonian, eager to reach Loch Lomond, offered the F & C $3\frac{1}{2}$ per cent on its ordinary stock and a complete overhaul of its track and rolling stock as the price of an amalgamation with the Caledonian. But the F & C opted to stay independent. A hard struggle lay ahead. There were too few people and too little potential freight in the district for the railway to have a chance of paying its way. The following table shows the population served by each station on the line (1881 figures) and the distance of each station from the village it purported to serve.

	Population	*Distance*
		(*miles*)
Gargunnock	698	¾
Kippen	403	1
Port of Mentieth	1,375	4
Buchlyvie	339	¾
Balfron	1,900	2
Drymen	1,619	2
Caldarvan	1,085	3
Jamestown	869	—

The figures for Kippen, Buchlyvie and Jamestown give the village population. The remaining figures give the population of the entire parish in which the station is situated. Thus the catchment area of the railway yielded 8,288 souls many of whom lived remote from the line. Of the eight intermediate stations only one was situated in the village it served.

After ten years of independent operation the directors leased the F & C to the North British, but the line remained a separate company until the amalgamations of 1923.

THE GLASGOW DUMBARTON & HELENSBURGH

The Clyde did not have a continuous line of railway along its north bank until the opening of the Glasgow, Dumbarton & Helensburgh in 1858. This line was a revival of the C & D proposal of 1844. From its junction with the Edinburgh & Glasgow at Cowlairs it was to run via Possil, Maryhill, Temple, Kilbowie and Old Kilpatrick to meet the C & D at Bowling. The GD & H trains were to have running powers over the C & D from Bowling to Dalreoch immediately west of the C & D bridge across the Leven at Dumbarton. From Dalreoch the route was to continue by Cardross to its terminus in Helensburgh. At the eastern end the Helensburgh trains were to have running powers into the E & G's Sighthill goods yard and Queen Street station.

The Act for the GD & H was obtained on 15 August 1855 and the proprietors were proud of the fact that the line was a local promotion. As the chairman pointed out, 'I need hardly remind you that this railway was got up on very different principles from any other. Most lines hitherto have been promoted by parties at a distance with a view to profitable investment of their funds, but the Glasgow, Dumbarton & Helensburgh was got up by the committee in the country at large for their own special convenience and advantage.' This was a dig at the English capital lavished on the south bank railways.

The GD & H was a railway of bits and pieces. The eastern section from Cowlairs to Bowling, $10\frac{3}{4}$ miles long, was divided from the western section of $7\frac{3}{4}$ miles from Dalreoch to Helensburgh by the Caledonian and Dumbartonshire. Enough ground was taken for double track but the prudent owners laid only single line at first, with spartan single-platform stations. A tunnel and cutting at Dalreoch required the removal of 130,000cu yd of red sandstone. The bridge over the Leven was ready-made, but the Helensburgh company agreed to pay the C & D one half the original cost of construction. On the eastern section of the line there was a nine-arch viaduct over the Kelvin (five arches collapsed during construction in 1857) and a four-arch viaduct over the Lussett Glen, Old Kilpatrick.

At the last minute the GD & H fell out with the E & G over terms for the use of Queen Street. The Caledonian was quick to offer better terms for the use of Buchanan Street with the result that when the line opened on 28 May 1858 the Helensburgh trains ran through Sighthill yard to reach the Caledonian terminus. This arrangement lasted until 30 June when improved E & G terms lured the GD & H to the more convenient Queen Street.

The C & D and the GD & H formed a committee of management and their joint announcements henceforth appeared under the heading The Dumbartonshire Railways. Since the GD & H had running powers over the C & D and both companies had running powers over the E & G to Queen Street most trains carried a portion for Balloch and a portion for Helensburgh between Glasgow and Dumbarton, the trains being divided at Dumbarton. Goods trains were similarly handled. With Dumbarton brought within 30 minutes of Glasgow the river boats were badly hit. The owners withdrew them from the railway pier at Bowling and switched their services to Dumbarton where they made arrangements with road hauliers to take their passengers and cargoes on to Vale of Leven destinations. At the same time they made drastic cuts in their fares, the passage from Glasgow to Dumbarton being reduced to 4d (1½p) steerage. The railway singles from Glasgow to Helensburgh were 1s 9d (9p) first class, 1s 3d (6p) third class with seats and 9d (4p) third class without seats.

The main purpose of the building of the line was the establishment of a rail and steamer route along the north bank with Helensburgh as a packet station. But when the Helensburgh board sought talks with the Clyde steamboat proprietors late in 1857 in anticipation of the opening of the line six months later they found that the wily Caledonian had earmarked all the available boats for the 1858 season. In particular it had organised a service from Greenock to the Gareloch ports right on Helensburgh's doorstep. The GD & H had to wait until 2 May 1859 before it could offer boat connections to Garelochhead, Row and Rosneath.

Helensburgh was unsuitable for a packet station. The railway station was some distance from the pier, and the people of Helensburgh, justly proud of their attractive, well-planned town, defeated every effort of the railway company to make a rail link between station and pier. On 14 August 1862 the E & G absorbed the C & D and the GD & H and on 31 July 1865 the combined system fell to the North British. At last a large company with powerful financial backing was in possession of a homogeneous north bank route to the coast. In 1866 the North British, through its subsidiary the North British Steam Packet Company, put two vessels on the Helensburgh station to ply to Rothesay, Kyles of Bute and Ardrishaig. The service failed to win support and was withdrawn after one season. Three years later a modest service between Helensburgh and the Holy Loch and Gareloch proved modestly successful, but it was 1882 before the North British risked a service to Rothesay. By that time it was clear that Helensburgh never could be made a satisfactory packet station, and the company decided to build a new station and pier at Craigendoran a mile east of the town. The pier came into use in 1883. In 1886 the Glasgow, City & District Railway was built under Glasgow to link the North British lines to the east and west of the city centre. A new route was thus provided from Edinburgh and the eastern suburbs of Glasgow through a new Queen Street Low Level station to the western suburbs and on to the coast. For the first time the North

British was fully equipped to offer a challenge to the Caledonian for the coast traffic.

THE CLYDEBANK COMPLEX

In July 1872 the Clyde Trustees obtained possession of the Clydebank shipyard of J. and G. Thomson at Govan on the south bank of the river for harbour improvement purposes. The Thomsons moved their yard to a new site on the north bank some 7 miles down river, a site not served by railways and without houses for the workers. The Thomson labour force still lived in Govan, and the problem was how to transport them daily to and from the new shipyard.

A free ferry linked Govan with Partick on the north side of the river, and through Partick passed the North British branch from Maryhill (on the Helensburgh line) to the docks at Stobcross. On 4 July 1878 the Glasgow, Yoker & Clydebank Railway got an Act to build a line from the Stobross branch down the north bank to the new shipyard. It was opened as a single line on 1 December 1882. There was a station at Partick convenient for the ferry from the south bank and an intermediate station at Yoker. The western terminus was named Clydebank. The service was an isolated one serving mainly the workers and the shipyard.

Within a year of the opening of the GY & C the Singer Manufacturing Company of New Jersey built a 46 acre factory for the manufacture of sewing machines adjoining Kilbowie station on the Helensburgh line, and $\frac{1}{2}$ mile from Thomson's shipyard. The shipyard later became John Brown's, producing some of the largest ships ever to float; the Singer factory expanded until it covered 110 acres—the biggest single industrial complex in Scotland. Clydebank grew round these two great industries and its railways shared in its prosperity.

THE LANARKSHIRE & DUMBARTONSHIRE

The Caledonian never had become reconciled to its exclusion from the north bank. By the late eighties it still had no stake in the north bank's abundant riches except for running powers to Stobcross docks grudgingly allowed by the NB and access to

Bowling by the Forth & Clyde Canal. The river bank from Glasgow down to Clydebank was a close-packed mass of engineering works, factories and shipyards all pouring traffic on to the North British. The Caledonian, sooner or later, was bound to demand a share in this bonanza.

The assault opened innocently enough in 1889 with the promotion in Dumbarton of the Dumbarton, Jamestown & Loch Lomond Railway which proposed to take a line up the east bank of the Leven to a pier at Aber Bay on Loch Lomond. Then came news of a bold scheme to build an entirely new railway from Glasgow to Dumbarton to join the proposed Loch Lomond Railway. The Lanarkshire & Dumbartonshire, independent but strongly backed by Caledonian men and money, was to hug the river passing the very doors of the shipyards and engineering factories. Passenger stations were to be planted as near as possible to corresponding stations on the parallel North British route, sidings pushed into yards and factories. At its eastern end, within the Glasgow city boundary, the L & D was to join the Glasgow Central Railway, a Caledonian counterpart of the Glasgow, City & District, a new underground railway passing the Central station and linking Caledonian lines east and west of the city centre. Also envisaged was a line that would encircle the north-west sector of the city through Maryhill and Possil (keeping close company with the Helensburgh line) and by joining existing lines would provide a freight route to the Lanarkshire coal and steel belt. The finished system would give the Caledonian control of a passenger route stretching from Coatbridge to Loch Lomond and a freight route that would carry shipbuilding materials direct to the north bank yards.

The L & D was strongly supported by the north bank shipbuilders, three of whom, John Denny, Sir Andrew McLean and James Thomason were on its board. The first meeting of directors took place on 13 November 1889, but so complicated were the preliminaries that it was not until 5 August 1891 that the company got its Act. The North British, the Forth & Clyde Junction and the newly-formed West Highland, all with a stake in Loch Lomond, opposed the Bill. The L & D on the other hand opposed the West Highland on the grounds that Ardlui station would take traffic away from the pier! It was generally agreed that two separate railways in the Vale of Leven and two terminal piers serving two separate fleets on Loch Lomond did not make sense. After much discussion the Dumbarton, Jamestown & Loch Lomond railway was dropped and the North British was forced to agree to the formation of a joint company, the Dumbarton & Balloch Joint Railway which would take over the railway from Dumbarton to Balloch and the Loch Lomond steamers. The D & BJR, in which the CR, NB and L & D were to be partners, was to start functioning on the day that the L & D opened for passenger traffic between Glasgow and Dumbarton.

The new railway was opened from Stobcross to Clydebank on 1 May 1896 and to Dumbarton East Junction, where it joined the Helensburgh line, on 1 October 1896. The stations on the riverside section were Partick Central, Partick West, Whiteinch, Victoria Park, Scotstoun, Yoker, Clydebank, Kilbowie Road, Dalmuir, Old Kilpatrick, Bowling and Dumbarton East. The L & D passed under the NB at Partick, crossed over it at Bowling and recrossed it at Dumbuck before joining it at Dumbarton East. With the advent of the L & D Bowling became the meeting place of five lines of communication; two railways, a trunk road, the canal and the river.

Clydebank was now intersected by three railways. The original Helensburgh line passed to the north of the Singer factory and the L & D to the south of it, while an extension of the GY & C passed south of the L & D. Under an Act of 1893 the GY & C was doubled and extended to join the Helensburgh line at Dalmuir. The new line left the original route about half-way between Yoker and Clydebank stations, the original Clydebank station being retained as a terminus for Glasgow suburban traffic, and a new station being built on the extension at Kilbowie Road. This was named Clydebank Central. The GY & C now became virtually a loop to the Helensburgh line and some of the through trains to Helensburgh and Balloch were routed over it.

Clydebank thus acquired five passenger stations: Central and East on the GYC, Kilbowie (to be renamed Singer) on the Helensburgh line, and Clydebank and Kilbowie Road on the L & D. In addition there were workers' platforms in Kilbowie Road opposite the Singer factory and at the L & D Clydebank station for the shipyard workers. All this passenger capacity was needed. Clydebank's population could not supply the enormous labour force required by its industries, and every day there took place a spectacular commuter operation without parallel in the country. Every morning a pattern of special trains converged on Clydebank from as far east as Airdrie and as far west as Balloch.

The 'Singer workers' became a feature of the morning and evening traffic pattern. On a typical morning between six and seven o'clock fourteen trains would be converging on Clydebank. They were easily distinguished from the ordinary suburban traffic by the guttering candles in the compartment windows; the carriages were unlit, and the workers carried their own illumination. Both the Caledonian and North British dispatched Singer trains from Balloch. They followed a common route to Dumbarton East Junction, the Caledonian train taking its own (L & D) metals to Kilbowie Road, the North British train running via the Helensburgh line to Singer. Both companies started trains at Airdrie and Coatbridge to run by their respective routes to their Clydebank destinations; Singer employees in the east end of Glasgow were catered for by three trains starting at the NB Bridgeton Cross station. Workers in the north of the city had a choice of three trains starting at Springburn. One ran via Duke Street and the Glasgow, City & District line, the other two via Cowlairs Junction and Maryhill.

The greatest single prize on the L & D route was the Singer factory, but the L & D found itself barred from it. The North British had entered on a 'thirling' agreement with Singers for the specific purpose of keeping the Caledonian out, and the agreement still had eleven years to run. The L & D, making the ingenuous plea that it was *not* the Caledonian, sought permission to put a branch into the factory. Singer's law agent replied that the L & D could put a siding into the works if they wanted provided the Caledonian would give an undertaking not to send traffic over it! The Forth & Clyde Canal separated the L & D from the Singer factory and in 1901 the directors decided to erect a swing bridge across the canal in anticipation of the time when a siding might be taken into the works, but Singer asked the company to delay construction of the bridge until they were free to allow the railway to enter their factory. Nevertheless, the L & D accepted a tender from Sir William Arrol to build the bridge.

If the Singer factory was barred to the L & D there were other pickings to be had along the line. The L & D invited industrialists to apply for branch lines which would be built to the factory gates free. Layouts inside the factories were offered at reasonable terms. Sidings costing £1,165 13s 7d (£1,165.68) were put in at Beardmore's Dalmuir engine works, Yarrow's new yard at Scotstoun was linked with the railway as was the Coventry Ordnance Works. Halley's International Motor Company acquired a loading bank at Yoker. When Rothesay Dock was built at Clydebank in the first years of the twentieth century to handle the bulk of the river's mineral traffic both the L & D and the NB ran branches to the dock. All in all the L & D developed into a busy freight line with heavy, all-year-round commuter traffic, and a brisk passenger trade with Loch Lomond in the summer. The railway was vested in the Caledonian on 1 August 1909.

THE DUMBARTON & BALLOCH JOINT RAILWAY

The D & BJR with its 6 miles of track and fleet of steamers on Loch Lomond was the most distinctive of the Scottish joint lines. The events of the months preceding its formation give an insight into what happened when two incompatible partners were forced into marriage. The D & BJR, of course, was to come into being on the day the L & D opened. During the construction of the L & D the Caledonian, fearing that the NB deliberately would neglect maintenance on the property to be handed over, insisted on inspections of the future D & BJR being made, and this included the Loch Lomond steamers.

On 25 August 1896 eleven NB senior officers and their exact CR counterparts met at Dumbarton station and moved in a body to a point 656yd east of the booking office. This was to be the starting point of the joint line. The NB men were on their own ground, and they had made up their minds in advance what they wanted. The East Junction signal box was *their* box, they told the Caledonian men; it would be worked by NB men who would be paid by the D & BJ. To this the Caledonian coldly replied, 'We will look into the matter and Mr Deuchars (NB superintendent) will be communicated with.' The party moved to the Dalreoch box where a similar interlude took place. By the end of the tour of inspection, with the NB claiming privileges everywhere, a fund of ill-will had been built up between the prospective partners.

On 26 September 1896, Thompson of the Caledonian wired Conacher of the NB, 'We will open the L & D on 1 October.' On the same day the Caledonian, without prior consultation with the NB, published its Glasgow–Dumbarton–Balloch timetables. Some of its trains, notably those connecting with steamers, rode roughshod over the existing NB timings. A hurried meeting took place between NB and CR representatives and the worst anomalies were ironed out.

When the D & BJ opened on 1 October it had neither a manager nor a secretary. Certain operating personnel had not been told whether they were working for the NB or the D & BJ. Booking clerks did not know where to send the money they collected. Eventually, they were told to send it to a Mr Reid in a Glasgow office. Every day Mr Reid was visited by representatives of the NB, CR and L & D who checked the takings.

The prospect of a new railway to Loch Lomond was welcomed by Glaswegians and residents in the Vale of Leven alike, for the long NB monopoly of Loch Lomond had led to higher than normal fares being charged. The return fare from Glasgow to Ardlui was 5s (25p) whereas the fare from Glasgow to Rothesay, a comparable distance, was 2s 6d (12½p). The new timetable doubled the number of trains leaving Vale of Leven stations, but the advantage to the travelling public was doubtful. Passengers entraining in the Vale of Leven or at Dumbarton had to specify whether they wanted to travel in an NB or CR train. The luckless passengers who got into a carriage of the wrong colour and arrived at a station on the Caledonian with an NB ticket were charged single fare from Dumbarton. A regular traveller wrote in the *Glasgow Herald* two days after the opening of the line,

> With baited breath we have awaited the labour of the mountain and behold the proverbial mouse. Instead of additional facilities we have the North British railway fares stereotyped and their trains merely duplicated by the Caledonian. Worst of all, in spite of newspaper announcements, the various station officials steadily decline to take each other's tickets, thereby causing endless confusion and chagrin. Conceive a partnership where the partners keep each a different set of books and protest each other's checks.

The Caledonian was to regret its precipitate action in forcing the opening of the D & BJ at short notice. There were only NB tickets at the joint line stations on opening day and all passengers for destinations beyond Dumbarton were forced to travel by NB trains. The Caledonian forthwith sent tickets printed 'D & BJR via Caledonian'.

William Fraser, formerly manager of the Loch Tay Steamboat Company was appointed manager of the D & BJ, and under his guidance order was wrought out of chaos. A list of staff for transfer from the NB to the new company was drawn up and distinctive uniforms provided. The Loch Lomond steamers lost their NB look and emerged in an attractive livery of red funnels, pink paddle boxes and silver-grey hulls. Fraser was responsible to a joint committee consisting of eight members, four from the NB and two each from the Caledonian and L & D. Fraser was obliged to buy his stores either from the Caledonian or North British, although he was at liberty to accept the lowest offer. In the event of offers being equal he had to buy half his requirements from the NB and half from the CR. He had to ensure that freight collected at joint line stations and consigned 'via CR' or 'via NB' in fact went by the correct route. Unconsigned freight was sent by Caledonian and North British on alternate weeks.

The Loch Lomond steamers gave a year-round service for passengers, mail, cargo and livestock, and played an important part in the lives of the lochside communities, to some of which the steamers provided the only reasonable means of communication. There was a world of difference between the *Prince of Wales* cruising round the sunlit islands packed with summer tourists and the *Empress* beating down a dark and sleet-swept loch on her 6.30 am sailing from Ardlui to Balloch on a December Monday morning. An *Empress* breakfast menu, still in existence, describes the fare offered the Edwardian merchants and business men on their $2\frac{1}{4}$ hour voyage down the loch; fish, ham and eggs, cold salami, cold joints, tea and coffee. And all for 2s (10p). The D & BJ boats developed a tradition of their own, and the loch skippers became as well known as their counterparts on the Clyde. The vessels were magnificently appointed. The D & BJ accounts show numerous items for dining-room plate and the French polishing of furniture and woodwork. The

vessels were frequently painted and always by small local firms
—one man to one boat.

In its first year of operation the company spent £45,252 in
providing additional platforms and berthage at Balloch Pier.
When the steamers arrived at the pier the passengers took their
seats in the train of their choice, Caledonian or North British,
and the rival companies vied with each other to provide an
attractive service. The NB had a train leaving Balloch Pier at
7.50 am due in Glasgow Queen Street at 8.30, while the Caledonian fixed its departure at 7.40 due in Glasgow Central at
8.25. The next NB train, the boat connection, left Balloch Pier
at 8.50 to arrive in Queen Street at 9.40. The rival Caledonian
train left Balloch 13 minutes behind the NB train, but it ran
express to Glasgow and arrived at Central also at 9.40.

The D & BJ fell heir to the freight traffic of the Vale of Leven.
The Cordale branch was built to serve the works of Messrs Wil-
liam Stirling. Prospects looked bright in 1907 when the motor
industry came to the vale with the establishment of Argyll
Motors at Alexandria. The D & BJ put two sidings into the works
at its own expense—£1,508—and subsequently got all the
Argyll traffic. But Argyll Motors were slow to settle accounts.
When their freight debt to the D & BJ stood at £500 a reminder
brought a cheque for £219 12s 7d (£219.63) dated 1 July 1908.
It was dishonoured by the bank and three days later Argyll
Motors went into liquidation.

The formation of the D & BJ had the curious result of depriving
the North British of a through route of its own between Glasgow
and Helensburgh. Between Dumbarton East Junction and
Dalreoch NB trains had to use the metals of the joint line, but
the NB had not anticipated that it would have to pay tolls to the
D & BJ for its through traffic. Litigation on the matter between
the NB on one hand and the CR and L & D on the other dragged
on for ten years until, in 1906, the court decided that the NB
must pay £250 a year, plus £2,500 back money, to the joint
line.

From 1 August 1909 the Caledonian and North British became the sole partners in the D & BJ. The joint line functioned
until nationalisation in 1948.

GOUROCK

In spite of improvements and developments on the north bank the south bank carried the bulk of the coast traffic. The G & SW had its direct route to Greenock; the Caledonian was doing well with the Wemyss Bay route, but rather poorly with its original Greenock route. The stage was set for the next episode in the tussle for traffic.

In 1877 a group of railway adventurers promoted a railway to run either from the Caledonian or the G & SW at Greenock round the coast via Gourock to Ravenscraig where a new pier to rival Wemyss Bay would be built. Gourock consisted of a few houses clustered round a headland flanked by two bays. There was a small stone pier on the headland. The plan was to take the railway across both bays on causeways, each causeway being pierced by a bridge giving access to the beach to small vessels. This proposal resulted in the formation of the Committee Opposed to the Railway Crossing the Bay, and the enterprise collapsed in a morass of parochial bickering.

In fact, the Caledonian had bought Gourock pier and the surrounding land in 1869 with an eye to future development. The Caledonian Railway (Gourock Branch and Quays) Bill of 21 March 1878 gave an indication of what that development entailed. Smithells of the Caledonian made it clear in his evidence that his company intended to create, not only a packet station, but an ocean terminal with wharfage for transatlantic liners and cargo ships. The rise of Gourock as an international port could take place only at the expense of Greenock. The Greenock authorities looked on the Caledonian proposals as treachery, for at that very moment they were spending money on cranes specially to accommodate the Caledonian at the new Garvel dock. The G & SW saw in the Bill the instrument that would give its rival a sweeping monopoly of the Renfrewshire coast. Between them Greenock and the Sou' West ensured that the preamble was not proved.

But the Caledonian was not to be kept out of Gourock. An Act was soon obtained to make a passenger pier at Gourock with a rail link to it from Greenock. The extension was a costly one to make. The railway could not be taken round the built-up coastline, and had to be driven under Greenock in the longest tunnel in Scotland. It was not until 1889 that the job was finished, but the Caledonian's £600,000 investment was to prove richly rewarding.

The new pier at Gourock was a masterpiece. It was bigger than Princes Pier, closer to the principal resorts, and express trains ran from the heart of Glasgow to the gangways. The private steamboat owners, who had been picking up a good livelihood at Princes Pier were apprehensive about the re-emergence of the Caledonian, and plotted to force the highest possible fee for serving Gourock. But the Caledonian created its own steamboat-owning subsidiary, the Caledonian Steam Packet Company, and had four vessels ready for service when the first train steamed into Gourock on 1 June 1889. The four steamers with their gleaming black hulls, white superstructures and yellow funnels, established a dynasty that was to become famous in Clyde steamer annals. Just as Princess Pier had ousted Custom House Quay twenty years before, so Gourock ousted Princes Pier in 1889. The Caledonian had turned the tables on the Sou' West. Captain Campbell, who had done so much for the Caledonian on the Wemyss Bay route regarded the coming of the Caledonian Steam Packet Company as an affront, and in 1890 he gave one week's notice of withdrawal of his steamers. The csp Co promptly put two brand new vessels on the route, and the Caledonian triumph was complete.

The G & sw retaliated by purchasing ground near Princes Pier from the Greenock Harbour Trust for £42,000 and on it built a new pier and station in the 'Spanish style blended with a treatment of the Renaissance'. Whatever it was, it was impressive especially when viewed from the sea. By establishing and running its own fleet of finely-appointed steamers the Sou' West managed to retain a worthwhile share of the traffic, and by building bigger and faster ships than the Caledonian it managed to win back some of the lost traffic. When the new Princes Pier station and pier were opened for traffic on 25 May 1894 the scene was set for a great triangular duel for the coast traffic.

Page 187 (above) A Caledonian Railway West Coast express ready to depart from Glasgow Central; (below) an interior view of Glasgow Central station

Page 188 (*above*) Locomotives and social history. The engine which headed Gladstone's train from Edinburgh to Glasgow when he was on his last campaign. The prime minister's bust is displayed on the buffer beam; (*below*) a Caledonian locomotive fitted with condensing apparatus to minimise pollution on the underground lines

By this time there were thriving residential villages round the shore of the Holy Loch and Loch Long—Hunter's Quay, Sandbank, Strone, Kilmun, Blairmore and Kilcreggan—and every morning steamers of the CSP Co, NB and G & SW called at the piers in quick succession and whisked away their respective shares of the commuter traffic to Gourock, Princes Pier or Craigendoran for transfer to express trains for Glasgow. There were also competing services from the larger towns of Dunoon and Rothesay. In the evening the process was reversed. Round 4 pm three trains left Glasgow and sped by their various routes to the coast with the first batch of returning commuters. Before the connecting steamers had delivered their passengers at their destinations three more express trains had set off from Glasgow with the second wave of homebound commuters. The following skeleton timetables show the pattern of the up morning runs from Rothesay and Dunoon in 1898.

	NB *via* *Craigendoran*	*CR* *via* *Gourock*	*G & SW* *via* *Princes Pier*
Rothesay dep	7.15	7.15	7.20
Dunoon dep	7.55	8.0	7.50
Train dep	8.26	8.19	8.20
Glasgow arr	9.3	9.0	9.0

The G & SW provided a second express from Princes Pier to Glasgow St Enoch at 8.25.

The down service in the evening was equally impressive.

	NB	*CR*	*G & SW*
Glasgow	4.10	4.13	4.3
Pier dep	4.41	4.48	4.40
Dunoon arr	5.12	5.8	5.3
Rothesay arr	5.52	5.48	5.40
Glasgow	5.10	5.20	5.5
Pier dep	5.52	6.0	5.43
Dunoon arr	6.23	6.20	6.15
Rothesay arr	7.3	7.0	6.55

The Clyde services of the period provided a classic example of keen competition giving the community high quality service at low fares. The Clyde commuters performed their daily

M

journeys in an atmosphere of pounding paddle wheels and belching funnels. The engineers kept the machinery in tiptop condition. The rival companies added bigger and faster vessels to their fleets and put locomotives of increasing power on the connecting trains. The routes to the coast, much of the mileage in built-up areas and abounding in curves and gradients, were not designed for sustained high speed, yet some spectacular running was achieved.

Even at its peak the Clyde coast traffic did not justify the elaborate triplication of services. Hard economic facts forced the contestants to seek agreements and the early years of the twentieth century saw a modification of the competition for traffic. But the three routes continued to offer excellent services until the outbreak of World War I when most of the steamers were sent on sterner duties, some of them never to return.

With the grouping of 1923 two railway fleets, LMS and LNER, handled the Clyde services, but there was no drastic change in the traffic pattern. Some LMS steamers began their sailings at Princes Pier in connection with trains on the former G & SW route before sailing to Gourock to collect passengers off the former Caledonian trains. The Second World War and nationalisation brought more sweeping changes. With a unified railway fleet now operating, rationalisation was possible. Steamers ceased to call at Princes Pier although the train service from Glasgow was maintained. For a period in the 1950s and 60s Princes Pier functioned as an ocean terminal, for liners from the USA and Canada, passengers being conveyed to and from Glasgow by special boat trains. The last boat train ran on 30 November 1965 and the passenger service beyond Kilmacolm was withdrawn on 14 February 1966, freight on 26 September 1966. Princes Pier station buildings have been demolished and the site utilised as a container terminal with rail connection to the Gourock line. Services on the Gourock and Wemyss Bay lines, as on the Craigendoran route, have been revolutionised by electrification.

Clyde excursion traffic fell away rapidly in the 1960s to be replaced by car-ferry traffic. The emphasis now is on catering for the car-owning visitor to the Clyde resorts rather than the passenger who wants a sail in the traditional style.

CHAPTER VIII

Glasgow

The rapidity of conveyance on railways, and the small cost at which trains are run are two elements which, if properly understood and worked together, seem to afford the means of enabling thousands who now live in cities to sleep every night in the pure air of the country. The working classes are not likely to be the first to enjoy the double benefit of city employment and wages and country residence to boot. There are thousands of persons of means superior to theirs who need country air as much as they. The working classes will be well off if the migration from the city of a large number of the wealthier classes gives to them a better choice of dwellings in the city. We do not wish to see cities deserted, but we wish to see some influence at work which will constrain the owners of property in cities, for their own sakes, to take effectual measures for the improvement of their houses; and that influence lies latent in the incorporated bodies of shareholders who own the lines of railway which, connecting city with town and town with country, offer facilities for travelling undreamt of in past times.

Thus did the *North British Railway and Shipping Journal* foresee the commuter age in December 1848.

If, in the opening decade of the nineteenth century the corporation of Glasgow was not railway minded, at least its members were disposed to listen to the views of their esteemed consulting engineer, Thomas Telford. The magistrates were preoccupied with the river, and Telford advised on the bridges and harbour; he was a Glasgow favourite. It was probably because he reported favourably on an 1809 scheme to build a horse tramway from Glasgow to Berwick that the corporation contributed £24 towards the survey. The tramway was to have wagons fitted with removable bodies which could be transferred to road vehicles at any part of the city served by the railway; surely the earliest version of rail-borne container traffic. When more money was sought for a re-survey of the route in

1810 the corporation refused to contribute on the grounds that the tramway was more a national than a local scheme.

In 1824 Telford reported on a scheme for canalising the Clyde above Glasgow as far as Carmyle, and running short railways from nearby villages to piers served by the river steamers. Nothing came of this typical product of canal age thinking. There was no demand for urban transport. Its citizens found it no hardship to walk, for Glasgow was a small city. For those who had to travel further afield there was the Clyde and the canals.

Kirkman Finlay, governor of the Company of Proprietors of the Forth & Clyde Navigation, privately informed the Corporation of Glasgow in March 1824 that the Monkland & Kirkintilloch was about to be promoted. He pointed out that the railway would feed coal to the canal and increase the canal's traffic. Since the corporation held stock in the canal would it not be prudent for the city to back the railway financially? The Glasgow magistrates were not deceived. They well knew that Monkland coal that reached the Forth & Clyde Canal went to Edinburgh, and the last thought in their minds was to subsidise coal for *Edinburgh*. They refused to support the railway, but sought to have a clause inserted in the Act ensuring that coal coming down the railway and bound for Glasgow would be charged no more than coal for Edinburgh.

A direct request for support from the Monkland & Kirkintilloch board in January 1826 was refused, but a similar request from the Garnkirk & Glasgow in May 1827 had better luck. By this time the corporation had appointed a committee on inland communications, and industrialists and ship owners, pleading the city's chronic shortage of coal, urged the corporation to give official support to the railway. They agreed on the grounds that the railway was 'a probable means of checking or counteracting the effect of future combinations among the workmen employed in producing that article'. In other words, they hoped the Garnkirk & Glasgow would tap new pits and help to cut out the coal strikes which the shortage of coal had encouraged.

THE FIRST STATIONS

The Townhead station of the Garnkirk & Glasgow remained for ten years the only station in Glasgow. Situated inconveniently on the fringe of the city, and with nothing to commend it architecturally, it played little part in the community life of the citizens. The transportation centre remained in Trongate, where the offices of the coach proprietors were situated. Patrons of the railway went by coach from Trongate to the distant railway station, or walked.

Bridge Street station, opened in 1841 to accommodate the GPK & A and the GP & G, was a different proposition. Its situation on the west side of Bridge Street, the main thoroughfare leading south from Glasgow Bridge, was convenient for the business and commercial centre; its imposing appearance with its fine Grecian portico and supporting pillars in cream stone, commanded attention. Queen Street, opened in 1842 as the gateway to Edinburgh, brought the railway still closer to the city centre. The function of all three stations and the railways that served them was to get people out of the city rather than provide transport within its boundaries. Urban development extended barely a mile beyond each of the terminals.

Bridge Street and Queen Street quickly developed character and became focal points of the community. Contemporary descriptions, not all of them flattering, portray the terminals as lively places. A guide book thus explained to Glaswegians the then novel process of buying a ticket at Bridge Street.

> Upon entering the traveller advances to the clerk, states the place to which he intends to journey, pays his fare, receives a ticket corresponding to the class of carriage he has chosen and takes his seat. Here all is bustle and activity. Crowds of travellers including gentlemen, manufacturers, merchants and others of every rank and profession down to the humble operative, ladies gay and buxom, country damsels, persons young, middle-aged and stricken in years, married and unmarried, are seen hurrying to and fro or anxiously taking their places in the different carriages. The officers, too, are assisting the travellers into the carriages, superintending the trains and taking care that everything is in proper order.

Edinburgh & Glasgow officials seemed to have been less

solicitous towards their passengers if the first-hand account of a
traveller between Queen Street and Edinburgh in July 1847 is
to be believed.

> On arriving at the station at nine o'clock I found the narrow passage
> or street in which it is situated crowded to suffocation till half an hour
> after the time the train ought to have started. The engine hissed and
> snorted, and the whole went round, but we were long, long in getting
> into daylight. When we got there I looked out and found we were
> merely crawling along; indeed, sometimes we stopped altogether. A
> good many got out of the carriages and a proposal was made that all
> should get out and shove it along.

If the Glasgow passenger stations of the early 1840s served the
city reasonably well the adjoining goods stations did not. Queen
Street goods station was hopelessly cramped. Townhead was
too far away from the city centre. But the cardinal fault was
that there was no goods station on either river bank, and freight
from the railway depots had to be carted through the city
streets to the Clyde. Between 1810 and 1846 the number of
vessels berthing in Glasgow harbour had increased sevenfold.
In 1810 all were sailing ships, now many were steamers that had
to be bunkered. The south bank of the river dealt with two-
thirds of the exports including all the coal and mineral traffic,
while the north bank concentrated mainly on imports. Masses
of traffic converging on the river caused the utmost congestion
in the Glasgow streets. Carts of coal from the Townhead depot
or the Monkland Canal basin jostled for a place on Glasgow
Bridge with carts of cotton goods from the east end mills. A herd
of cattle being driven through a city street from the harbour
was likely to encounter heavy lorries laden with machinery for
export. Glasgow's crying need was for an efficient goods station
on either river bank.

On 1 August 1811 William Dixon, coalmaster, bought
1,242sq yd of ground from the corporation of Glasgow for the
purpose of building a tramway on which to convey coal from
his Govan pits to the Ardrossan Canal basin at Port Eglinton.
Nearly twenty years later Dixon promoted the Polloc & Govan
Railway which was in effect a partial realignment of the tramway and its extension to Rutherglen in one direction and to
Windmillcroft on the south bank of the Clyde in the other

direction. The object of the railway was to carry coal from the Dixon pits to the river for export to other parts of Scotland and beyond.

Windmillcroft was described as 'one of the most important and valuable appendages of the Corporation' and the magistrates fiercely opposed its despoliation by a railway. They argued, too, that a railway designed to export coal to other parts of Scotland would not benefit the citizens of Glasgow, and anyway the land might be required in future for quays and docks. Dixon fought for the Polloc & Govan off and on for a decade, but it was not until 22 August 1840 that the railway was opened 'from Rutherglen to the Broomielaw Harbour'. The promoters found themselves with 2,100yd of the line still to construct four days before the deadline set by the Act, but the job was completed and the opening took place as planned. It was very much a Dixon family occasion with William Dixon's son and his friends riding in open wagons and the pit band blaring suitable music.

Extravagant opening day speeches envisaged the extension of the line to the Monklands, Wishaw, Coltness and Hamilton with the Broomielaw becoming a central coal depot. But the Polloc & Govan remained little more than a colliery tramway. Its life was short. On 14 March 1867 an Act was obtained authorising the lifting of the railway from West Street down which it passed on its way to the Clyde.

The Glasgow Harbour Union Railway was an 1846 scheme to get coal down to the north bank of the Clyde. The line was to leave the Edinburgh & Glasgow at the approaches to Queen Street and drop partly in tunnel under the city to emerge on the quay a short distance below Glasgow Bridge. Along 1,300 linear yards of the river front were to be erected coal staithes, two of them built out in the river, and two on the passenger quay at the Broomielaw. Three local engineers reported on the scheme for the Clyde Trustees and roundly condemned it. Their report painted a grim picture of the harbour under a constant cloud of coal dust smothering the passengers and permeating the sheds and warehouses containing the grain, spices, textiles and other exports and imports. The report concluded with the engineers' views of the relationship that should exist between any proposed railway and the harbour authorities.

We again express our sincere hope that the Trustees shall never permit a single square inch of either the streets or the quays, or the water
surface of the harbour to be occupied by coal staithes; and most re-
spectfully advise that no railways of any kind be permitted to be
placed upon any part of the sheds or the streets of the quays of the
harbour of Glasgow, but that those railways with their termini and
also their depots, shall be placed on ground adjacent thereto, and at a
convenient distance from the sheds and streets of the quays, so that the
traffic may be carried on to or from the harbour in a manner similar
to the general traffic which is now carried on in this Port.

In spite of this depressing report the deputy chairman and
five members of the board of the Clyde Trustees saw fit to take
shares in a company which sought to make a coal depot out of
1,200 linear yards of the south bank. This was the General
Terminus & Glasgow Harbour Railway authorised in 1846 to
build a line from the Polloc & Govan Railway to the Clyde and
link it with the Glasgow & Paisley Joint, the Glasgow Paisley
Kilmarnock & Ayr, the Glasgow Barrhead & Neilston, and the
Clydesdale Junction. With such a line in operation coal from
the Lanarkshire and Ayrshire collieries could be taken direct to
the Clyde over railways either completed or authorised.

The General Terminus was planned in detail to handle export coal. A hydraulic crane by Armstrong of Newcastle, the
first of its kind in Scotland, was built on the quay to lift coal
wagons and empty them into the holds of ships. Power for the
crane was provided by the recently-formed Gorbals Gravitation
Water Company. The hydraulic crane was augmented by two
conventional steam cranes.

The General Terminus Railway was ready for use by
December 1848. Its main feeder, the Clydesdale Junction, did
not open until 1 June 1849, and the GT officials used the gap to
test their equipment and perfect their loading technique. On
16 February 1849 a demonstration coal train was run from
Dixon's Govan colliery and its load was taken on by the *Visitor*
of Waterford. It was found that the hydraulic crane could
handle one wagon every three minutes. Clearly the General
Terminus proprietors had a coal handling plant much more
efficient than anything yet seen in Scotland.

The opening of the Glasgow Barrhead & Neilston Direct
Railway on 29 September 1848 saw the establishment of South

Side station at the southern end of Main Street, Gorbals. Then, on 1 November 1849, the Caledonian opened a terminus at the head of Buchanan Street on the north bank to replace the unsatisfactory Townhead station. The Glasgow Garnkirk & Coatbridge had already spent £20,000 on arches over which it hoped to extend the line from Townhead to a point nearer the city centre, but when the GG & C fell to the Caledonian that company's engineer vetoed the scheme on the grounds that the new terminal would stand too high above street level. Access to Buchanan Street station was gained by taking the approach line off the GG & C at Milton Junction about 2 miles short of the terminal and dropping it down through St Rollox and under the Forth & Clyde Canal. Part of the line was cut through deep deposits of chemical waste from the Tennant works. The 'pestilential effluence' of which the first passengers by the new route complained was still in evidence when the line closed 118 years later.

Both Buchanan Street and South Side were little more than wooden sheds. The Caledonian had hoped to give Glasgow a station worthy of the city on the north bank close to the river into which its principal trains from the south would run. But opinion in Glasgow was such that a railway bridge across the Clyde was unacceptable, and the Caledonian had to be content to terminate its south trains at South Side, which at least was marginally better than Townhead. When Buchanan Street was opened the English traffic was transferred back to the north side.

CROSSING THE CLYDE

In 1846, just before the opening of the North British, there were 105 miles of railway representing a capital outlay of £2,751,827 north of the Clyde while the 73 miles of completed railway south of the Clyde accounted for £1,870,971. Glasgow needed a railway bridge across the Clyde for two reasons; to bring the south side lines into a central station on the north bank and to link the systems north and south of the river. But any railway company that suggested building a bridge faced opposition from four sources: the inevitable rival scheme; the corporation of Glasgow which was jealous of preserving the amenities of the river; the River Trustees who feared that traffic would flow from river to railway and so diminish their revenue; and the Bridge Trustees who foresaw a fall in road bridge tolls following the building of a railway bridge. Between March and August 1846 a Parliamentary Select Committee produced 1,470 pages of notes on the subject, but no bridge.

The West of Scotland Junction Railway thought it had got over most of the objections by proposing to build a railway bridge on top of Glasgow Bridge, thus creating a double-decked structure. It was an Edinburgh & Glasgow scheme, Learmonth the chairman of the WSJ being also chairman of the E & G. But the Caledonian also had plans to bridge the Clyde. Both companies promised generous compensation, even offering to take over the future upkeep of the city's road bridges in exchange for the *sole* right to build a railway bridge. The Bridge Trustees played off one railway against the other. 'Before the Trust agrees to accept this arrangement', said one of its members, 'they ought to exhaust every means of arranging with other railway companies who desire to cross the Clyde. Such terms might be procured as would throw the bridges at once free of debt.'

The WSJ proposal to build on top of Glasgow Bridge sparked off an unholy row. The bridge, the widest in Britain and 5ft longer than any Thames bridge, was held in special affection by Glaswegians. It was Telford's last masterpiece, a monument 'illustrative of the munificence and taste of Glasgow, at once the ornament and boast of the city'. To add insult to injury Edinburgh gave parliamentary support to the WSJ Bill. 'Why, having a fine city of their own', bewailed the *Glasgow Argus*, 'should they, for their own convenience or love of gain spoil ours? What would they say if some Glasgow scheme were in contemplation to build a railway station with a tall belfry or steeple to it within a yard of their beautiful Scott monument?' When the Bill reached the House of Commons it was described as a scheme to give John Miller, CE, power to do what he liked with the city of Glasgow. The preamble was not proved.

The Caledonian scheme fared no better although for a different reason. In 1844 the Clyde Trustees had bought 61 acres of undeveloped land on the north bank at Stobcross a mile down the river from Glasgow Bridge, with a view to making a large new dock. In the same year a government deputation condemned the scheme and recommended that the upper reach of the Clyde between Glasgow Bridge and Stockwell Bridge be converted into a harbour capable of taking the largest ships. Such a harbour would have enclosed fifteen acres of water in the centre of the city and would have been convenient to the Customs House and warehouses. It was across this harbour, between the two city bridges, that the Caledonian proposed to take a railway bridge to a terminus on the corner of Argyle Street and Dunlop Street. The Admiralty refused to sanction the bridge unless the Caledonian agreed to include an opening span. The railway company undertook to build an opening bridge provided an assurance was received that the Bridge Trustees would rebuild Glasgow Bridge with an opening span. But there was no enthusiasm for the harbour in Glasgow and nothing more was heard of the scheme.

The Glasgow, Airdrie & Monklands Junction (Chapter II) overcame the opposition by offering to build its bridge well to the east of the city bridges. But a long approach viaduct on the north side was to profane Glasgow Green, an area prescribed by parliamentary statute as 'an open space for the use of the common citizens for washing, drying, bleaching and making their walks and sports.' Amid howls of protest the company erected two full-sized specimen arches in wood and stucco on the Green to show the citizens what the finished bridge would look like. More than a year later the arches were still in place, monuments to a lost cause, and the company was under pressure from the corporation to remove them.

The bridge question lay dormant for twenty years, to re-emerge in the sixties with an urgency that demanded an early answer. By 1864 the Caledonian was handling 2,760,000 passengers at its Glasgow terminals, the G & SW 780,000 and the E & G 1,570,000 in stations that were becoming increasingly inadequate. A new situation had been created by the friendly relationship which had arisen between the Edinburgh & Glasgow and the Glasgow & South Western. The two companies were cut off from direct physical contact by the unbridged Clyde and their common enemy the Caledonian. Rather than send freight to the east over the Caledonian the Sou' West had been known to route it via Gretna! It was natural, then, that

E & G and the G & SW should unite to promote the City of Glasgow Union Railway.

The new scheme entailed the building of a SW–NE diagonal line from the Glasgow & Paisley Joint line near West Street to the Sighthill branch of the Edinburgh & Glasgow at Springburn. The suggestion was that the river bridge and a new station on the north bank would be available to all comers, and attention was drawn to the fact that the South Eastern, the London Chatham & Dover and the Great Western co-existed peacefully under one London roof. But Glasgow was not London. When the Caledonian learned that only two of the proposed nine directors of the CGU would be Caledonian appointees it lost interest in the scheme and concentrated on plans to cross the Clyde on a bridge of its own.

Following the 1865 amalgamations the NB became the second partner in the CGU. Many amending Acts were passed to meet local difficulties before the line took its final shape. Its southern starting point was moved 315yd west of Shields Road to Pollok Junction. From there the line was to pass to the north of South Side station, cut through Gorbals mainly on arches and cross the river at Hutchesontown. Immediately north of the river (Clyde Junction) a branch was to swing round parallel with the river and run into a new terminal station which was to be of outstanding architectural distinction and stand in spacious lawn-flanked grounds with frontages in St Enoch Square and Argyle Street. The main line was to run straight on from Clyde Junction to join the projected Coatbridge branch. This line, the successor to the abortive Glasgow, Airdrie & Monklands Junction, was the final link in the chain that was to establish the route from Edinburgh to Glasgow via Bathgate. The long delayed transfer of the university to the West End had at last been arranged and the NB had acquired ground for a passenger and goods station—to be named College—on the site of the old university, immediately west of the junction of the CGU and the Coatbridge line. CGU trains were to use Coatbridge branch metals as far as Bellgrove Junction where the CGU main line would swing to the left and continue to climb steeply through Duke Street, Alexandra Park and Barnhill to its planned junction with the NB at Springburn.

The building of the CGU, 6¼ miles long, took eleven years and cost £2,000,000 compared with the £1,470,000 it had cost to build the two major systems it joined. The site on which the bridge was built had silted up and the engineers had to go down 80ft to find a foundation for the piers. There were five central spans of 75ft each and two side spans over riverside streets of 63ft 9in each. The Bellgrove to Springburn section ran through a succession of short tunnels and deep walled cuttings which demanded much time and money in their execution.

In the city centre there was endless difficulty over the acquisition of land. The cGU's fine plans for an elaborate station in St Enoch Square were delayed by resident tenants who refused to vacate their properties. The company stopped the branch short at Dunlop Street where a temporary four-platform station was established, while the fight for ground was continued. It was to be six years before St Enoch came into use. It was all that the cGU had promised. With its hotel (the largest in Scotland) it was a great Gothic castle of a place. Passengers who alighted there on 1 May 1876 after having travelled from St Pancras by the first train over the Settle and Carlisle route must have seen something of Midland splendour in St Enoch's glazed arch, 504ft long, 80ft high and with a clear span of 198ft. Glasgow's first really great terminal station received the royal accolade, and a ceremonial opening, on 17 October 1876 when the Prince and Princess of Wales arrived in the royal train. In 1883 the station and its approach lines were taken over by the G & SW and St Enoch became the headquarters of that company.

The cGU's first service was a modest passenger shuttle between Shields Road and the temporary Dunlop Street station. It was significant in that it provided the people of the south side with the first rail link to the city centre. There were no intermediate stations at first, but Main Street, Gorbals was opened on 1 January 1872. The shuttle service was extended to Bellgrove on the Coatbridge line calling at Gallowgate on 1 July 1871. The trains worked into Dunlop Street and were propelled out over Clyde Junction to resume their journey. On 1 September 1872 through services to Edinburgh via Bathgate from Greenock, Ardrossan and Ayr were inaugurated.

The northern section of the cGU from Bellgrove to Springburn was not opened until 16 August 1875 and then only for goods and minerals. The CGU partners were more interested in freight than passengers. It was six years after the opening of the line before the first two passenger stations, Duke Street and Alexandra Park, were brought into use on 1 July 1881. Four years later passenger trains got as far as Barnhill, serving an intermediate station at Garngad—known as Blochairn for the first fourteen days of its existence. It took the passenger service another two years to bridge the last quarter mile between Barnhill and Springburn.

The service, established with such lethargy, eventually proved successful. Springburn was the centre of the Scottish locomotive building trade with four large factories employing upwards of ten thousand men. At the southern end the passenger service had been extended to the Govan branch to serve a concentration of shipyards and engineering shops and to Renfrew where there was also much industrial activity. There was considerable exchange of workers between the districts in which the railway played its part. A workers' service was run from Springburn to Paisley where part of the large labour force in the mills was drawn from Glasgow suburbs served by the line.

The usefulness of the CGU was enhanced by the construction of various spurs and branches. Links were made to the Caledonian Barrhead line and to the General Terminus line. A spur from Haghill Junction just south of Alexandra Park station to Parkhead gave direct access from Springburn to the Coatbridge line, and a spur from Stockwell Junction to Saltmarket enabled trains from the north to run direct into St Enoch.

On 7 August 1896 the CGU was partitioned between its partners. The North British took over the section north and east of College West Junction, and the Glasgow & South Western absorbed the lines south and west of that point. Each company retained running powers over the portion retained by the other. The G & SW continued to run suburban trains to Springburn.

NORTH BANK DEVELOPMENTS

By the mid 1860s the Broomielaw still provided the main berthage on the Clyde, but there was as yet no rail access to the north bank berths. Then, after more than twenty years of deliberation, the Clyde Trustees decided to construct a new wet dock at the site purchased in the 1840s at Stobcross. Railway communication was essential and since the North British Helensburgh line was the nearest railway to the site of the dock that company took the opportunity to promote a line from Maryhill to Stobcross. Unfortunately, from the railway's point of view, Glasgow was expanding westward and much of the farmland across which the line was to be taken had been earmarked for a superior type of suburban development. Faced with fierce opposition from landowners the NB routed its line further west and took it in a wide south-easterly sweep towards the river.

An Act was obtained for the Stobcross branch in 1870 and construction occupied three years. As the CGU had already found, building a railway in an urban area was a costly business. Owners of postage stamp plots along the route produced development plans and claimed high prices from the promoters. James Hozier of Partick had been getting £10 a year rental for his plot but demanded £2,700 from the NB plus compensation for the despoliation of the streets he had not yet built. James McLean's four old tenements yielded £94 11s (£94.55) per annum, but his price to the railway was £1,600. Robert Black's 2 acre site had cost him from 3s 6d (17½p) to 5s (25p) a square yard; he demanded 50s (£2.50) and got 30s (£1.50). The NB had hoped to acquire 200 individual plots for £75,000, but by the time it had spent £75,498 it was in possession of only forty plots.

The engineering works included a 30 chain diversion of the Forth & Clyde Canal, a viaduct over the Kelvin and several street bridges. The yard at Stobcross was 70ft above the dock, and a connecting line was dropped on a steep gradient to quay level. Preparation of the ground in this area called for the removal of 350,000cu yd of material.

It was understandable that the Caledonian and G & SW should want a share of the traffic generated by the new dock. The G & SW plan was to continue the CGU from Dunlop Street to Stobcross on a route parallel with the river. This would have meant bridging St Enoch Square, demolishing a large amount of property, some of it nearly new, and crossing at right angles the site on which the Caledonian hoped to build the approach lines to its north bank station. In the face of daunting opposition the preamble was not proved. The Caledonian demanded and got running powers to Stobcross, joint ownership of the line from the yard to the quay and goods depots of its own at Stobcross and Partick. Caledonian traffic was routed through Sighthill yard across Cowlairs Junction and then by the Helensburgh line to the Stobcross branch. The arrangement was unsatisfactory. The NB too often found excuses for delaying Caledonian traffic passing over its territory so that the 6 mile trip from Sighthill to Stobcross could take on occasion 6 hours. The NB added a further pinprick by refusing to house Caledonian engines at its Stobcross shed overnight, which resulted in the Caledonian having to work light engines to and from the depot night and morning.

Around 1870 an isolated pocket of industrial activity formed on the north bank at Whiteinch about a mile downstream from Stobcross. Among the establishments founded about that time were the shipyards of Barclay Curle & Co Ltd, and Charles Connell & Co Ltd and the cabinet factory and sawmill of Wylie & Lochhead. The Whiteinch site was surrounded by rural estates and was without railways. Local industrialists, estate owners and, oddly enough the United Presbyterian Church, Dowanhill contributed finance for two separate companies to take a line down through the estates to the riverside factories and yards. The Whiteinch Railway Company was to construct a short branch off the Stobcross line near Crow Road to the Glasgow–Dumbarton trunk road, while the Whiteinch Tramway Company was to continue the line across the road and through the fields to the river. Both companies got Acts of Incorporation on 1 July 1872 and the complete system came into use in September 1874. The NB worked the traffic down to Dumbarton Road where it was taken over by James and William Wood who conveyed it over the tramway to the various yards and works. For the first year the Wood brothers used horse haulage, but the trade, mostly in coal, coke, sand, rivets and plates supplied by the hauliers in their capacity as merchants, justified the purchase of a locomotive by 1875. The Woods also provided a shunting service for factories on the tramway.

From the beginning the NB had a covetous eye on the White-inch lines. In 1878 it made an attempt to oust the Woods from the tramway, but the local proprietors beat off the attack. Another assault on the tramway made in 1891 was also un-successful, but on that occasion the NB succeeded in purchasing the railway. By this time the rural estates had disappeared and Whiteinch had become a residential and industrial suburb of Glasgow. The Woods' engine steamed not through fields but along a street of three-storey tenements. The NB intention was to make the railway a passenger branch with a terminal station on the north side of Dumbarton Road. A new connection to the branch was made from a point on the Glasgow, Yoker and Clydebank line west of Crow Road and passenger traffic to Whiteinch (Victoria Park) began on 1 January 1897.

The fortunes of the Whiteinch tramway began to decline with the opening of the Lanarkshire & Dumbartonshire in 1896. The new railway ran close to the works served by the tramway and offered a service that the Wood brothers could not equal. Traffic dwindled to the point where revenue did not cover the cost of the tramway engine. In May 1914 the Woods went into voluntary liquidation and a firm of coalmasters, A. and G. Anderson, took over the management of the line although the NB supplied engine and crew and took full re-sponsibility for maintenance of the track. In 1916 the NB was given the right to work the tramway in perpetuity.

Other branches to the west of Glasgow completed about this time included the line from the Stobcross line to the pits and brickworks of Knightswood opened in 1875, and a later exten-sion to Cowdenhill stone quarries. Earlier, on 28 August 1863, a 3 mile 14 chain branch had been opened as a single line from the Helensburgh line to the textile town of Milngavie. There was an intermediate station at Bearsden. The district was lightly populated, but prospects of early development as a high class residential area had motivated its sponsors.

In the early 1870s the civic authorities were gravely dis-pleased with the station facilities offered by the Glasgow rail-ways, and much acrimonious correspondence passed between the corporation and the various railway headquarters. The complaints were justified. The long-awaited new station at Dunlop Street was only temporary. Buchanan Street had been

N

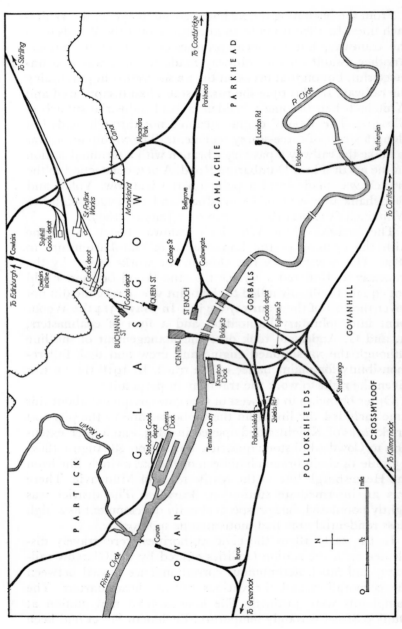

Plan of Glasgow showing the location of the Glasgow stations in 1882

'temporary' since its opening in 1849—and was to remain so until 1933! Queen Street, with goods and passengers huddled in a confined space, was chaotic. South Side was too far away to be generally useful while Bridge Street, although reasonably central, required its patrons to cross a river bridge from the city centre and, anyway, was inadequate for the traffic offered. Speaking on the subject at a town council meeting in July 1874 the Lord Provost said,

> No effort will be spared to bring about a reform in the present station arrangements in the city.

The announcement was met by loud cries of approval, and Councillor Dreghorn commented,

> The whole of the stations in Glasgow are a disgrace to the city. I am not aware if the North British is worse than the others, but while the magistrates are at it they might as well stir up the others.

To which the Lord Provost replied, 'I think the North British is certainly the worst in the city.'

The North British considered expiating its sins by running a line from Stobcross citywards to a new terminus in Bothwell Street. This station would take all the Helensburgh, Balloch and Milngavie trains and ease the situation at Queen Street. But the ultimate solution was very different. Through its subsidiary the Glasgow City & District Railway, the NB provided two stations on one site and 2½ miles of new line within the city without unduly ruffling the owners of city properties. The GC & D, in short, linked the Coatbridge line and the CGU east of the city to the Stobcross line in the west by means of a tunnel which included in its course a low level station under the existing Queen Street station.

The GC & D was only the fourth underground railway in Britain. Its construction posed many engineering problems not the least of which was the excavation of a four-platform station without interrupting traffic in the main line station overhead. The line of the tunnel under Kent Road was occupied by a main sewer which had to be moved to a new position in sections as the tunnel advanced. Patches of wet sand alternated with boulder clay and freestone, and great caution had to be observed in conducting blasting operations under occupied city offices. There was little disturbance to surface property. A crescent of fine houses had to be demolished to clear the site for Charing Cross station, and east of Queen Street some properties had to be demolished and rebuilt after the completion of the tunnel. At its eastern end the new line was diverted immediately to the north of the existing College station and driven under High Street.

The GC & D was opened on 15 March 1886. A new through College station was built and the original station closed. The other stations on the line were Queen Street Low Level, Charing Cross and Finnieston. On the same day a branch ½ mile long was opened between Partick Junction and Hyndland to serve a developing residential area. On 1 August 1886 the opening of a spur from the Stobcross line to the Helensburgh line made through running from the GC & D to the coast possible. Queen Street goods station was closed and the NB was accommodated at the G & SW College station until it built a goods depot of its own at High Street.

In January 1884 a pamphlet *Suggested Railway Connections in the East End of Glasgow* was published by Mr A. Wilson who advocated the construction of several railways in Bridgeton, a busy, populous textile centre employing many thousands in its mills and which had been missed by the north bank railway network. Wilson's main line was to run at the back of Monteith Row to Moir Street near Glasgow Cross where it was to join the CGU, while a secondary line was to link the CGU near Bellgrove. Bridgeton got its railways, but not on the Wilson pattern. On 1 June 1892 the NB opened a branch from the east end of College station to a terminus at Bridgeton Cross, with an intermediate station at Gallowgate Central. The G & SW tunnelled through from St Johns on the CGU to a point on the NB branch near Gallowgate Central and opened a passenger service into the NB's Bridgeton Cross station on 1 April 1893. The G & SW trains were little used except at rush hours and the service was withdrawn on 1 February 1913 and the tunnel sealed.

The opening of the Glasgow City & District, together with its associated spurs and branches, existing or contemplated, secured for the north bank a comprehensive system of urban railways. Terminal points in the west, Hyndland, Milngavie, Victoria Park and Maryhill, and their counterparts in the east,

Bridgeton Cross, Springburn and Airdrie, made possible many permutations of shuttle services. Hyndland became a popular, although not exclusive, reception point for through trains from Edinburgh via Bathgate, while Bridgeton Cross functioned as the main starting point for Helensburgh and Balloch trains. Residents in the Airdrie and Coatbridge area found that they could get to the Clyde coast and Loch Lomond without change of train or with one simple change. There was direct access to the Kelvin Valley line from Queen Street Low Level. At busy times incoming main line trains, which formerly would have congested Queen Street High Level, could be routed round the CGU via Springburn, drop their passengers at Queen Street Low Level and return empty stock to Cowlairs carriage sidings via Maryhill. Or the direction could be reversed. Purely local trains did not make a complete circuit as a booked working. Usually they originated at Maryhill and ran via the GC & D to Bridgeton Cross or Springburn, or started from Hyndland and ran to Maryhill via Springburn.

SUBURBAN TRENDS

It was not until the opening of the City of Glasgow Union Railway that Glasgow felt a real need for inner suburban services. Earlier efforts to establish such services had met with little success. In 1843 the Glasgow & Paisley Joint Railway opened two intermediate stations, Bellahouston and Moss Road, but they were closed two years later for want of patronage. The Glasgow Barrhead & Neilston provided a passenger service between Kennishead and Spiersbridge in September 1848; it lasted six months.

The *North British Railway and Shipping Journal* made the point that railways could not hope to generate suburban traffic at stations planted in open country and advocated that the railway companies should build their own villages and provide all civic services and amenities. The companies would profit from rents and from traffic to and from the towns. The E & G took up the idea in a modified form with the introduction of villa tickets. These were free season tickets granted to people who agreed to build houses at any undeveloped location on the railway. The tickets were valid for a minimum of five years with a year added for every additional £100 spent on a house above £1,000. The venture was most successful at Lenzie where a community of substantial villas rose round what had been a junction on an empty moor. Although the breadwinners travelled free, members of their families had to pay and freight attracted to the new town was charged the normal rates.

The E & G encouraged country people to visit Glasgow on shopping expeditions by providing a unique parcels service. Customers could purchase railway labels at ½d each from shop-keepers, and parcels with these labels affixed were collected from the shop by railway carters and conveyed to the station where they were picked up by the returning passengers before they boarded their trains.

For many years suburban operations were confined to weekday only; the Sunday traffic potential was ignored, a policy which was to throw considerable traffic on the roads on Sundays. In September 1867 the *Glasgow Herald* conducted a survey of traffic on the Glasgow–Paisley road on Sundays. On a typical Sunday fourteen omnibuses each way, employing forty-two horses, carried 932 passengers. The *Herald* wrote scathingly of over-crowded omnibuses and overworked horses, and blamed the Sabbatarian railway directors for 'Sunday cruelty to animals'. The *Evening Citizen* joined in the campaign against what it called 'a social grievance and a crying nuisance'. One train between Glasgow and Paisley morning and night, the news-papers said, would wipe out the evil. But the Glasgow railways had to wait nearly a hundred years before they were to see a really comprehensive Sunday service.

THE SOUTH SIDE LINES

One of the earliest south side lines, the Busby Railway, was a good example of a small company promoted by men with local knowledge with the object of exploiting purely local industries. The hamlet of Giffnock lying some 2 miles to the south of the Glasgow Barrhead & Neilston line between Pollokshaws and Kennishead had two extremely valuable quarries in its imme-diate vicinity. One produced a fine-grained, whitish sandstone known as liver rock, a favourite with the builders of the best villas and the sculptors who were adorning the new public buildings with elaborate Victorian decorations. The other quarry yielded Eastwood pavement, a fine foliated limestone ideal for stairs, hearths and above all for the pavements of the new Glasgow streets. The transport of the riches of these quarries to the Glasgow building sites was the main reason for the promotion of the railway.

The Busby Railway Company was authorised on 11 May 1863 to build a railway of 3 miles 43 chains from Busby Junction on the Neilston line through Giffnock and Clarkston to the thriving textile town of Busby. While the line was under construction the directors decided to push on to East Kilbride, a farming village lying 504ft up in the Cathkin Hills. The railway, worked by the Caledonian, was opened to Busby on 1 January 1866 and to East Kilbride on 1 September 1868. In 1882 the line was absorbed by the Caledonian, and in the following year the new owners extended it across the hills from East Kilbride to join the Hamilton–Strathaven line near High Blantyre. That was a mistake. There was little population on the extension and the services varied between two and four trains a day. The line was closed in 1914.

At the outset the Busby Railway ran only three trains each way a day with an extra one on Saturday evenings. The trains ran into South Side station until it closed in 1877. Until June 1879 they terminated at Gorbals on the extension to St Enoch, and on the opening of the Central station that year they found a home there.

The wealthier Glaswegians, fleeing from the industrialisation of the inner suburbs, tended to build their new homes on the East Kilbride branch. Thornliebank station was opened on 1 October 1881 to serve a rising community. In the same year the increase in traffic justified the doubling of the line as far as Busby. By the end of the century a dozen passenger trains daily were running each way. But as passenger activity increased, freight traffic diminished. In 1898 a bleach works at Busby which merited a branch closed down. Over the next few years the quarries became worked out, but the railway got quarry traffic in reverse when William Beardmore & Co Ltd of Parkhead Forge began to send train loads of ash to be deposited in the abandoned workings.

The south side's most successful venture in urban railway

EAST KILBRIDE RAILWAY

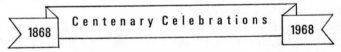

| 1868 | Centenary Celebrations | 1968 |

SATURDAY SEPT. 14th

to commemorate the opening of the Busby to East Kilbride section in Sept.1868 and the Thornliebank to Busby section in Jan.1866, and to express the need for improvement and extension, now and in the future.

You are invited to join the 09 02 train from East Kilbride at your local station

10 a.m Glasgow Central Station

Passengers in 1868. Costume seen off by Mr.R.M. Shand, station manager

Mr R.M. Ross. Chairman, Renfrewshire Eastwood District Council and others will join at stations en route

Central Station	dep 1018	Thornliebank	dep 1031	Busby	dep 1041
Crossmyloof	dep 1024	Giffnock	dep 1034	Thorntonhall	dep 1045
Pollockshaws West	dep 1027	Clarkston	dep 1038	Hairmyres	dep 1048

THIS TRAIN IS OPEN TO ANYONE (AT NORMAL FARES)

10.53 a.m.
East Kilbride Station

Presentation of a
CALEDONIAN RAILWAY KEY

by Mr. A.B. ALLISON
Glasgow Divisional Manager, British Railways

to Provost J. WRIGHT, East Kilbride
on behalf of users at all stations on the line

11.15 a.m.
PROCESSION

from East Kilbride Station via Kittoch St., Main St., Churchill Ave., Cornwall St.

to site of proposed new

TOWN CENTRE
RAILWAY STATION

(near footbridge to swimming pool)

Sale of Caledonian Railway relics etc. at East Kilbride Station,

Exhibition and free British Rail film show at former Council Chambers, Princes St.

KNOW THE PAST -
CREATE THE FUTURE

Issued by the Glasgow-East Kilbride Railway Development Association, 92 Hillview Dr. Clarkston, Tel.Giffnock 4721

Printed by PRODUCT SUPPORT (GRAPHICS) LIMITED - EAST KILBRIDE

When the East Kilbride branch was threatened with closure, the East Kilbride Railway Development Association fought successfully for its retention, even printing timetables at its own expense and distributing them in the district. This reproduction is of a poster advertising the Centenary Celebrations of the line organised by the association transport was the Cathcart District Railway, a scheme which aimed to encircle and serve the prosperous new suburbs built largely of Giffnock stone. The Cathcart Circle became a Glasgow institution. In a very amusing book written about the railway, its staff and passengers (*Snooker Tam of the Cathcart Railway*) R. W. Campbell had this to say:

> God made the country, man made the cities and the railways made the suburbs—hence the growth of Suburbia and the rise of the Cathcart Railway. This railway is as famous as the Grand Trunk Road or Watling Street. To be ignorant of the Cathcart Circle is akin to saying that the Thames is in Germany and the Tweed in Alaska. After the Polis Force the Cathcart Railway is the greatest thing in Glasca.

The first section of the Cathcart District Railway was authorised in 1880 from Pollokshields East to Cathcart, a distance of 2¼ miles. The line was opened to Mount Florida on 1 March 1886 and to Cathcart on 25 May, and there were also stations at Queens Park and Crosshill. The CDR, an independent company but under the suzerainty of the Caledonian, faced a much easier task than the builders of the CGU across the river. No large-scale demolition of expensive property was involved; the engineers could pick a path across open spaces and between streets in the still developing suburbs.

The Cathcart line was run as a branch, the trains starting from Glasgow Central. In 1887 the company got an Act to complete the circle by bringing the line back from Cathcart to the city via Langside, Shawlands, Maxwell Park and Pollokshields West to Muirhouse Junction. On 2 April 1894 a service was started on the two 8 mile concentric circles thus created. There had been forty-two trains a day to the Cathcart terminal station; eighty-nine operated on the Circle. Island platforms were provided at the stations so that passengers who missed a train could pick up the next one without changing platforms. At Glasgow Central the Circle trains had their own special platform with an approach stairway from Argyle Street as well as the usual entrance from the concourse. Passenger traffic built up rapidly with the steady increase of south side population, and the Circle, as Campbell said, became an institution. Skylarking schoolboys, the bane of Snooker Tam and his colleagues, graduated into sober commuters who in turn supplied a new generation of schoolboys to the Circle trains. Crosshill and Mount Florida stations were adjacent to large football stadiums which attracted huge Saturday crowds. The Circle was an ideal medium for handling the processions of football specials and expeditiously disposing of the stock.

Nevertheless, at the meeting of the CDR shareholders after the first full year of the Circle's operation, they were given the disconcerting information that the Circle had earned less than the half circle in its last year. This was due to the depredations of the tramcars. The chairman explained that Glasgow Corporation, who had newly acquired the horse trams, had concentrated on the area served by the railway to the detriment of all other districts. But he was confident that the low tramcar fares would saddle the ratepayers of Glasgow with such a debt that the corporation would be forced to raise the fares and allow fair competition by the railway.

When the Lanarkshire & Ayrshire extension to the city opened on 1 May 1903 the line skirted Cathcart station, but did not serve it. However, two stations, Kirkhill and Burnside, were established on the L & A east of Cathcart in comparatively open country which the L & A rightly decided was ripe for development, while Muirend, Whitecraigs and Patterton west of Cathcart were L & A stations in the Glasgow outer suburban zone. Both groups of stations were served by separate services from Glasgow Central.

The usefulness of the lines entering Glasgow from the south was greatly enhanced by the opening in 1879 of the Caledonian Central station at the culmination of more than thirty years struggle to gain a footing on the north bank.

The Act authorising the bridging of the river and the construction of the station was obtained in 1873. That was the period when the corporation was chiding the railways over the inadequacy of their city terminals, and the Caledonian set out to provide something on a grand scale. Glasgow Bridge was to be widened and a railway bridge constructed on top of the widened part. Financial prudence had dictated acceptance of the scheme that had infuriated the lieges thirty years before; the Bridge Trustees needed money to repair Glasgow Bridge and under the latest agreement the Caledonian agreed to pay the whole cost of restoring the bridge. The company purchased ground for the station on the east side of Hope Street close to the site of the NB Bothwell Street terminal then proposed in connection with the Stobcross and Helensburgh lines. Indeed, the Caledonian had plans to link up with the coast line and for running a line down from Buchanan Street to the new station.

The Caledonian dream evaporated when the cost of buying existing property was counted. The alignment of the bridge extension meant that the approach lines to the station would have to cut through the buildings on the west side of Jamaica Street. In 1875 a new Act was obtained authorising the construction of an entirely new bridge about 50yd downstream from Glasgow Bridge and an approach line behind the buildings to a modest station situated between Gordon Street and Argyle Street.

Simultaneously with the construction of the Central station an extensive reconstruction of Bridge Street was begun, so that by the end of 1879 Glasgow had two stations, virtually on the same line, one north, the other south of the river. In the reconstructed Bridge Street station there were four bay platforms catering for the G & SW suburban services and the Caledonian Wemyss Bay and Gourock trains, and two through platforms with lines running on to the Central station. Trains from Carlisle and the south and from Edinburgh, which had been using Buchanan Street, now ran into the Central.

The new Clyde bridge was William Arrol's first great bridge; he went on to build the Tay, Tower and Forth bridges. It was 700ft long, 55ft wide and carried four tracks. Glasgow did not like it at first because it completely blocked the famous view from Glasgow Bridge down the harbour, but the critics had to admit that it was necessary.

The long-awaited Central station was a bad station. The eight platforms were short and narrow. Long trains in some platforms bottled in shorter trains in neighbouring platforms. There were no proper carriage sidings. The concourse was too cramped to allow free movement of passengers. The Caledonian planners had failed completely to see that the new lines they were already building would result in the trains entering the station doubling in number in seven years.

The bridge that spanned Argyle Street was widened by 20ft and a ninth platform added, and alterations in layout made for

a smoother flow of traffic through from Bridge Street. But these
were makeshift measures. The Caledonian had to rethink the
whole problem of a Central station. The first scheme envisaged
the creation of an eight-line station at Bridge Street, the lines
feeding across a new Clyde bridge to a fifteen-platform re-
designed Central station. The actual plan, which was completed between 1901 and 1905, resulted in the closure of Bridge
Street and the concentration of all the Caledonian traffic in a
thirteen-platform Central station greatly widened and extended
over Argyle Street and on to the new eight-track Clyde bridge.
Some of the former Bridge Street through lines were converted
into much-needed carriage sidings. The widening of the bridge
over the part of Argyle Street between Hope Street and Union
Street converted most of the popular thoroughfare into a
covered way. Glaswegians rose in arms against the creation of
this gloomy tunnel in the city centre, but it proved to be a
blessing in disguise. The covered way was lined with attractive
shops where the populace could window gaze and shop sheltered from the rain in bad weather. The covered way soon became the favourite meeting place, especially on Sunday nights,
of Highlanders exiled in Glasgow. To this day it is known in
Glasgow as 'the Heilanman's Umbrella'.

By the time the new station opened it was handling (with its
low level platforms serving the Glasgow Central Railway),
22,000,000 passengers per annum.

THE GLASGOW CENTRAL RAILWAY

The Caledonian, with a covetous eye on the North British
cross-city link via the Glasgow, City and District, had long
yearned for a share in the north side suburban traffic. When a
private syndicate promoted the Glasgow, Central & Suburban
railway in 1887 the Caledonian gave its moral support and a
promise to back the scheme to the tune of £2,000,000. The
line, like the GC & D, was to run from the east end of the city
across the city centre to the western suburbs keeping close to the
river most of the way and passing through the Central station.
It was to be an elevated railway after the style of the Liverpool
Overhead.

Rumours of the venture caused a tumult among Glasgow

property owners and speculators. The railway was to pass through the business and commercial heart of the city and the promoters would have to acquire many properties. Interested parties waited eagerly for publication of the plans. Gardiner & Company, the Glasgow lithographers, completed the plans on a Saturday morning and they were given immediately to two messenger boys for delivery at the office of Crouch & Hogg the engineers. During their short walk through the streets of Glasgow the boys were stopped by a well-dressed, middle-aged man who, after satisfying himself that the boys were carrying railway plans to Crouch & Hogg, took them up a close (an entry leading into a building) where he got down on his knees and inspected the plans. In due course he made off with one sheet. This episode led to the appearance in court of Robert Macdougall, property agent, on a charge of theft of a plan which contained information of very great importance to him in his line of business. His two-day prison sentence was served in vain, for the Caledonian, sensing the tremendous wave of opposition to the elevated railway, instructed the Glasgow Central & Suburban to withdraw its Bill. The scheme presently reappeared as an underground railway.

The Glasgow Central Railway was authorised on 10 August 1888; its purpose was to provide a $6\frac{1}{4}$ mile underground link between Strathclyde Junction on the Dalmarnock branch of the Caledonian in the east and the projected Lanarkshire & Dumbartonshire at Stobcross in the west. From Stobcross the line was to turn north to reach Dawsholm and Maryhill in the north-west of the city. There were to be stations at Dalmarnock, Bridgeton Cross, Glasgow Green, Glasgow Cross, Glasgow Central (Low Level), Anderston Cross, Stobcross, Kelvin Bridge, Botanic Gardens, Kirklee, Maryhill and Dawsholm. On 31 May 1890 the GCR was absorbed by the Caledonian, and on 25 July of that year a line was authorised from Bridgeton Cross on the GCR to run via Carmyle to Newton on the main line to the south. The new line was to cross the Rutherglen–Coatbridge line (Chapter VI) by a double junction at Carmyle.

The construction of the CGU, and the legal difficulties which preceded the start of the work, presented fearsome problems. From Glasgow Cross to Anderston Cross the railway was to pass under Argyle Street and Trongate, two of the busiest thoroughfares in the city. Cut and cover methods were to be used to make the tunnels, and the railway company had to guarantee an uninterrupted passage to the tramcars and provide access to all shops. The engineers had to resort to elaborate underpinning to prevent the collapse of buildings along the route. Even so claims for compensation from business premises formed a major item in the final total account for the railway. Some tenement property had to be demolished, and the GCR had to find alternative accommodation for the displaced tenants within a mile of their places of employment. Existing sewers and drains had to be sealed and relaid.

The passage of the railway under the west-end parks, too, was fraught with difficulties. In taking the railway under Kelvingrove Park the company was instructed by the corporation to avoid disturbing growing trees. Every blade of grass removed had to be replaced. Vigilant citizens kept an eye on proceedings, and the GCR was quick to learn of any liberties taken by the contractors. When the company sought permission to sink a ventilating shaft in the Botanic Gardens the owners, the Glasgow Botanic Institution, assented but claimed the right to order the closing of the shaft at any time. Stations in the gardens were required to be 'of such ornamental character as will harmonise with the surroundings thereof, all at the sight and to the satisfaction of the Corporation and of the President of the said Institution.' The station subsequently erected at Botanic Gardens would not have been out of place in the Kremlin.

The GCR, when it was opened throughout for all traffic on 10 August 1896, gave the Caledonian a huge stake in the Glasgow suburban traffic. More than 260 trains a day passed through Central Low Level station. The service ran from Rutherglen through the city centre stations to Stobcross thence to Dawsholm and Maryhill; or they could continue on the L & D to Partick East Junction and run via the L & D's Crow Road and Kelvinside stations to rejoin the GCR at Bellshaugh Junction, Dawsholm. The L & D had continued its line beyond Maryhill for 1 mile 58 chains to join the Caledonian branch from St Rollox to the Forth & Clyde Canal basin at Hamiltonhill, and a station was built at Possil near the NB station, Possilpark. On 1 February 1897 the GCR service was extended to Possil for workers' trains and on 1 October 1897 for all traffic.

During the building of the underground railways in the 1890s, Glasgow feared that its famous buildings would collapse into the new railway tunnels. This cartoon from *The Bailie* expresses Glasgow's fears

OUR MODERN TRAVELLING FACILITIES.

By 1896 Glasgow had two steam underground railway systems, a cable subway, horse trams, motor cabs and cluthas (passenger steamers which plied on the Clyde between Glasgow and White-inch). A bewildered stranger is here seen seeking a policeman's help to escape the plethora of transport facilities on offer

(a cartoon from *The Bailie*)

The new railways gave Caledonian freight traffic from all parts to the north bank an enormous boost. No longer was the company dependent on NB charity to reach the Stobcross area. Traffic approaching Glasgow from the south and east and bound for the docks and shipyards west of the city had a choice of three routes. It could be taken on to the GCR via Rutherglen or Newton, or it could be sent round the northern outskirts via London Road Junction and Balornock Junction. Freight coming down from the north could run via Robroyston West Junction on to the Possil line and thence to the Clyde. That the Caledonian facilities duplicated most of those already provided by the North British scarcely mattered; there was traffic enough for both.

THE GLASGOW 'CAUR'

In 1898, two years after the opening of the Glasgow Central Railway, Glasgow Corporation electrified two of its horse tram routes as an experiment, and it was significant that both routes ran to Springburn, a railway stronghold. Within a few years electric cars were whining merrily along the streets and out into the surrounding countryside creaming traffic away from the hard-won suburban lines. Glasgow loved its *caurs*. The routes multiplied until they were carrying 225,000,000 passengers a year. And on the night in September 1962 when the cars ran for the last time, more than a quarter of a million citizens lined the streets in a torrential rainstorm to witness their passing.

Passengers waiting for trains in the Central Low Level station could hear the tramcars rumbling along Argyle Street above their heads. It was the sound of doom for the expensive new railway. The Central line stations, with tunnels at each end belching sulphurous smoke on to their platforms, were not pleasant places. Regular travellers had already learned the trick of using a paper bag as a glove to grip soot-coated door handles. More and more passengers defected to the clean, frequent and cheap trams. Soon it was possible to board a tram outside the Central station and travel west all the way to Loch Lomond with only one change or east to the Lanarkshire towns of Hamilton, Bothwell and Motherwell, and at fares that left change out of a shilling. In due course the Glasgow fare scale

o

ranged from ½d to 2d and for 2d a passenger could travel from Airdrie to Paisley, a distance of 21 miles. Railway directors repeatedly assured their shareholders that the Glasgow tramway venture would end in financial ruin; instead the tramway department made imposing and increasing profits.

The suburban service operated by the G & SW between Govan and Springburn on the CGU line was the first to capitulate to the trams. The single fare from St Enoch to Springburn (3 miles 40 chains) was 1½d and to Govan (4 miles 2 chains) it was 2d. The season ticket rates worked out at 1½d per day to Springburn, 2d per day to Govan. The tramcars charged fares of 1d to Springburn, 1½d to Govan. The trains ran every ½ hour, the trams every 3 minutes. The G & SW board admitted that the service it offered was completely outclassed by the trams and on 30 September 1902 it was withdrawn. The withdrawal was the subject of leading articles in the railway and lay press and troubled meetings in the boardrooms of those companies that had made heavy long-term investments in suburban lines. The G & SW continued to run a few workers' trains over its suburban lines but by and large it opted out of inner suburban traffic and concentrated instead on fast commuter services to the coast.

THE PAISLEY LINES

The spate of suburban railway construction round Glasgow in the 1890s had its counterpart in nearby Paisley. To the immediate south of Paisley the ground rose to the pleasant Gleniffer Braes, a favourite area for picnickers and a likely site for future urban development. Some 3½ miles up in the hills was Barrhead, a busy town with textile mills, bleachfields and a large new sanitary porcelain factory. Paisley, of course, was served by the Caledonian and G & SW and Barrhead by the Glasgow, Barrhead & Kilmarnock Joint line, but the towns had no direct railway communication with each other. The G & SW and the Caledonian embarked on a scramble to exploit this promising territory. Both companies produced schemes which were in effect circular routes embracing Paisley and Barrhead and the rural areas likely to be developed. A third project, sponsored by the Glasgow & Paisley Joint line, was for a second line from Glasgow to Renfrew. This line was to leave the Joint line at Cardonald and run by the south bank of the Clyde to Renfrew. All the lines when built gave the district a comprehensive network of suburban railways, which was at once caught up in the tramcar era and destroyed.

The opening of the Canal line in 1885 sparked off the Paisley suburban mania. The new line, skirting as it did the southern outskirts of Paisley was an excellent base from which to assault the Gleniffer Braes. By February 1886 the G & SW had pushed a line 1 mile 30 chains into the hills to reach Potterhill. The branch made a triangular junction with the Canal line at Corsebar Junction (for Glasgow) and at Meikleriggs for Ayrshire. The line was opened for goods on 5 February 1886 and for passengers on 1 June 1886.

Just over a mile further up the slope of the Braes stood a large textile mill owned by William Fulton and Sons. Transport to the mill had been a problem. Coal had to be carted up the steep narrow road from Paisley and the finished cloth returned by the same route. The Fultons had bought an 8 horsepower Aveling & Porter road locomotive which became an accepted sight roaring up the Glen road with a 'train' of coal. Now the time was ripe for the railway to take over the job. By 1899 the branch had been taken up the Braes to Glenfield coal depot conveniently sited for the mill. The next stage took it into Barrhead, the Glenfield line in the process becoming a short branch from the newly created Thornly Park Junction. To get into Barrhead the G & SW had to burrow under the GB & K north of the existing station. A new station, Barrhead Central, was built on the new line almost alongside the GB & K station. Where the new line and the Joint line intersected two spurs were built: one from Blackbyres Junction linking the new line with the Joint line at Barrhead North Junction enabled trains on the new line to run on the Joint line, while a second spur from the Joint line at Barrhead South Junction enabled trains coming from Glasgow via Pollokshaws to run into the new Barrhead Central station. The G & SW was now in a position to operate a circular service embracing Glasgow, Paisley and Barrhead. The Inner Circle trains ran from St Enoch by the Canal line and Potterhill to Barrhead Central and returned by Pollokshaws. The Outer Circle trains traversed the same route in the reverse direction. All trains reversed in Barrhead Central station. The circle service opened on 1 October 1902, the ominous day on which the Govan–Springburn services ended.

In 1902 the Caledonian took over the affairs of the Paisley & Barrhead District Railway, a local venture that had been authorised on 6 August 1897 to exploit the supposed riches of Barrhead and the Gleniffer Braes. The line was to form a wide circle beginning on the Gourock line at St James west of Paisley, sweep in a circle south and east to pass across the face of the Braes and south of Barrhead and turning north drop down the Braes to a junction with the Glasgow & Paisley Joint line at Greenlaw east of Gilmour Street station. From the top of the circle a line was to cut into Barrhead (where there would be two new stations, South and New) and then climb into the hills to join the Lanarkshire & Ayrshire at Lyoncross.

The planned new lines opened up exciting possibilities for the Caledonian. A circular service covering Paisley, Barrhead and intermediate stations would rival the G & SW service. Like the G & SW circle trains the Caledonian trains would have to reverse in Barrhead. The Caledonian trains on the circle would join the coast line at St James, pass through Gilmour Street and regain the circle line at Greenlaw Junction. By introducing certain spurs still wider circuits could be accomplished. For instance trains could be run from Glasgow to Barrhead via Greenlaw and return via St James. An even wider circle would be possible if trains were sent out over the Lanarkshire & Ayrshire to Lyoncross and then down the new line through Barrhead to Paisley.

Construction of the line began on 15 August 1898, and the Caledonian forthwith embarked on the Battle of the Braes. Almost immediately the Paisley & Barrhead board received an imposing petition from the merchants and manufacturers of Johnstone asking that a branch be run to their town. The petitioners made the point that an outlet to Ayrshire and Lanarkshire via the new line and the Lanarkshire & Ayrshire would break the G & SW monopoly of Johnstone. The petition was rejected, but on 9 August 1899 the Paisley & Barrhead decided to double the portion of their line lying between the Lanarkshire & Ayrshire and the Glasgow & Paisley Joint line in anticipation of heavy coal traffic from the L & A.

The line was run without difficulty round the western outskirts of Paisley and up the Braes towards Barrhead. Stations were built at Ferguslie, Stanley and Glenfield. The line was then taken into Barrhead (New) station (on the way being linked with the G & SW line at Blackbyres Junction) and over the town on a massive stone viaduct. Then followed a stiff climb up the slopes to the junction with the L & A at Lyoncross. From Blackbyres Junction the eastern half of the circle ran back down the Braes to Greenlaw on the Glasgow–Paisley line.

The Caledonian and the G & SW came into direct conflict at the approaches to Barrhead. The G & SW so planned the Barrhead extension to its Potterhill branch that the Caledonian was forced to make an alteration in its levels, an embankment becoming necessary where none had been planned. Charles Forman, the engineer, complained that the Potterhill–Barrhead line 'has evidently been laid out to interfere with and hem in this company's line as much as possible'. However, the Caledonian forced the G & SW to pay the cost of the materials for the embankment.

The Battle of the Braes ended in farce. Both the Caledonian and the G & SW were driven from the field by the electric tram. The Caledonian admitted defeat when its line was nearing completion. Passenger stations, some of them almost ready for service, were abandoned before they had issued a single ticket. The G & SW venture fared little better. The circular service was withdrawn on 1 October 1907. On 1 February 1913 services ceased between Potterhill and Barrhead Central, but services were maintained from St Enoch to Potterhill via Paisley and from St Enoch to Barrhead Central via Pollokshaws until 1 January 1917. On that date the last remnant of the G & SW's short-lived Paisley suburban system vanished.

The ill-fated Paisley railways left the district, and especially Barrhead, with ugly, decaying railway properties. The town centre of Barrhead was a clutter of mouldering stations, rusty abandoned bridges and weed-covered embankments, memorials to the suburban service that never was. In the end the local council dumped the town refuse on the abandoned railway site.

While the Caledonian and Glasgow & South Western were squabbling over routes to Barrhead they were jointly (as proprietors of the Glasgow & Paisley Joint line) pushing a new railway into Renfrew.

By 1897 all the territory facing the navigable channel on the

north side of the Clyde from Glasgow down to Erskine Ferry, a
distance of 10 miles, was occupied by shipyards, wharves and
engineering shops. On the south bank, which did not have
railway lines close to the river, development stopped at Shieldhall some 3 miles from the centre of Glasgow, except for a small
pocket of industry at Renfrew. There were those who believed
that all the south bank needed was a railway, and development
would follow. The original plan was to take the new line off the
Joint line at Cardonald and run it close to the river through
Renfrew, across the Black Cart and White Cart and through
the Blythswood estate to Erskine. Lord Blythswood admitted
that such a railway would be to the benefit of the county, but
he was not prepared to see it built during his lifetime.

The scheme which eventually was authorised was the Glasgow & Renfrew District Railway. The line ran from Cardonald
to Renfrew where the main station, Kings Inch, adjoined the
Paisley–Renfrew Ferry road. It then crossed both the road and
the original Paisley & Renfrew Railway before making a U-
turn to run parallel with the branch to a terminus at Porterfield
adjoining the existing branch station at Renfrew South. Deanside station was established in empty fields half-way between
Cardonald and Renfrew as an act of faith in anticipation of
development locally. Passenger traffic on the line opened on
1 June 1903. Deanside station was closed on 2 January 1905.

In 1906 Charles Forman secured the tentative agreement of
Lord Blythswood to an extension of the G & RD to the west end
of Bishopton tunnel where it would link up with the Gourock
line. The idea was rejected by the board who decided that the
time was not financially opportune.

The Renfrew Railway suffered from having too many cooks.
The Glasgow & Paisley Joint was the nominal owner, but
officials of the Caledonian and G & SW also had power to interfere in the company's affairs. For instance, an oil store at Kings
Inch was passed by Caledonian and G & SW inspectors only to be
condemned as badly sited by a Joint Line inspector. On 25
November 1903 Donald Matheson of the Caledonian had a
trip over the line, and that same afternoon he sent a scathing
report to the Joint Line board. 'I am of the opinion that the
permanent way be described generally as being in an unsatisfactory condition particularly that part between the junction

with the Shieldhall branch and Deanside station which is dis-
gracefully bad. Indeed, the part to which attention is specially
directed, to the south of Deanside station, is in a condition
dangerous for traffic working, so much so that I have no hesitation in advising that the speed of trains passing over it should be
restricted to ten miles an hour.'

As far as passenger traffic was concerned the Glasgow &
Renfrew District Railway had to be content with the crumbs
left by the tramcars plying on the Renfrew road. The service
was withdrawn on 19 July 1926. The engineering works in
Renfrew, however, yielded sufficient freight traffic to justify
the retention of the line.

THE FINAL PATTERN

During the 1914–18 war a few of the less-used stations in the
suburban area were closed as a war economy measure, never to
be reopened. Passenger services were withdrawn from the
Govan branch on 9 September 1921. But the basic services
remained unaltered, although reduced in frequency, until after
the 1939–45 war.

The great post-war event in the Glasgow suburban scene was
the electrification of the former North British north side and
Clyde coast lines on 5 November 1960. On the previous day,
a Sunday, a preview of the full weekday service was offered to
the public. Passengers who had bought season tickets valid
from the Monday were carried free, others paid cheap day
fares. In spite of the fact that it was wintertime Glaswegians
poured in thousands through the bright, refurbished stations
into the clean, attractive blue trains. It was a gala day remini-
scent of the opening days of pioneer lines long ago. An abiding
memory was the satisfied smiles of passengers and railwaymen
alike. Never had staff morale been so high. And traffic on the
bread-and-butter trains in the following week was up 400 per
cent on steam days.

The jubilation was short lived. A serious fault in the electrical
switchgear forced the withdrawal of the trains and the old
steam service was reintroduced on 19 December 1960. It was
not until ten months later that the electric service was resumed.
There were three basic services: Airdrie–Helensburgh, Bridge-

ton Central–Balloch, and Springburn–Milngavie, with short-working shuttle services providing additional trains in the central area at rush hours. The new trains served high density housing estates east and west of the city, and a combination of cheap fares and fast and frequent services soon forced competing bus operators to reduce their services.

The success of the electrics hastened the end of the steam services on the parallel Glasgow Central Railway. Individual stations on the line had been disappearing one by one. Botanic Gardens was the first to go on 6 February 1939, followed by Kirklee on 1 May 1939. Kelvinside was closed on 1 July 1942, Kelvin Bridge on 4 August 1952. Anderson Cross and Stobcross, both in the busy hub of the city, lost their passenger services on 3 August 1959. The few remaining dingy trains were withdrawn from stations carrying the soot of more than half a century on 5 October 1964 and the whole expensive underground system was abandoned. Shortly afterwards the associated ex-Caledonian freight lines from the east of the city round the north-west to the docks were abandoned and their traffic diverted to the parallel ex-North British lines.

The south side electrification was inaugurated on 29 May 1962. The services affected were the Cathcart Circle, Neilston and Motherwell via Kirkhill lines. The higher proportion of car owners and the absence of large working-class housing schemes were two of the reasons given for the relative lack of success of the south side scheme.

Castlemilk, the huge south side council estate, was just out of range of the railway, and on 5 November 1962 Glasgow Corporation and British Railways joined in an experiment to make the now famous blue trains available to dwellers in the estate. A special bus service was run from Castlemilk through Croftfoot to King's Park station where there was an immediate blue train connection. The fare from Castlemilk to Glasgow by bus and rail (a through ticket was issued) was 8d (3½p) compared with 10d (4p) by the direct Castlemilk–Glasgow bus. The time by each route was the same—29 minutes.

The experiment failed because the people of Castlemilk found a change of vehicle in the course of a short journey unacceptable. Accommodation was provided for 75,000 passengers per week, but only 10,000 used the service; a utilisation of 13 per cent in rush hours, 6 per cent off peak. In a typical four-week period revenue was £1,264, expenses £2,842, resulting in a loss of £1,578. The service was withdrawn in May 1964.

The last major change in the Glasgow transport scene was in 1966 when, on 27 June, St Enoch station closed and its traffic was transferred to Central, and on 7 November, Buchanan Street closed and its traffic went to Queen Street.

The last Paisley 'suburban' line to lose its passenger service was, oddly enough, the oldest line in the district, the Paisley & Renfrew Railway, opened on 3 April 1837. It ran from a station at Hamilton Street, Paisley to a wharf on the south bank of the Clyde at Renfrew. Its main purpose was to take passengers and freight from Paisley down to the wharf where steamers would connect with the trains. But the River Cart was navigable up to Paisley Harbour and coastal vessels preferred to sail direct to the town. The railway was built to the 4ft 6in gauge, and although the company started off with locomotives, these were sold and horse haulage adopted on 7 March 1842. Although the line was purchased by the GPK & A on 24 July 1847 and taken over by the G & SW on 21 July 1852, it remained an isolated, horse-operated system. It was not until 1 August 1866 that it was re-gauged and linked with the parent system. Hamilton Street station was closed and replaced by a new station at Abercorn. The junction with the main line was at Gallowhill, a short distance east of Paisley, Gilmour Street, and faced Glasgow. In 1874 the junction was moved further east to Arkleston. A passenger service was operated from Glasgow (St Enoch) to Renfrew Wharf, and the line also served the shipyards and factories on or near the river bank. Passenger services between Arkleston Junction and Renfrew Wharf ceased on 5 June 1967.

CHAPTER IX

Edinburgh

THE EDINBURGH & DALKEITH

A visitor to Edinburgh in 1824 who had climbed to the summit of Arthur's Seat would have found the city spread out at his feet. Down below to the north-west the old medieval town 'grandly fretted with towers and crowned with heaven-pointing spires and defiant battlements' climbed up the mile-long ridge to the castle. Beyond the old town rose the elegant squares and terraces of the new town and beyond the new town was the blue line of the sea where the Firth of Forth merged with the German Ocean. The vista to the south was scarcely less impressive. Rolling countryside dotted with farms and coal pits stretched to the horizon. Smoke curled up from Edinburgh's myriad of chimneys; *Auld Reekie* had been Scott's favourite name for his country's capital. But there were days in winter when the coal barges from Lanarkshire were frozen in the Union Canal and heavy seas closed the port of Leith to the Northumbrian colliers, and even the Lothian coalfield right on Edinburgh's doorstep was inaccessible because of the state of the roads. Edinburgh was in desperate need of coal.

The men who met one day in September 1824 in the Royal Exchange Coffee House in Edinburgh were investigating the possibility of building a railway from the Lothian coalfield to the city. Some of them had met at the same place and for the same purpose seven years earlier, but their meeting had been abortive. Now the Lothian coal lords, Buccleuch, Lothian and Rosebery, gave their support to the railway. Thomas Grainger produced plans and the Edinburgh & Dalkeith Railway got its Act on 26 May 1826.

The Lothian coalfield was intersected by the rivers North Esk and South Esk lying in deep valleys like twin moats separat-

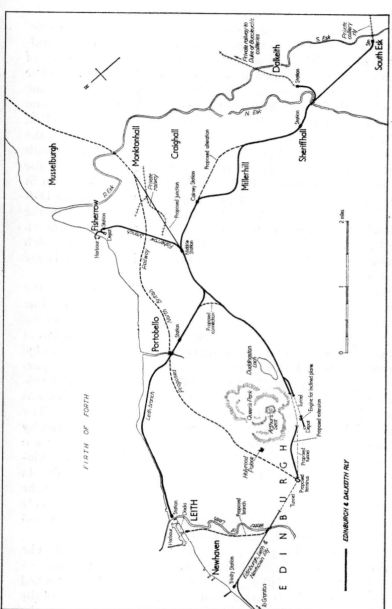

Edinburgh & Dalkeith Railway. This is a copy of a map published with the prospectus of the
North British Railway

ing the best of the coal from Edinburgh. The E & D established a base depot at St Leonards on the southern fringe of the city. The promoters took their line down through a steeply descending tunnel (1 in 30) from St Leonards to the plain south of Arthur's Seat, continued it by Duddingston Loch to Niddrie and the nearest coal pit, Craighall. From Niddrie the line struck south through Millerhill village and Hardengreen, then it was taken across the first of the river barriers, the North Esk, on a viaduct 6oft high to a temporary terminus between the rivers at Dalhousie Mains. At the same time a branch was built from Niddrie eastwards to Fisherrow on the west bank of the Esk opposite Musselburgh. The main line was opened from St Leonards to Craighall on 4 July 1831. The whole line to Dalhousie Mains and the Fisherrow branch were opened in the following October. The main line was double, the branch single, and the gauge the Scottish gauge of 4ft 6in which Grainger had established with his railways in the west. Horse haulage was used throughout.

While the first phase of the E & D was being completed the Marquis of Lothian concerned himself with extending the line 1½ miles from Dalhousie Mains to the South Esk and across the river to Arniston, the site of his pits. He made the extension at his own expense, building in the process a spectacular bridge across the South Esk. It was 1,011ft long and its timber superstructure was supported on stone pillars and cast iron Gothic arches. Because of the high cost of this bridge the marquis was allowed to pass his coal over the North Esk bridge free. The Duke of Buccleuch was equally eager to exploit his collieries by giving them the benefit of railway connection. When the E & D made a branch from near the south end of the North Esk viaduct into the town of Dalkeith (which stands on a peninsula formed by the confluence of the North and South Esk) the duke extended the line across the South Esk on a viaduct scarcely less spectacular than the one built by his noble neighbour and so gained access to his Smeaton and Cowden pits.

The Dalkeith branch opened in the autumn of 1838. The Arniston branch had already been functioning since 21 January 1832. In 1838 a 4 mile branch from Niddrie reached Leith harbour. Single throughout, it ran by the west side of the Duddingston–Portobello road before turning west to cross the

Craigentinny Marshes to Seafield. When finally completed the
E & D formed a compact $12\frac{1}{2}$ mile horse-operated system linking
Edinburgh with the Lothian coalfield, the great port of Leith
(although by a roundabout route) and the fishing port of
Fisherrow. Direct services were also offered between Dalkeith
and Leith and Leith and Musselburgh.

As a mineral railway the E & D was superb. In a short time the
coal traffic built up to 300 tons a day. The commercial policy of
the company, as much as its operating efficiency, secured its
immediate acceptance as an Edinburgh asset. Hitherto coal had
been carted through the streets from Leith or Port Hopetoun on
the Union Canal. The coal merchants and carters, notoriously
dishonest, made a practice of selling coal illicitly from consignments in transit. A customer never knew whether he was getting
the quality and quantity of coal for which he had paid.

The E & D installed a recently invented weighbridge at St
Leonards and appointed Robert Gibb Company Weigher.
Gibb's job was to issue a certificate with every cart of coal dispatched from the depot, giving the quality, weight and time of
departure. Railway inspectors patrolled the streets keeping an
eye on carters. The coal was advertised as *railway* coal. It was
given what a century later would have been called a brand
image. Press advertisements told purchasers to look for the
name of Robert Gibb on their delivery certificates. They were
also asked to check the departure time from St Leonards and to
refuse delivery if 'you find that more time than enough has been
spent on the journey'. The E & D kept its promise 'to secure to
the consumer what he has hitherto been little accustomed to, a
knowledge of what kind of coal he buys, and of what price he
really pays for it'.

A typical advertisement ran, 'Michael Fox, 1 St Leonards
Street begs to intimate to his Friends and the Public that he
delivers the Marquis of Lothian's Coal at the following ready
money prices.

Diamond	13s	(65p)
Jewel	11s 6d	(57½p)
Household	10s 6d	(52½p)
Churls	7s	(35p)
Dross	5s 6d	(27½p)
English	19s	(95p)

English coal always was about double the price of local coal and some advertisements offered it as a special treat. 'Any families requiring a cart of Scotch coal can have a bag of English coal sent along with it.'

The E & D was paid a back-handed compliment when fraudulent vendors began selling non-railway coal as railway coal. The E & D had an impression of its inspector's stamp printed in the Edinburgh Directory, and the purchasers were asked to look for the stamp in red on their receipts.

Following his success selling railway coal Michael Fox decided to try the passenger business. By arrangement with the E & D management he put an old stagecoach on the line and on 2 June 1832 began a service of three return trips a day between St Leonards and the North Esk depot. The response was startling. In the first full month of operation 14,392 passengers travelled on the line, and in the following month the total rose to 20,615. Fox extended his services, and in the first year more than 150,000 passengers were carried. In 1834 the E & D obtained powers to run its own passenger traffic and by 1836 it had taken over the entire operation. By 1838 forty vehicles were in use carrying 299,201 passengers—469 per mile of track. Passenger density on the steam operated Liverpool & Manchester in the same year was 378, on the Stockton and Darlington 105. An analysis of traffic on the various sections gave the following results.

Edinburgh and Dalkeith	157,860
Edinburgh and Fisherrow	82,249
Edinburgh and Leith	11,005
Leith and Dalkeith	31,166
Leith and Fisherrow	16,921

In addition to timetable trains, private coaches could be hired from any station to any station at any hour of the day or night. Between 6 am and 9 am the charge was 14s (70p), between 9 pm and midnight it was 20s (£1) and between midnight and 6 am 25s (£1.25).

It is likely that the E & D's traffic returns were accurate, for the company's system of accountancy was nothing if not thorough. The coach drivers issued tickets and collected fares, but the guard was required to count the passengers entraining at each stop and enter the appropriate figure in his waybill. At the end of each trip the driver handed over the fares to the guard who checked them with his waybill. As an extra check inspectors were employed at St Leonards and Niddrie to count the passengers on the coaches.

Dr Robert Chambers, reflecting on the E & D trains jogging their leisurely and profitable way round the southern outskirts of Edinburgh and comparing them with trains on more sophisticated railways, wrote, 'In the very contemplation of the innocence of the railway you find your heart rejoiced. Only think of a railway having a board at all the stations forbidding the drivers to stop by the way to feed their horses!' The name The Innocent Railway entered the history books and the legend grew that the line was so called because it never killed or injured a passenger. In fact injuries, whether to passengers alighting from trains in motion or to pointsboys taking chances at loops were numerous; the manager himself got a leg injury that left him with a limp for life.

Mr Rankine, the enterprising manager of the E & D, who has been described as 'an intelligent engineer', found time to conduct experiments to determine the relative efficiency of wheels with cylindrical and conical tyres. In his subsequent report Rankine concluded that on straight track cylindrical wheels presented only half the resistance of conical wheels, but conical wheels fared better on curves. But Rankine found that when he elevated the outer rail above the inner rail on a curve the resistance to the cylindrical wheel was greatly reduced. The E & D main line from the foot of the St Leonards inclined plane was 11,740yd long of which 8,349yd were straight and 3,391yd were on curves, some of them 'very quick'. Rankine's report gives an interesting glimpse of the motive power on the line. 'The horses are not at all deterred by the work they perform,' he wrote. 'Indeed, passengers often remark, that at the end of a journey the horses seem little more fatigued than if they had run the distance at the same speed unloaded.'

The E & D served its public well for more than fourteen years. But a railway of the first railway decade was ill-fitted to meet the demands of the second. Its innocence was against it. By 1846 the E & G had penetrated to the heart of Edinburgh, the Caledonian was coming from the south-west and the North

British from the south-east. On 21 July 1845 the NB was authorised to purchase the E & D, and the sale for £113,000 was completed in October 1845. A year later began the work of converting the gauge and otherwise bringing the railway up to main line standards. Thus did Edinburgh's first and highly original railway vanish into the maw of a coming giant. But it still had a useful part to play in the story of the capital's rail transportation.

The former E & D was reopened by the North British for goods traffic on 7 July 1847 and for passengers on 14 July 1847. The line had now become a branch off the main line. A service of eight trains daily was given between Edinburgh (North Bridge) and Dalkeith. With E & G and NB trains converging at North Bridge this became the centre for passenger traffic and patronage of the outlying station at St Leonards no longer justified its retention as a passenger station. It was closed on 1 November 1847. A service from Dalkeith, Portobello and Leith to St Leonards was re-introduced on 1 June 1860, but the demand for it was so small that it was discontinued on 30 September of the same year.

LEITH

Of the 299,201 passengers who used the E & D in 1838 only 11,005 travelled between Edinburgh and Leith. The reason for this was that the route from central Edinburgh to Leith was 8 miles long and involved an omnibus journey to St Leonards. The direct route by road from the centre of Edinburgh to Leith was 1¼ miles.

In 1650 Sir A. Leslie, commander of the Scottish forces opposing Cromwell, built a broad breastwork of earth between Edinburgh and Leith and this became the basis of a means of communication. By 1678 public conveyances were running on it, and taking 1½ hours on the journey. By the coming of the railway age the breastwork had developed into Leith Walk and supported an excellent competitive service of omnibuses.

There were, in fact, three ports strung along less than 3 miles of the Forth foreshore, each with a special function and character, and all within 3 miles of Edinburgh. Leith stood at the mouth of the Water of Leith, and was split into North Leith and

Page 237 (*above*) The Glasgow Central Railway in the course of construction through the heart of Glasgow; (*below*) original entrance to Glasgow Central Low Level station in Argyle Street

Page 238 (*above*) Botanic Gardens station, Glasgow Central Railway;
(*below*) Maryhill station when first opened, Glasgow Central Railway

South Leith by the river, although West Leith and East Leith would have been more apt geographical descriptions. The port had two docks sustaining coastal, continental and foreign traffic. Granton, $2\frac{1}{4}$ miles west of Leith was a terminus for ferries to Fife, but vessels for London and other British ports also used its jetty. Between Leith and Granton stood Newhaven, a fishing port, and close-by was Newhaven chain pier. There was ready-made passenger and goods traffic in plenty for any promoter who was willing to link Edinburgh and one or all of the ports with a railway.

On 13 August 1836 the Edinburgh, Leith & Newhaven Railway got an Act to connect the points in its title. From a station in Canal Street, Edinburgh (between the North and Waverley bridges at the east end of Princes Street) the line was to run down to Leith and then continue along the shore to Trinity and Newhaven. Canal Street station was to be built in the valley between the old and new towns and the railway had to be driven in tunnel through the ridge on which the new town was built to emerge on the open slopes leading down to the Forth. Owners of properties, among which were the newest and most valuable in Edinburgh, were perturbed at the prospect of engineers burrowing under their foundations, and the railway found itself involved in costly, time-wasting litigation. Some of the shareholders lost confidence, and lack of money forced alterations in the original plans. By an Act of 1 July 1839 the line to Leith was abandoned. From the north end of the tunnel the route now took a more westerly course and headed straight for Trinity where there was to be a terminus near the chain pier and a branch to Leith. The extension to Newhaven was abandoned.

During the protracted preliminaries to the construction of the railway the status of Granton underwent a significant change. The harbour was reconstructed and the irregular sailing ferries were replaced by regular steam ferries plying between Granton and Burntisland in Fife. It was as a ferry station that Granton was to make its name. It did not take much imagination to see that trunk lines would extend from the Border to Edinburgh and that these lines would be continued north into Fife. The Forth ferries would be a vital link in the east coast chain of railways, and a company owning a line from Edinburgh to the ferry port would command a lucrative traffic.

P

The Edinburgh Leith & Newhaven Railway recast its plans to meet the new situation. An Act was obtained to extend the line to Granton harbour and the title was changed to Edinburgh Leith & Granton Railway. The *Liverpool Standard*, which had advised the Lancashire railway speculators that the Edinburgh Leith & Newhaven's chances were only 'fair', now described the reconstituted railway as 'a very profitable and valuable link in the grand chain which connects England and Scotland'. The *Railway Record* commenting on the line said, 'Probably there is no instance on record of a railway company having encountered so many difficulties and living. The shares which once could be had for literally nothing now rose to within £2 of par.'

The line between the north end of the tunnel, from a station known as Canonmills (later Scotland Street) and Trinity was opened on 31 August 1842, which happened to be the day on which Queen Victoria arrived in state in the Firth of Forth and made a ceremonial landing at Granton. If the railway directors had hoped to bask in the afterglow of the royal visit they were disappointed; the next issue of *The Scotsman* contained columns of print about the royal festivities, but not a word about the new railway. A branch from Bonnington Junction east of Trinity to Leith was opened in May 1846 and the extension from Trinity to Granton came into use on 19 February 1846. The whole system, from Canal Street station through the tunnel, was opened on 17 May 1847.

The muddle and confusion which bedevilled EL & G affairs extended to its motive power policy. The directors had intended to open the original section with steam locomotives; tenders were invited, but the engines were never ordered. Rolling stock suitable for locomotive haulage, however, was ordered and these vehicles proved to be much too heavy for the horse haulage which the company employed and the trains consistently ran late. The directors ordered lighter carriages and for a year tried to sell the original stock to the GPK & A and the E & G. In the end they got rid of two third class carriages to the Wishaw & Coltness for £262 16s (£262.80).

At one time the EL & G directors thought of employing the atmospheric principle and a representative was sent to Croydon to make on-the-spot investigations. This situation was forced on the company by the sudden appearance of two companies

A share certificate of the Edinburgh & Leith Atmospheric Direct Railway which proposed to build atmospheric railways between Edinburgh and Leith, one of them strongly supported by the North British.

The war of the 'atmospherics' which went on for several weeks is serio-comic in retrospect, but it caused alarm in the EL & G board room at the time. In the early hours of 19 October 1845 a representative of the Edinburgh & Leith Atmospheric Railway nailed parliamentary notices to the doors of the city churches. But when first light came it was found that the notices had been replaced by almost identical notices advertising the Edinburgh & Leith Atmospheric Direct Railway. The Edinburgh & Leith Atmospheric Railway offered a reward of £50 for information leading to the apprehension of the perpetrator of the outrage. The 'Direct' office denied complicity and maintained that the whole thing was a publicity stunt. The Edinburgh & Leith Atmospheric Direct Railway was much more concerned in revealing the alleged defects of its rival than in extolling its own virtues.

'It would be wise', cautioned one of its spokesmen, 'if investigators and speculators were to pause before involving themselves as stockholders of a concern so absolutely doomed. The Provisional Committee beg leave again to call attention to the fact that *this* railway was the first projected to Leith on the atmospheric principle, that the rival company are the plagiarists of the scheme and that not with a view to serve the public, but their own interests, nearly half of their original stock having been divided among their Provisional Committee, a proceeding generally reprobated, and which has excited popular indignation to a great degree. The public are therefore now called upon to support the present Company in connection with which there is no jobbing; and if they do so heartily and promptly the Provisional Committee pledge themselves immediately to place this undertaking upon higher ground than the rival scheme can ever attain notwithstanding of the vauntings and boastings of their supporters.

The Canal Street station of the EL & G stood at right angles to the North Bridge station of the E & G which was opened on the same day. It had two very short platforms. At the outset of their journey travellers faced a precipitate plunge on a gradient of 1 in 27 down the tunnel that took them under Princes Street, St Andrew Street, Duke Street and Dublin Street to emerge at Scotland Street station. The trains freewheeled down the slope held in check by brake trucks and by brakesmen sitting on the roofs of the carriages. Steam engines took over the trains at the tunnel mouth. Ascending trains were pulled up to Canal Street by a stationary engine.

In the first timetable trains were timed to leave Canal Street 20 minutes before the departure of the various steamers from Granton. The management in their advertisements suggested that the journey would take 7 or 8 minutes but regretted that they could not give more precise times until they had had a few days' experience of running the railway! On 3 June 1847 a new timetable giving intensive regular interval services came into use. Between 8.30 am and 9 pm there were twenty-five trains in each direction between Edinburgh and Granton and from 8.25 am to 9.25 pm there was a half-hourly service between Leith and Granton. Through coaches were provided between Edinburgh and Leith. In addition to the regular interval trains, special boat trains were run from Canal Street to Granton at 5.30 am and 6 am to connect with the Aberdeen and Kirkcaldy steamers. At 6.45 am there was a bathers' train to Trinity and Granton.

The EL & G should have prospered; in fact, it was beset by difficulties. Excessive expenditure, repeated changes of policy and amateurish management combined to prevent its expected success. Francis Cockshott the first manager (at the age of twenty-two!) was to say that officers and staff never knew if and when they would be paid their salaries. Inside a few weeks the manager and locomotive superintendent resigned, the assistant locomotive engineer was dismissed for an unspecified neglect of duty and the engineer of the stationary engine was dismissed for breach of regulations. Pathetic entries in the minute books spoke of the company's financial plight. The manager, pleading with the E & G to settle an account for lease of rolling stock said, 'The directors request that the account be paid by Saturday as the money is particularly required for weekly payments.' 'Mr Hawthorn of Newcastle requires payment of account,' was a typical minute book entry. 'Mr Bruce, who built the Chimney Stalk (for the stationary engine) requires his money and has been a long time kept of it,' was another. By the end of the first half year when the unpaid bills were laid on the board room table they were found to amount to £8,331 8s 1d (£8,331.40½).

The EL & G sought salvation by amalgamation. The E & G showed some interest, but nothing came of it. On the other hand the Edinburgh & Northern was in the peculiar position of having an office in Edinburgh and all its mileage across the Forth in Fife. In June 1847 the E & N bought the Granton–Burntisland ferries and on 27 July acquired the EL & G, so establishing a reasonably homogeneous transport system for eastern Scotland. The new company thus formed was known as the Edinburgh Perth & Dundee Railway.

After its colourful beginning the story of the Edinburgh railways settled into a pattern of steady development, a pattern in which the rising port of Leith played a major part. In the competition to serve Leith the North British and Caledonian saturated the port area with railways. The Caledonian, with its station inconveniently situated at the west end of the town, had been overshadowed in Edinburgh by the North British. The North British, which had inherited all the early local lines and so acquired a ready-made suburban system, was first challenged by the Caledonian when the company, encouraged by the Duke of Buccleuch who owned Granton harbour, on 28 August 1861 opened a branch from its main line at Slateford to Granton harbour. By 1 September 1864 the Caledonian was in Leith, a branch having been pushed out from Crew Junction on the Granton line. At the same time a spur was run from the main line at Dalry Junction to Coltbridge on the Granton line. The Caledonian was now in a position to run traffic direct from Leith to points west of Edinburgh. To get traffic away from North Leith the North British had to haul it up the 1 in 27 incline through Scotland Street tunnel and run it round the spur at Canal Street station on to the west-bound main line.

The North British improved its access to Leith by building a line from Piershill Junction, on the main line east of Edinburgh, to Trinity, thus creating a direct route from North Leith to the east and south. This line was opened for goods on 2 March 1868 and for passengers on 22 March 1868. Two spurs, one from Easter Road on the Piershill–Trinity line to the main line south, just east of the Calton tunnel, the other from Bonnington South Junction to Bonnington Junction made it possible for traffic from North Leith to run direct to Waverley station. A station was opened at Abbeyhill on 1 May 1869. The new North British route from the Forth ports enabled the company to close Scotland Street tunnel and the rather inconvenient Canal Street station.

The Caledonian used its Leith line for freight and minerals only until 1 August 1879 when a passenger service was opened from the company's Lothian Road station to Leith calling at Murrayfield, Craigleith, Granton Road and Newhaven. Railway activity in the area was spurred by the opening of the Edinburgh Dock in 1881. Some 54 acres of reclaimed ground associated with dock construction were shared between the Caledonian and North British. By 1 August 1903 the Caledonian drive to the east had reached Seafield. Seafield was served already by the South Leith branch of the North British from Portobello—the original Niddrie–Seafield branch of the Edinburgh & Dalkeith Railway. The Caledonian planned a passenger service for its Seafield branch and three platforms were built—Newhaven, Ferry Road and Leith Walk—but never used.

OTHER DEVELOPMENTS

By 1880 new suburbs were taking shape to the south of Edinburgh and to cater for their needs the Edinburgh, Suburban & Southside Junction Railway was opened on 1 December 1884. The main section of the line ran from St Leonards Junction (on the original E & D) westwards to Haymarket with stations at Duddingston, Newington, Blackford Hill, Morningside Road and Gorgie. A further station was opened at Craiglockhart on 1 June 1887. The suburban trains used the original E & D between St Leonards Junction and Niddrie West Junction, from which point a spur took them to Niddrie North Junction on the Waverley route, thence by the main line to Waverley station. It was thus possible for the trains to complete the circle Waverley to Waverley in either direction. The new railway also served as a by-pass by means of which trains could pass between the Edinburgh and Glasgow and East Coast main lines without going through Edinburgh.

Up to the 1890s Edinburgh had little to show in the way of railway architecture. The grand station in the Italian style that had been promised by the Caledonian in 1845 still had not

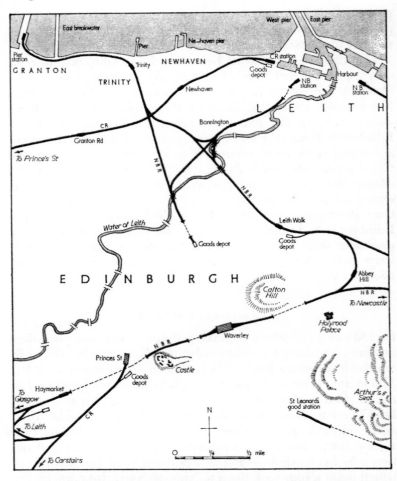

Plan of Edinburgh showing the layout of railways around
Leith in 1882

materialised half a century later. The company's Lothian Road
terminus was little more than a wooden shanty. The North
British Waverley station, confined in a narrow valley between the
old and the new towns, was prevented from expanding outwards by geography and upwards by the law of servitudes or
ancient lights, which kept the station buildings to a maximum

height of 30ft above rail level. The rival railway establishments stood at opposite ends of Princes Street, perhaps the most distinguished street in the world; for what other street is fronted by a mile of magnificent gardens and has as a backcloth a spectacular castle set on a high rock? The North British Railway ran unobtrusively at the foot of the gardens; its trains, sending an occasional whiff of steam up the face of the castle rock, interfered not at all with the majesty of the scene.

The gardens, so beloved by the people of Edinburgh, were a nightmare to the North British board. With the opening of the Forth Bridge in March 1890 traffic from Perth, Fife and the North, from Glasgow and Bathgate and off the Suburban line converged on Haymarket and somehow had to be threaded through the gardens to Waverley. It was like fitting a quart into a pint pot.

A 'new accelerated service' was advertised to begin on 6 September 1890 between Aberdeen, Edinburgh and the south. The new express train in the up direction took 2 hours to get from Corstorphine to Waverley with the result that the connecting trains for the south were late in departing. The East Coast trains due away at 10.30 and 10.40 pm did not leave until the early hours of the 7 September. That same night the train due in Waverley from Glasgow at 7.20 did not arrive until 9.30 having taken nearly $3\frac{1}{2}$ hours for the $47\frac{1}{4}$ mile journey. Chaos on this scale lasted for weeks. The station and its approaches were chronically jammed with trains, and the platforms were crowded with travellers looking for trains that had not arrived. 'Railway officials, guards and porters ran hither and thither in a state of excitement,' said a contemporary report. John Walker, the general manager, and some of his directors, jostled with the crowds on the platform 'and were baffled in their endeavour to cope with the confusion'.

The North British directors knew the cure for their ills—the quadrupling of the line through Princes Street Gardens and an extension of the Waverley station. Any threat of an encroachment on the gardens was bound to lead to a public outcry. The board had their eyes on the Waverley Market, which stood at the north boundary of the station, as a site for their station extension. The ground could be used for carriage storage at rail level and the upper part could serve as a parcels depot, thus releasing space for additional platforms in the station area.

At this time the Caledonian, too, had its eyes on the Waverley Market. Determined to get a site in the centre of the city the company planned to acquire the market as a station, and to get there from Lothian Road it proposed a tunnel under the whole length of Princes Street. The line was to be continued to Leith to link with the existing Caledonian Leith branch and form a suburban circle complementary to the North British south side circle.

When details of the various schemes were published there was an unholy uproar. The town council thought the Caledonian was claiming the right to build a double line through Princes Street Gardens. With the North British proposing an additional double line the famous gardens would have become a six track main line railway. The underground scheme was no more acceptable. Visions of underground stations with air vents belching smoke into the gardens horrified the city fathers. Lord Provost Russell declared that the city would not yield ground in the gardens to the railway companies even if they covered the ground with gold.

But so serious was the transport problem that a strip of the gardens had to be sacrificed. An Act of 5 July 1891 authorised the North British to quadruple its line from Corstorphine through Haymarket and Princes Street Gardens to Waverley and eastwards from Waverley through the Calton Hill to Abbeyhill. This involved the cutting of new tunnels between Haymarket and Princes Street Gardens and through the Mound and Calton Hill. Waverley station was rebuilt round a central island containing the booking and administrative offices. The finished station covered 23 acres. Its nineteen platforms with an aggregate length of 13,980ft could accommodate 358 carriages at one time. A count taken on 6 June 1908 showed that 1,319 trains left or entered the station on that day. The Caledonian, resigned to its site at the West End, at last built a station, Princes Street, with nine platforms, worthy of the city. Both companies provided hotels which were to become city landmarks.

In the event it was the North British that got the short line to Leith, with the opening of the Leith Central branch from London Road Junction on 1 July 1903. A spur was built between Lochend Junction and Lochend North Junction on the Leith Central line to enable Suburban line trains to operate to and from Leith Central.

The Caledonian turned its attention to exploiting the outer suburbs to the west of the city, left the main line at Slateford and climbed up the winding valley of the Water of Leith to rejoin the main line at Ravelrig Junction, serving on the way, Colinton, Juniper Green, Currie and Balerno. The pleasant little valley, so close to Edinburgh, had both passenger and freight potential. There were three paper mills, two stone quarries, a salt works and a tannery on the line. As well as residential traffic the Balerno branch attracted a considerable volume of 'picnic' traffic in summer. On 1 March 1894 the company opened a branch from Craigleith to Davidson's Mains and Barnton, then growing residential areas. In 1895 the Caledonian gave consideration to a plan to complete a circle line by extending the Barnton branch south-west almost to the North British Edinburgh–Glasgow main line before turning east to Corstorphine. The plan did not fructify. When Corstorphine got its railway it was a short North British branch from Haymarket West Junction opened on 1 February 1902. There was an intermediate station at Pinkhill.

The North British operated an intensive outer suburban service east and south of the city. One of the railway sights of Edinburgh was the east end of the Waverley station at the evening rush hour with its platforms packed with trains ready to set off. The destinations, described on curved boards carried in front of the engine chimneys, included Musselburgh, Macmerry, Glencorse, Dalkeith, Polton and Penicuik.

The Musselburgh branch was opened on 16 July 1847 as an extension of the Fisherrow branch of the E & D. Passengers were first carried on the Monktonhall to Macmerry branch on 1 May 1872. From Ormiston on the Macmerry line a light railway was opened to Giffard on 14 October 1901, serving Pencaitland, Saltoun and Humbie. The Dalkeith branch, which left the Waverley route at Glenesk Junction, had been part of the E & D. From Millerhill, also on the Waverley route, a branch to Roslin promoted by the Edinburgh, Loanhead & Roslin Railway was opened on 23 July 1874 and extended to Glencorse (then Glencross) on 2 July 1877. The intermediate stations were Gilmerton, Loanhead and Roslin. The Esk Valley Railway was opened from Esk Valley Junction on the Peebles line to serve Lasswade and Polton on 15 April 1867. The branch from Rosewell and Hawthornden station, also on the Peebles line, to Rosslyn Castle and Penicuik was opened by the Penicuik Railway on 2 September 1872. Most of the lines were promoted as independent companies and partly financed locally by people anxious to bring the benefits of railway travel to their own small communities. Worked from the start by the North British they became branches of that company when they were absorbed by it. They prospered for many years when they provided the only form of public transport between the outlying towns and Edinburgh.

In the six months ending December 1913 the North British issued 11,929 season tickets at its Edinburgh stations. In the corresponding period of 1920 the number rose to 21,368, giving a revenue of £88,529. In the same period North British stations in Glasgow issued 28,849 tickets for a return of £68,888. The longer distances involved and a higher percentage of first class fares accounted for the favourable Edinburgh position. In the last six months of 1920, 435,035 passengers were booked at Leith Central, 491,598 at Musselburgh and 431,559 at Portobello. In the 1920 timetable Waverley dispatched ninety-five suburban trains per day, Princes Street sixty. Fifty years later all that was left of the crowded, bustling suburban system were Slateford and Haymarket.

The Edinburgh railways were less subject to the ravages of town transport than were the Glasgow railways. The cable-operated Edinburgh trams were slower than their Glasgow counterparts and their field of operation was more restricted. In Edinburgh the railway companies could extend their lines out of range of the trams. When the Edinburgh tramway system was electrified in 1922 it proved a formidable rival to the inner suburban lines, just at a time when the new buses were attacking the outer suburban services. At first only a few less prosperous stations were closed, but in time whole services began to disappear from the timetable. The Macmerry branch closed to passengers on 1 July 1925 and passenger services ended on the Glencorse line on 1 May 1933.

In spite of the general trend the railway companies did what they could to retain and encourage suburban traffic. Sunday excursions at very cheap rates were run to the Barnton and Balerno branches, and were well patronised. On 26 September 1927 a halt was opened at Hailes on the Balerno line to cater for patrons of the local golf course, and East Pilton was given a halt on 1 December 1934 to encourage the residents in a new housing estate to travel by train. When the LNER introduced Sentinel steam rail cars in the late twenties one of these vehicles was put on exhibition at Waverley station and presented to the public as the last word in modern suburban travel.

Dalkeith lost its passenger service on 3 January 1942, Balerno on 30 October 1943. The North British withdrew passenger trains from the North Leith line on 16 June 1947, and from Leith Central on 7 April 1952. The awkward pedestrian approach to the Waverley station was partly responsible for the demise of the Leith Central service. Few people could be induced to climb the Waverley steps at the end of a 1½ mile journey when an Edinburgh Corporation bus would deposit them at street level. The ex-Caledonian service to Leith survived until 30 April 1962. On 10 September 1962 passenger services on the Suburban Circle ended. The last of the Edinburgh branches, that to Corstorphine, saw its final passenger train on 30 December 1967.

Efforts to induce the authorities to include railways in plans for future urban development failed. The capital had turned its back on the railway—almost. In 1970 an energetically conducted public campaign resulted in a British Rail decision to reopen the closed station at Kingsknowe which had become the centre of a housing development. The station was still *in situ* although overgrown and in poor shape. Refurbished and fitted out with electric lighting it was reopened on 1 February 1971.

Conclusion: Towards the New Railway

The railways gave the region life. There are those who would have it that when a railway died the community it had served died with it. That was seldom true. It was the railway that died, not the community. The community simply had found an alternative source of mobility—usually the motorcar.

There was much talk in the 1960s of the effects of the Beeching axe by people who refused to recognise that the implement wielded by the doctor was not an axe but a scalpel. The good work of the 1960s, so roundly condemned at the time, expunged the branch lines and wayside stations that almost nobody wanted, leaving the main lines as clean and uncluttered as motorways — and much safer. They were exactly the right medium for the high-speed traffic of the seventies.

When in 1906 the North British inaugurated a service of express trains taking 3 hours for the journey between Edinburgh and Aberdeen it called its new trains the Inter-City Expresses. Inter-City! More than half a century later British Rail used the phrase to popularise a new concept of fast, uninterrupted travel between cities.

The region's prestige line was and is the Glasgow–Edinburgh route via Polmont. The North British put much money and effort into promoting its inter-city services at a time when there was little competition. But the old company had to contend with difficulties not immediately apparent to the passengers. The route crossed successively coalfields, fireclay beds and shale mines which created a warren of tunnels under the railway. The company's records make constant mention of the purchase from the mine owners, often at high cost, of 'stoops'—pillars of coal, fireclay or shale left *in situ* in the workings to prop up the roadbed. The stoops did not always function and frequent subsidences meant speed restrictions and the limping progress of trains which were nominally expresses.

Slow trains dawdling along the main line, stopping at all stations, traffic coming off branches, engines pottering about the numerous colliery and works sidings all helped to impede the inter city service. Then there was the crippling bottleneck of Queen Street station. When a train arrived the engine had to be released to go to Eastfield $1\frac{1}{2}$ miles away for servicing. An engine that had spent 70 minutes on a journey from Edinburgh might spend 3 hours on shed and in transit between shed and station between trips, a process as wasteful in line occupation as it was in money.

With so many obstacles to overcome it is remarkable that the North British managed to operate a prestige service, even if the trains ran at intervals of an hour and took more than 70 minutes for the $47\frac{1}{4}$ miles when track conditions were bad. Now that the old underground workings have been abandoned the track has been consolidated and made secure. New techniques have been used to reinforce the old stone viaducts that gave trouble for years. The wholesale elimination of branch lines and sidings with their facing points, and the disappearance of inter-mediate stations with their stopping trains have made faster, smoother running possible. The end of steam and the introduc-tion of diesel powered trains made for the more economical use of motive power and reduced line occupation. At last there was space for more trains. British Rail enhanced the value of the Edinburgh–Glasgow service to the public by the simple ex-pedient of halving the length of the trains and doubling their number. The North British did its best with the tools at its disposal, and often it was a very good best. But it did not have the mechanical or operational facilities to run a train from Glasgow to Edinburgh in 43 minutes. Such is the measure of progress on the prestige route.

The crests of the old Scottish companies were as complex as they were ornate. Usually, among their embellishments, they embodied the coats of arms of the principal towns they served. It is doubtful if a traveller looking casually at a crest could have named the company it represented. The simple, bold emblem of British Rail is instantly recognisable wherever it appears— and it appears in divers places—on Freightliner containers, on express parcels trains, on the funnels of the finest cross-channel ships in the business, on the trains of the motor-rail system, on the fastest passenger trains that ever ran on British rails. In spite of the hard knocks they take, the men who serve the region today are no less inventive and versatile than the railway managers of the past.

Page 255 (above) East end of Waverley station, Edinburgh, in 1850; (below) east end of Waverley station in 1906, with suburban train waiting to depart

Page 256   The main hall of Waverley station built in 1897, as
reconditioned in 1970

Chronology: A Note

A comprehensive chronology of the complex region covered by this book would require a volume in itself. The following tables of dates are merely intended to provide a time scale, and to make reference to some of the more important dates easy. Railway chronology is a field fraught with difficulties. At the former British Railways Board Historical Records Office in Edinburgh, inquirers were shown a book ruled in two columns, one headed 'our Dates' the other headed '——'s Dates'; —— being a chronologer of high repute. The differences were daunting to a historian in search of accuracy. In the following tables the official dates are given unless *conclusive* proof has been produced to refute them. It is true that even primary sources are at times wrong. For instance, a writer who found that the minute books of the Lanarkshire & Ayrshire Railway and the directors' report to the shareholders of that company gave 2 June 1890 as the opening date of Montgomerie Pier, Ardrossan, would feel justified in accepting that date as being absolutely accurate. But if the writer were to examine the files of *The Glasgow Herald* he would find a railway announcement advertising the opening of the pier for 30 May 1890, and a subsequent report describing the opening of the pier on that day. Again, that 'Bible' of Scottish chronologers, the official Caledonian chronology compiled by Andrew Brand, nods more than once; and it can never be taken for granted that a station opened on a particular day on the strength of an official staff notice to that effect. There have been cases of openings being cancelled after the issue of the official notice.

Such are the pitfalls that await the railway historian. If any reader disagrees with the dates given, the author would be glad to hear from him, *provided he gives the source of his information.*

Q

Chapter 3   Inter-City

21 February 1842	Edinburgh & Glasgow Railway opened.
28 August 1847	Shieldhill branch (E & G) opened.
15 February 1848	Carstairs–Edinburgh–Glasgow (Caledonian Railway) opened.
12 November 1849	Edinburgh & Bathgate Railway opened.
1 April 1858	Denny branch (Caledonian Railway) opened.
5 July 1858	Campsie branch (E & G) opened.
1 October 1864	Bathgate–Morningside branch opened.
1 March 1866	Ratho (Queensferry Junction)–Kirkliston–Dalmeny opened.
11 August 1866	Bathgate & Coatbridge Railway opened.
5 November 1866	Blane Valley Railway opened for goods.
1 July 1867	Blane Valley Railway opened for passengers.
1 June 1868	Dalmeny–South Queensferry opened.
9 July 1869	Cleland–Midcalder opened.
28 July 1870	Milngavie Junction Railway opened.
1 February 1871	Glasgow & Coatbridge Railway opened.
1 April 1871	Edinburgh–Glasgow (College) through passenger service inaugurated.
1 June 1878	Kelvin Valley Railway: passenger service Glasgow (Queen Street)–Kilsyth via Lenzie inaugurated.
1 October 1878	South Queensferry–Port Edgar opened.
1 June 1879	Kelvin Valley Railway: opened from Kilsyth to Maryhill for goods. The line at first was not connected to the NBR at Maryhill.
1 October 1879	Kelvin Valley Railway: Kelvin Valley Junction (Maryhill) brought into use.
1 October 1882	Strathendrick & Aberfoyle Railway opened.
1 August 1885	Kelvin Valley Railway absorbed by NBR.
1 October 1885	Alloa branch and bridge opened.
2 August 1886	Bonnybridge branch (Caledonian Railway) opened.
1 February 1888	Denny branch, south fork, opened.
2 June 1890	Dalmeny–Saughton Junction; Dalmeny–Winchburgh Junction, opened. Forth Bridge connecting lines.
5 August 1891	Strathendrick & Aberfoyle absorbed by the NBR.
1 February 1899	Glasgow (Buchanan Street)–Bo'ness passenger service inaugurated (Caledonian Railway).

1 July 1899	Bo'ness passenger service (Caledonian Railway) withdrawn.
1 May 1930	Bathgate–Morningside closed to passengers.
28 July 1930	Bonnybridge branch (Caledonian Railway) closed to passengers.
1 February 1935	Kilsyth–Bonnybridge passenger service ends.
9 January 1956	Edinburgh–Glasgow passenger service via Bathgate discontinued.
7 May 1956	Bo'ness branch closed to passengers.
4 May 1964	Twechar–Banknock closed.
7 September 1964	Lenzie Junction–Kirkintilloch closed to passengers.
20 July 1965	Denny West Junction–Carmuirs Junction closed.
7 February 1966	Ratho–Kirkliston–Dalmeny closed.
4 April 1966	Kirkintilloch Basin–Middlemuir Junction; Lennoxtown–Kelvin Valley West Junction; Twechar–Lenzie Junction closed.
6 November 1967	Dalmeny Junction–South Queensferry closed.
29 January 1968	Grangemouth branch closed to passengers.
22 February 1968	Broxburn Junction–Broxburn closed.
6 May 1968	Grangemouth Junction–Fouldubs Junction closed.

Chapter 4 *The South-east Triangle*

22 June 1846	North British Railway opened from Edinburgh to Berwick with branch from Longniddry to Haddington.
13 August 1849	North Berwick branch opened to Williamstown.
1 November 1849	Hawick branch opened.
11 December 1849	Tranent colliery branch opened.
17 June 1850	North Berwick branch opened throughout.
29 August 1850	Royal Border Bridge opened.
1 June 1851	St Boswells–Kelso opened.
4 July 1855	Peebles Railway opened.
5 April 1856	Selkirk Railway opened.
17 July 1856	Jedburgh Railway opened.
7 October 1856	Haddington branch singled.
23 June 1862	Border Union Railway and Border Counties Railway opened for goods and minerals.
1 July 1862	BU and BC opened for passengers.

16 November 1863	Berwickshire Railway: Dunse (Duns)–Earlston opened.
18 April 1864	Riddings Junction–Langholm opened.
4 July 1864	Leadburn–Dolphinton opened.
2 October 1865	Berwickshire Railway: Earlston–St Boswells opened.
13 April 1891	Eyemouth Railway opened.
1 May 1898	Gullane branch opened.
2 July 1901	Lauder Light Railway opened.
12 September 1932	Lauder Light Railway closed to passengers.
1 April 1933	Dolphinton branch closed to passengers.
12 August 1948	Jedburgh branch; Duns–Earlston; closed following severe flood damage.
10 September 1951	Reston–Duns; Galashiels–Selkirk: closed to passengers.
5 February 1962	Eskbank–Peebles–Galashiels: Eyemouth–Burnmouth; closed to passengers.
18 May 1964	Polton–Esk Valley Junction closed.
15 June 1964	St Boswells–Kelso closed to passengers.
2 November 1964	Galashiels–Selkirk closed.
7 November 1966	Reston–Duns closed.
18 September 1967	Riddings Junction–Langholm closed.
1 April 1968	St Boswells–Kelso closed. Longniddry–Haddington closed.
6 January 1969	Waverley route closed.

Chapter 5   The South-west Triangle

27 May 1808	Kilmarnock & Troon Railway authorised.
6 July 1812	K & T opened from St Marnocks Depot, Kilmarnock to Troon Harbour.
14 June 1827	Ardrossan & Johnstone Railway authorised.
15 July 1837	Glasgow, Paisley, Kilmarnock & Ayr Railway authorised.
5 August 1839	GPK & A opened Ayr to Irvine.
23 March 1840	GPK & A opened Irvine to Kilwinning.
21 July 1840	GPK & A opened Kilwinning–Beith.
21 July 1840	GPK & A opened Paisley–Howwood.
20 August 1840	Ardrossan–Liverpool sailing inaugurated by *Fire King*.
4 April 1843	Dalry–Kilmarnock opened.
16 July 1846	Glasgow, Dumfries & Carlisle Railway authorised.

1 March 1847	Irvine harbour branch opened. Swinlees branch opened.
22 May 1848	Crosshouse–Irvine opened.
9 August 1848	Kilmarnock–Auchinleck opened.
23 August 1848	Dumfries–Gretna (GD & C) opened and worked by GPK & A.
27 September 1848	Glasgow, Barrhead & Neilston Direct Railway opened to Barrhead.
15 October 1849	Closeburn–Dumfries opened.
20 May 1850	Auchinleck–New Cumnock opened.
28 October 1850	New Cumnock–Closeburn opened. GPK & A and GD & C amalgamate to form G & SWR.
5 October 1855	GB & N opened to Crofthead.
15 May 1856	Ayr & Dalmellington Railway opened for goods.
7 August 1856	Ayr & Dalmellington Railway opened for passengers.
15 September 1856	Ayr & Maybole Railway opened for goods.
13 October 1856	Ayr & Maybole Railway opened for passengers.
7 November 1859	Castle Douglas & Dumfries Railway opened.
24 May 1860	Maybole & Girvan Railway opened.
12 March 1861	Portpatrick Railway: Castle Douglas–Stranraer opened.
28 August 1862	Portpatrick branch opened.
1 October 1862	Stranraer harbour branch opened.
1 September 1870	Ayr–Mauchline opened.
27 March 1871	Glasgow, Barrhead & Kilmarnock opened to Stewarton.
11 June 1872	Annbank–Cronberry opened for goods.
1 July 1872	Annbank–Cronberry opened for passengers.
26 June 1873	GB & K opened Stewarton–Kilmarnock. Beith branch opened.
3 April 1875	Wigtownshire Railway: Newton Stewart–Wigtown opened.
2 August 1875	Wigtownshire Railway: Wigtown–Millisle opened.
3 April 1876	Millisle–Garlieston opened.
9 July 1877	Millisle–Whithorn opened.
5 October 1877	Girvan & Portpatrick Junction Railway (Girvan–Challoch Junction) opened.
1 May 1878	Ardrossan–West Kilbride opened.
1 June 1880	West Kilbride–Fairlie opened.
1 July 1882	Fairlie–Fairlie Pier opened.

1 June 1885	Fairlie Pier Junction–Largs opened.
4 September 1888	Lanarkshire & Ayrshire Railway: Barrmill–Ardrossan opened.
3 November 1888	L & A: Ardeer branch opened.
30 November 1888	L & A Link to G & SW and Ardrossan harbour opened.
1 November 1889	L & A: Kilbirnie branch opened for goods.
2 December 1889	L & A: Kilbirnie branch opened for passengers.
30 May 1890	L & A: Montgomerie Pier, Ardrossan brought into use.
2 June 1890	L & A: Irvine branch opened.
3 March 1892	Monkton–Annbank opened for goods.
1 June 1896	Darvel–Newmilns opened.
14 July 1902	Gatehead–Hurlford opened for goods and minerals. Riccarton passenger station was built on this line but never used for regular passenger traffic.
1 March 1903	Millisle–Garlieston closed to passengers.
1 April 1903	L & A: opened Giffen–Cathcart for goods.
1 May 1903	L & A: opened Giffen–Cathcart for passengers.
1 September 1903	Brackenhill Junction–Catrine opened.
6 June 1904	Kay Park Junction–Bellfield Junction (Riccarton Loop) opened for goods and minerals.
1 March 1905	Cairn Valley Light Railway (Dumfries–Moniaive) opened.
1 May 1905	Strathaven–Darvel opened for passengers.
1 June 1905	Cart Junction–Brownhill Junction (Dalry and North Johnstone loop) opened.
17 May 1906	Alloway Junction–Girvan (Maidens & Dunure Light Railway) opened.
25 July 1930	L & A: Kilwinning East–Irvine (Bank Street) closed to passengers.
1 December 1930	Alloway Junction–Turnberry closed. Re-opened between 4 March 1932 and 31 May 1933.
4 July 1932	L & A: Local passenger service Uplawmoor–Ardrossan ceases. Boat and excursion trains continued to use the line.
2 March 1942	Girvan–Turnberry closed to passengers.
3 May 1943	Dumfries–Moniaive closed to passengers.
3 May 1943	Brackenhill Junction–Catrine closed to passengers.
6 February 1950	Portpatrick branch closed.
6 April 1964	Ayr–Dalmellington; Crosshouse–Irvine;

	Hurlford–Darvel; passenger services withdrawn.
5 October 1964	Beith Town–Barrmill closed.
5 October 1964	Wigtown–Whithorn–Garlieston closed.
14 December 1964	Lugton Junction–Neilston High closed.
14 June 1965	Dumfries–Challoch Junction closed. (PP & W) Stranraer Harbour boat trains diverted via Mauchline.
11 October 1965	Crosshouse–Irvine closed.
7 March 1966	Stranraer Harbour Junction–Stranraer Town closed to passengers.
18 April 1966	Ardrossan, Castlehill Junction–Parkhouse Junction closed to passengers.
18 April 1966	Barassie Junction–Lochgreen Junction (Troon avoiding line) closed to passengers except for one train.
18 April 1966	Stevenston No 1–Ardrossan Montgomerie Pier closed to passengers.
27 June 1966	Cart Junction–Brownhill Junction closed to passengers.
6 May 1968	Stevenston No 1–Ardrossan Montgomerie Pier closed.
12 September 1968	Alloway Junction–Heads of Ayr closed.
3 March 1969	Kilmarnock No 2–Barassie Junction closed to passengers.

Chapter 6   The Central Trunk

15 February 1848	Caledonian Railway opened from Carlisle to Garriongill with a branch from Carstairs to Edinburgh.
1 June 1849	Motherwell–Rutherglen opened.
17 September 1849	Newton–Hamilton opened.
5 January 1855	Lanark branch opened as single line for goods.
1 December 1856	Motherwell–Lesmahagow opened for minerals.
8 October 1857	Motherwell deviation line (from the Wishaw & Coltness Railway to the Clydesdale Junction Railway) opened.
9 August 1860	Hamilton–Strathaven opened to Quarter for goods.
5 November 1860	Symington–Broughton opened.
16 June 1862	Hamilton–Strathaven opened throughout for goods.

2 February 1863	Hamilton–Strathaven via Quarter opened throughout for goods and passengers.
1 February 1864	Broughton–Peebles opened.
1 April 1864	Lanark branch doubled. Lanark–Douglas opened.
20 September 1865	Rutherglen–Coatbridge opened for goods.
8 January 1866	Rutherglen–Coatbridge opened for passengers.
1 December 1866	Lesmahagow lines: Ferniegair–Brocketsbrae opened for passengers, also Stonehouse and Blackwood branches.
1 March 1867	Carstairs–Dolphinton opened.
1 April 1868	Ferniegair–Lesmahagow Junction opened to passengers.
13 September 1869	Solway Junction Railway: Annan branch opened for goods.
8 August 1870	Solway Junction Railway opened throughout.
26 October 1871	Whifflet–College passenger service commenced.
10 October 1872	Strawfrank curve opened.
1 January 1873	Douglas–Muirkirk opened for goods.
1 June 1874	Douglas–Muirkirk opened for passengers.
18 September 1876	Hamilton and Ferniegair connecting line opened for minerals.
2 October 1876	Hamilton and Ferniegair connecting line opened for passengers.
1 November 1877	Shettleston–Bothwell opened for goods. (Glasgow, Bothwell, Hamilton & Coatbridge Railway.)
1 April 1878	Shettleston–Hamilton opened for passengers.
1 October 1878	Uddingston–Fullwood opened for goods.
1 November 1878	Whifflet–Bothwell Castle (GB & H) opened for goods.
30 December 1878	Mossend branch opened for goods.
1 May 1879	Mossend branch opened for passengers.
1 May 1879	Whifflet–Bothwell Castle opened for passengers.
1 June 1879	Uddingston Junction–Fullwood Junction opened for passengers.
1 June 1880	Law Junction–Holytown opened.
2 April 1883	Moffat branch opened.
2 April 1883	Poniel Junction–Alton Heights opened. Muirkirk & Lesmahagow Junction Railway.
1 March 1885	Blantyre–East Kilbride opened for goods.
2 July 1885	Blantyre–East Kilbride opened for passengers.

19 April 1886	Airdrie branch (Caledonian Railway) opened for goods.
1 June 1886	Airdrie branch opened for passengers.
1 September 1887	Cairnhill Junction–Chapelhall opened.
2 July 1888	Newhouse–Chapelhall opened.
1 October 1901	Elvanfoot–Leadhills opened.
19 September 1902	Leadhills–Wanlockhead opened for goods.
12 October 1902	Leadhills–Wanlockhead opened for passengers.
4 July 1905	Strathaven and Darvel opened for goods.
1 May 1905	Strathaven–Darvel opened for passengers.
1 June 1905	Merryton Junction–Stonehouse; Stonehouse–Blackwood–Strathaven Central; Blackwood–Alton Heights; opened. Mid Lanark lines.
22 February 1951	Strathaven–Darvel lifted.
6 June 1961	Shettleston–Bothwell closed.
6 April 1964	Moffat branch closed.
4 May 1964	Wilsontown Junction–Wilsontown closed.
4 October 1965	Hamilton–Coalburn and Stonehouse–Strathaven closed to passengers; Coalburn–Auchlochan Colliery: closed.
18 October 1965	Lanark Racecourse–Simyllum West Junction closed. Used for turning engines until 19 December 1965.
7 January 1966	Coatbridge–Carmyle–Rutherglen closed to passengers.
4 April 1966	Symington–Broughton closed.
4 April 1966	Chapelhall–Bellside Junction closed.
18 April 1966	Lanark Junction south curve closed to passengers. (Edinburgh–Carstairs–Lanark service.)
18 November 1966	Lockerbie–Dumfries closed.
20 October 1968	Lanark south curve closed.
4 November 1968	Larkhall (Central)–Haughhead Junction closed.

Chapter 7   The River Clyde and Loch Lomond

15 July 1837	Glasgow, Paisley & Greenock Railway authorised.
March 1841	GP & G opened.
15 July 1850	Caledonian & Dumbartonshire Railway opened from Bowling to Balloch.

18 March 1856	Forth & Clyde Junction Railway opened from Stirling to Buchlyvie.
26 May 1856	Forth & Clyde Junction Railway opened throughout.
31 May 1858	Glasgow, Dumbarton & Helensburgh Railway opened.
14 August 1862	GD & H absorbed by Edinburgh & Glasgow Railway.
13 May 1865	Wemyss Bay Railway opened.
1 June 1869	Greenock Victoria Harbour branch opened.
1 September 1869	Greenock & Ayrshire opened for goods.
23 December 1869	Greenock & Ayrshire opened for passengers.
1 August 1872	Greenock & Ayrshire vested in G & SW.
1 December 1882	Glasgow, Yoker & Clydebank Railway opened.
5 August 1886	James Watt Dock (Greenock) branch opened.
1 June 1889	Gourock station and pier opened.
1 August 1893	Wemyss Bay Railway absorbed by Caledonian Railway.
25 May 1894	New Princes Pier opened.
1 May 1896	Lanarkshire & Dumbartonshire opened from Stobcross to Clydebank.
1 October 1896	L & D opened from Clydebank to Dumbarton East. Dumbarton & Balloch Joint Railway formed by CR, NBR and L & A to operate railway between Dumbarton East and Balloch Pier and Loch Lomond steamers.
25 April 1907	Formal opening of Rothesay Dock, Clydebank.
1 October 1934	Forth & Clyde Junction Railway closed to passenger traffic.
2 February 1959	Local passenger service between Kilmacolm and Princes Pier ends.
6 July 1964	King's Inch–Porterfield–Renfrew South closed.
1 September 1964	Balloch (Forth & Clyde Junction)–Jamestown closed.
5 October 1964	Old Kilpatrick–Bowling (Dunglass Junction) closed.
30 November 1965	Last boat train ran to Princes Pier.
26 September 1966	Princes Pier–Kilmacolm closed.
29 October 1966	Port Glasgow Junction–Port Glasgow Harbour closed.

Chapter 8   Glasgow

May 1831	Garnkirk & Glasgow opened for minerals.
1 June 1831	G & G opened for passengers.
27 September 1831	G & G ceremonial opening.
14 July 1840	Glasgow & Paisley Joint Railway opened.
12 August 1840	Bridge Street station (temporary) opened.
4 April 1841	Bridge Street station (permanent) opened.
21 February 1842	Queen Street station (Edinburgh & Glasgow Railway) opened.
1 July 1843	Moss Road station (Glasgow & Paisley Joint line) opened. (Closed about 1845.)
6 November 1843	Bellahouston station (Glasgow & Paisley Joint line) opened. (Closed about 1845.)
29 September 1848	South Side station opened. (Glasgow, Barrhead & Neilston Direct Railway.)
1 June 1849	Clydesdale Junction Railway opened. Trains from Motherwell ran into South Side station. Gushetfaulds Junction–West Street Junction opened.
1 November 1849	Buchanan Street station (Caledonian Railway) opened for passengers.
1 January 1850	Buchanan Street station opened for goods.
24 June 1861	Dalmarnock branch (Caledonian Railway) opened.
29 July 1864	City of Glasgow Union Railway authorised.
1 January 1866	Busby Railway opened.
1 May 1868	Govan branch opened for goods.
1 September 1868	Busby Railway extended to East Kilbride.
2 December 1868	Govan branch opened for passengers.
12 December 1870	City of Glasgow Union Railway opened between Pollokshields and Dunlop Street. Dunlop Street station opened. G & SW main line trains used the station from this date, but local trains continued to use Bridge Street.
19 December 1870	Gallowgate station (CGU) brought into use as terminus for North British trains pending opening of College station.
1 March 1871	Ibrox station opened.
1 April 1871	College station opened (for all trains).
1 June 1871	G & SW bus trains (Shields Road–Bellgrove) inaugurated.
1 January 1872	Main Street station (Gorbals) opened.

26 June 1873	Glasgow, Barrhead & Kilmarnock Joint line opened.
20 October 1874	Stobcross Railway opened.
29 October 1874	Whiteinch Railway and tramway opened.
16 August 1875	CGU. Bellgrove–Springburn opened for goods; Haghill Junction–Parkhead Junction opened.
1 May 1876	St Enoch station opened. St Pancras–St Enoch express service inaugurated. Link between CGU and GB & K opened.
17 October 1876	Ceremonial opening of St Enoch.
29 January 1877	Cathcart Road Junction–Langside Junction opened for goods.
1 February 1877	Cathcart Road Junction–Langside Junction opened for passengers.
12 April 1877	London Road station opened for goods.
1 September 1877	Gorbals station (GB & K) opened.
1 December 1877	Strathbungo station opened.
1 April 1879	London Road station opened to passengers.
1 July 1879	South Side station closed.
3 July 1879	St Enoch Hotel opened.
12 July 1879	Bridge Street station (rebuilt) opened.
1 August 1879	Central station opened.
1 September 1879	Carlisle and Edinburgh trains (Caledonian Railway) transferred from Buchanan Street to Central.
1 October 1879	Cardonald station opened.
29 June 1883	St Enoch station vested in G & SW.
1 August 1883	St Rollox station opened.
1 July 1885	Paisley Canal line opened for passengers.
17 August 1885	London Road–Parkhead opened for goods.
25 January 1886	Maxwell Junction–Bellahouston Junction opened. (CR–GSW connecting line.)
1 March 1886	Cathcart District Railway opened to Mount Florida.
15 March 1886	Glasgow City & District Railway opened. Hyndland station opened.
25 May 1886	Cathcart District Railway opened to Cathcart.
1 June 1886	Potterhill station opened.
2 August 1886	London Road–Blochairn Junction opened for goods.
13 December 1886	Barnhill (CGU) opened for passengers.
1 January 1887	Springburn (CGU) opened for passengers.
1 June 1888	Crossmyloof station opened.

1 February 1892	G & SW cease using Bridge Street station.
2 April 1894	Cathcart Circle opened.
1 May 1894	Hawkhead station opened.
26 November 1894	Balornock Junction–Hamiltonhill branch (Caledonian Railway) opened: Blochairn–Blackhill opened; Maryhill–Stobcross opened for goods.
1 April 1895	Caledonian Railway branch from Hamiltonhill branch to Saracen Foundry opened. Closed early in 1896 by court order, the branch having been built in breach of agreement with NBR.
1 November 1895	Glasgow Cross–Strathclyde Junction opened. London Road passenger station closed.
11 March 1896	Balornock Junction–Robroyston opened.
1 May 1896	Lanarkshire & Dumbartonshire Railway: Bellshaugh Junction–Partick West Junction opened for goods.
1 June 1896	Partick North Junction–Partick East Junction opened for goods.
15 June 1896	L & D opened to Dumbarton for goods.
7 August 1896	CGU partitioned between NBR and G & SW.
10 August 1896	Galsgow Central Railway opened throughout. Central Low Level station opened.
1 December 1896	Corkerhill station opened.
29 January 1897	Bridgeton Cross–Carmyle opened for goods.
1 February 1897	Bridgeton Cross–Carmyle opened for passengers.
1 February 1897	Possil station (Caledonian Railway) opened for passengers.
1 May 1897	South Renfrew station opened.
1 June 1897	Paisley West station opened.
30 September 1899	Through carriages between Edinburgh and Ayr (NBR–G & SW) discontinued.
1 October 1900	Eglinton Street station (later Cumberland Street) opened.
1 October 1902	G & SW bus trains cease.
1 October 1902	Potterhill–Barrhead Central, G & SW, opened. Circular service started, St Enoch–Potterhill–Barrhead Central–Pollokshaws–St Enoch.
26 June 1904	Kirkhill–Carmyle (Lanarkshire & Ayrshire Railway) opened for goods.
1 August 1904	Kirkhill–Carmyle opened for passengers.
1 October 1907	Barrhead Central circle service discontinued.
1 May 1908	Dawsholm station closed.

28 February 1909	Eglinton Street widening and new station completed.
14 June 1909	Buchanan Street new goods station opened.
1 January 1917	Passenger service withdrawn from Potterhill and Barrhead Central.
9 May 1921	Govan station closed to passengers.
6 February 1939	Botanic Gardens station closed.
1 May 1939	Kirklee station closed.
1 July 1942	Kelvinside station closed.
2 April 1951	Whiteinch (Victoria Park) closed to passengers.
4 August 1952	Kelvinbridge station closed.
2 November 1953	Glasgow Green station closed.
3 August 1959	Anderston Cross and Stobcross stations closed.
5 November 1960	North bank electrification inaugurated. Steam services were resumed on 19 December following a defect in the electrical equipment.
19 November 1962	Blackhill Junction–Germiston Junction closed.
20 July 1963	Ruchill Hospital branch (Caledonian Railway) closed. Robroyston Hospital branch closed.
28 October 1963	Barrhead (South)–Chain Road, Ferguslie closed.
2 March 1964	Service from Springburn to Singer Works platform ends.
29 July 1964	Milngavie–Ellangowan Paper Mills closed.
7 September 1964	Balornock Junction–London Road Junction closed.
5 October 1964	Glasgow Central Low Level and associated lines closed; Strathclyde Junction–Kelvin Hall; Tollcross–Bridgeton Cross Junction.
5 October 1964	Dumbarton East–Possil; Coatbridge–Whifflet (Upper)–Rutherglen; passenger services withdrawn.
1 March 1965	Paisley Abercorn–Cart Harbour closed.
3 May 1965	Jordanhill–Whiteinch closed. Used by electrification maintenance trains until 6 February 1967.
6 September 1965	Possilpark–Ruchill closed.
22 February 1966	Partick West Junction–Possil–Balornock Junction closed.
27 June 1966	St Enoch station closed. St Enoch–Shields Junction; St Enoch–Saltmarket Junction closed.

27 June 1966	Shields Junction–Bellahouston No 2 opened Spur to enable trains formerly using St Enoch to use Central.
7 November 1966	Buchanan Street station closed; Buchanan Street–Sighthill East closed.
28 November 1966	Germiston Junction–Balornock Junction–Robroyston West Junction closed.
5 June 1967	St Enoch–Clyde Junction closed.
5 June 1967	Arkleston Junction–Renfrew Wharf closed to passengers.
15 July 1968	Kelvinhaugh Junction–Stobcross closed.
24 July 1968	Port Dundas West–St Rollox West closed.
30 September 1968	Paisley, Chain Road–Rootes siding closed.
30 November 1968	Sighthill East Junction–Germiston Junction closed.

Notes

The original Kilbowie station on the Helensburgh line had its name changed in unusual circumstances. The NBR provided wagons painted with the name of the Singer Manufacturing Company whose large factory adjoined the station. Since the use of the special wagons was restricted to the firm and therefore uneconomical from the railway company's point of view, an arrangement was reached whereby Singer agreed to relinquish the wagons provided that Kilbowie station was renamed Singer.

When College station (Glasgow, City & District) was renamed the first name chosen was 'City', but this was abandoned when the board decided that it might be mistaken for a London station. When the station was designated 'High Street' the general manager of the North Eastern Railway objected on the grounds that there were already too many High Streets. However, his objection, although considered by the North British board, was overruled.

The Lanarkshire & Ayrshire Railway Act of 15 July 1897 provided for a spur from the East Kilbride line to Clarkston East Junction and also a spur to Clarkston West Junction. The eastern spur was intended to give traffic from the Cathcart line direct access to the East Kilbride line but, in fact, it was used only for the storage of stock. Clarkston West Junction, however, was brought into use on 1 April 1903 and allowed Lanarkshire traffic to run via the East Kilbride line to the L & A. With the opening of the Newton extension of the L & A some nine months later, the Lanarkshire traffic was diverted to that line and the short-lived Clarkston East and West junctions were closed, eventually to be removed in 1907. Williamwood station was opened on the site of Clarkston West Junction on 9 July 1929.

An excursion platform was opened at Calderwood Glen on the East Kilbride line in 1907 and closed in September 1939. Passenger service between East Kilbride and Hamilton was withdrawn on 1 October 1914, but between 1 October 1923 and 14 July 1924 one passenger train weekly used the route.

Chapter 9   Edinburgh

26 May 1826	Edinburgh & Dalkeith Railway authorised.
4 July 1831	E & D opened from St Leonards to Craighall. (Horse operated.)
21 January 1832	Arniston branch opened.
2 June 1832	E & D passenger service started.
13 August 1836	Edinburgh, Leith & Newhaven Railway authorised.
21 February 1842	Haymarket station (Edinburgh & Glasgow Railway) opened.
31 August 1842	Edinburgh, Leith & Granton Railway (formerly Edinburgh, Leith & Newhaven Railway) opened from Canonmills to Trinity.
4 July 1844	North British Railway authorised.
21 July 1845	NBR authorised to purchase E & D.
19 February 1846	EL & G Trinity–Granton opened.
10 May 1846	EL & G Bonnington Junction to Leith opened.
18 June 1846	North Bridge (Waverley) station opened. North British Railway opened.
1 August 1846	E & G extended from Haymarket to North Bridge.
17 May 1847	EL & G opened to Canal Street station. (Scotland Street tunnel.)
7 July 1847	E & D reopened for goods following regauging and upgrading by NBR.
16 July 1847	Musselburgh branch opened.
27 July 1847	EL & G absorbed by Edinburgh & Northern. Name of parent company changed to Edinburgh, Perth & Dundee in April 1849.
1 November 1847	St Leonards station (E & D) closed to passengers.
15 February 1848	Lothian Road station (Caledonian Railway) opened.
4 July 1855	Hardengreen Junction to Hawthornden Junction opened.

1 June 1860	St Leonards station reopened for passenger service to Dalkeith, Portobello and Leith.
30 September 1860	St Leonards station finally closed to passengers.
28 August 1861	Slateford–Granton (Caledonian Railway) opened.
1 September 1864	Leith branch (Caledonian Railway) opened for goods.
2 March 1868	Piershill–Trinity (NBR) opened for goods.
2 March 1868	Waverley–Abbeyhill–Easter Road opened. This spur gave the NBR direct access to Leith from Waverley for the first time. Canal Street station (hitherto the terminus for Leith), and Scotland Street tunnel were closed. Between 1868 and 1887 the tunnel was used for wagon storage, between 1887 and 1929 for mushroom cultivation and more recently for car storage by a dealer.
22 March 1868	Piershill Junction to Trinity opened for passengers.
1 May 1869	Abbeyhill station opened.
1869–73	Waverley station extended.
2 May 1870	Caledonian station (temporary) at west end of Princes Street opened.
1 May 1872	Macmerry branch opened.
2 September 1872	Penicuik Railway opened.
23 July 1874	Edinburgh, Loanhead & Roslin Railway opened to Roslin.
1 August 1874	Balerno branch opened.
3 July 1876	Wester Dalry branch opened.
2 July 1877	EL & R extended to Glencorse.
1 August 1879	Leith branch (Caledonian Railway) opened for passengers.
1 July 1882	Merchiston station opened.
1 December 1884	Edinburgh, Suburban & Southside Junction Railway opened.
1 June 1887	Craiglockhart station opened.
1892–1900	Reconstruction of Waverley station.
1 March 1894	Craigleith–Davidson's Mains–Barnton (Caledonian Railway) opened.
1894	Princes Street station (rebuilt) opened piecemeal.
2 July 1900	Dalry Road station opened.
14 October 1901	Gifford & Garvald Light Railway opened.

R

1 February 1902	Haymarket West Junction–Corstorphine opened.
15 October 1902	North British Hotel opened.
1 August 1903	Newhaven–Seafield (Caledonian Railway) opened.
21 December 1903	Caledonian Hotel opened.
15 August 1913	Lothian Lines authorised.
26 September 1915	Lothian Lines opened.
1 July 1925	Macmerry branch closed to passengers.
29 January 1934	Balgreen Halt opened.
1 December 1934	East Pilton Halt opened.
1 February 1937	House o' Hill Halt opened.
3 January 1942	Dalkeith branch closed to passengers.
30 October 1943	Balerno branch closed to passengers.
16 June 1947	North Leith branch closed to passengers.
7 April 1952	Leith Central closed. (Converted to diesel depot.)
30 April 1962	Leith branch (Caledonian Railway) closed to passengers.
10 September 1962	Suburban Circle closed to passengers.
8 April 1963	Niddrie North–Wanton Walls closed.
23 December 1963	Niddrie North–Niddrie West closed.
9 March 1964	Dalry Road–Coltbridge Junction closed.
9 March 1964	Dalry Middle Junction–Haymarket West Junction closed.
6 July 1964	Kingsknowe station closed.
7 September 1964	Abbeyhill and Piershill stations closed.
7 September 1964	Portobello and Joppa stations closed.
7 September 1964	Musselburgh station closed.
7 September 1964	Duff Street spur opened (Haymarket–Slateford connection).
2 August 1965	Crew Junction–Pilton West Junction closed.
6 September 1965	Princes Street station closed.
4 January 1966	Newhaven Junction–Leith Walk West Junction closed.
15 August 1966	Slateford–Dalry Junction–Morrison Street goods closed.
9 January 1967	Niddrie South (Millerhill)–Niddrie North–Leith South Junction (Portobello); Wanton Walls–Niddrie South closed. (Lothian Lines.)
27 March 1967	Penicuik–Hardengreen Junction closed.
24 July 1967	Easter Road Park halt closed.
4 September 1967	Granton Junction–Newhaven Junction closed.
4 December 1967	Balerno–Balerno Junction closed.

30 December 1967	Haymarket West Junction–Corstorphine closed.
28 February 1968	Newhaven Junction–North Leith closed.
6 May 1968	Leith Walk West–Leith East closed.
5 August 1968	St Leonards–Duddingston closed. (Edinburgh & Dalkeith.)
2 December 1968	Bonnington goods–Bonnington South Junction closed.
1 February 1971	Kingsknowe station reopened.

Bibliography

Minute Books of the following railway companies:

Aberlady, Gullane & North Berwick Ry. 1893–1900
Berwickshire Ry. 1861–76
Dumbarton & Balloch Joint Line Committee. 1894–1929
Edinburgh & Dalkeith Ry. 1824–45
Edinburgh, Leith & Granton Ry. 1836–48
Edinburgh, Suburban & Southside Junction Ry. 1880–5
Eyemouth Ry. 1883–1900
Forth & Clyde Junction Ry. 1852–1923
Glasgow & Renfrew District Ry. 1883–7
Glasgow Central Ry. 1888–95
Glasgow City & District Ry. 1883–7
Greenock & Ayrshire Ry. 1865–71
Greenock & Wemyss Bay Ry. 1865–75
Lanarkshire & Ayrshire Ry, 1881–1923
Lanarkshire & Dumbartonshire Ry. 1889–1909
North British Railway. 1842–1923
Paisley & Barrhead District Ry. 1896–1902
Strathendrick & Aberfoyle Ry. 1879–91

Appleton, J. H. *The Geography of Communications in Great Britain*
    Bradshaws Railway Manual
The Glasgow & Ayrshire Railway Guide (1841)
Kellett, R. J. 'Glasgow Railways 1830–1880, a Study in Natural
    Growth', *The Economic History Review*, 17 no 2 (1964)
Lewin, H. G. *The British Railway System; its Early Development
    to 1884*
Monkland Railways Company. *Rules and Regulations for Con-
    ducting of Traffic* (1863)
O'Dell, A. C. *Railways and Geography*

Sidney, J. *History of the Railway System* (1846)
Stephenson Locomotive Society Journal
Stephenson Locomotive Society. *The Glasgow & South Western Railway*
Warden, John. *The Glasgow & Ayr and Glasgow & Greenock Railway Companion* (1842)
Whishaw, F. *Railways of Great Britain and Ireland* (1840)
Willox, J. *A Guide to the Edinburgh & Glasgow Railway* (1842)

Books of circulars and cuttings relating to the G & SWR
Public and working timetables of the NBR, CR and G & SWR

SUGGESTIONS FOR FURTHER READING

Acworth, W. M. *The Railways of Scotland*
Dott, G. *Early Scottish Colliery Waggonways.*
Dow, G. *The First Railway Across the Border*
Handley, J. E. *The Navvy in Scotland*
Highet, C. *The Glasgow and South Western Railway*
Hunter, D. G. L. *Edinburgh's Transport*
Lindsay, J. *The Canals of Scotland*
McAdam, W. *The Birth, Growth and Eclipse of the Glasgow and South Western Railway*
McIlwraith, W. *The Glasgow and South Western Railway—Its Origin, Progress and Present Position*
Nock, O. S. *The Caledonian Railway*
Smith, D. L., *The Little Railways of South West Scotland*
Smith, D. L. *The Dalmellington Iron Company: Its Engines and Men.*
Thomas, J. *The Springburn Story*
Thomas, J. *The North British Railway*
Thomas, J. *Scottish Railway History in Pictures*
Thomson, D. L. and Sinclair, D. E. *The Glasgow Subway*

Acknowledgements

In the preparation of this book I owed much to Robert M. Hogg and his staff at the former BRB Historical Records Office, Edinburgh, to the Keeper of the Records of Scotland and his staff at General Register House, Edinburgh and to C. W. Black, City Librarian, Glasgow and his staff at the Mitchell Library. I am particularly indebted to George Barbour for his patience in tackling an intricate task of proof reading, and to Alastair Harper who was equally patient in preparing the index. W. A. C. Smith helped with the checking of part of the chronology and made useful suggestions concerning text material. William Caldwell of BR Public Relations Department (Scottish Region) gave ready assistance in locating illustrations.

Index

(Page references in bold-face numerals denote illustrations)